THE LIBRARY OF POLITICAL ECONOMY

POLITICAL ECONOMY is the old name for economics. In the hands of the great classical economists, particularly Smith, Ricardo and Marx, economics was the study of the working and development of the economic system in which men and women lived. Its practitioners were driven by a desire to describe, to explain and to evaluate what they saw around them. No sharp distinction was drawn between economic analysis and economic policy nor between economic behaviour and its interaction with the technical, social and political framework.

The Library of Political Economy has been established to provide widely based explanations of economic behaviour in contemporary society.

In examining the way in which new patterns of social organization and behaviour influence the economic system and policies for combating problems associated with growth, inflation, poverty and the distribution of wealth, contributors stress the link between politics and economics and the importance of institutions in policy formulation.

This 'open-ended' approach to economics implies that there are few laws that can be held to with certainty and, by the same token, there is no generally established body of theory to be applied in all circumstances. Instead economics as presented in this library provides a way of ordering events which has constantly to be updated and modified as new situations develop. This, we believe, is its interest and its challenge.

Editorial Board

Lord Balogh, University of Oxford
Andrew Graham, University of Oxford
Keith Griffin, University of Oxford
Geoffrey Harcourt, University of Cambridge
Roger Opie, University of Oxford
Hugh Stretton, University of Adelaide
Lester Thurow, Massachusetts Institute of Technology

Volumes in the Library

Dangerous Currents: The State of Economics — Lester Thurow
The Political Economy of Nationalism — Dudley Seers
Women's Claims: A Study in Political Economy — Lisa Peattie and Martin Rein
Urban Inequalities under State Socialism — Ivan Szelenyi
Social Innovation and the Division of Labour — Jonathan Gershuny

Dangerous Currents

The State of Economics

Lester C. Thurow

OXFORD UNIVERSITY PRESS

Oxford University Press, Walton Street, Oxford OX2 6DP

London New York Toronto
Delhi Bombay Calcutta Madras Karachi
Kuala Lumpur Singapore Hong Kong Tokyo
Nairobi Dar es Salaam Cape Town
Melbourne Auckland

and associated companies in
Beirut Berlin Ibadan Mexico City Nicosia

Oxford is a trade mark of Oxford University Press

Published in the United States
by Random House, Inc., New York

First published 1983
Reprinted 1984

Grateful acknowledgement is made to Data Resources, Inc., for
permission to reprint a table from 'Why Inflation Became Worse'
by Robert Gouch and Robin Siegel. Reprinted by permission of
Data Resources, Inc., Lexington, Mass.

British Library Cataloguing in Publication Data
Thurow, Lester C.
Dangerous currents.
1. United States—Economic policy—1981-
I. Title
338.973   HC106.7
ISBN 0-19-877183-5
ISBN 0-19-877214-9 Pbk

Printed in Great Britain
at the University Press, Oxford
by David Stanford
Printer to the University

For Ethan, Torben, and Gretchen

In the course of writing this book I have received more than the normal amount of helpful comments from: Sandra Del Boca, Andrew Graham, Keith Griffin, Robert Heilbroner, Edwin Kuh, Eli Shapiro, Lester Taylor, Peter Temin, and Martin Weitzman.

Contents

Introduction

Charting the Currents of Economics

For more than a decade now the engines of the world's economic ship have been slowing down, with growth occurring at an ever slackening pace. Meanwhile, the ship has been battered repeatedly by both inflation and recession. What started as inflation after the Vietnam war and the 1973 OPEC price hike developed into stagflation. Unemployment soared and inflation got worse as recessions got longer and hit the economy ever more frequently. By the early 1980s, talk of another Great Depression could no longer be dismissed as kooky; it had become a genuine possibility. Economic growth had stopped everywhere: east-west, north-south. Unemployment was in double digits in both America and Europe, with the rate in Great Britain above levels reached in the 1930s. And everywhere one looked—American savings-and-loan institutions or the Mexican banks—ominous financial cracks had begun to appear.

Yet our navigators, the economists of the world—the people with the charts and compasses—cannot seem to agree on what course should be followed. And nothing tried so far seems to work. Compare the routes chosen by American President Reagan and French President Mitterrand, whose disagreement with each other is nearly complete. One called for a hard turn to the right; the other, a hard veer to the left. Reagan lowered taxes on the rich, while Mitterrand did the opposite. Mitterrand expanded the social safety net; Reagan did the opposite. Reagan deregulated the economy; Mitterrand embarked on a program of nationalization. Reagan opted for a monetarist contraction, Mitterrand for a Keynesian expansion. How could two governments with intelligent economic advisers come to such different conclusions about what policies to pursue? Even more troubling after two years: both programs have to be pronounced failures. Neither is performing the way its architects said it would, and both electorates are unhappy with the results.

Meanwhile, Keynesianism—the once dominant mode of practice among economists—lapsed into disrepute. Not so long ago, Richard Nixon asserted that "we are all Keynesians now," but that school is currently associated with the policy-making failures of the 1960s and 1970s. In July 1982 I attended a conference of economists from all over the world in Tokyo.[1] The intellectual disarray among them was complete—no shared ideas about what was going on, why, and what could be done about our ailing economies.

The Keynesians there argued that the world-wide slowdown was caused by the excessively tight fiscal and monetary policies being used to fight inflation. The cure was to find another way to deal with inflation (tax-based incomes policies, among other vehicles), and to reflate our economies with lower taxes, larger government expenditures, and lower interest rates. Doubters immediately pointed to the example of France, where Keynesian reflation had not worked.

The monetarists at the conference said that our economic woes were brought on by a too rapid rate of growth of the money supply in the late 1960s and early 1970s, and could be addressed by a slow and gradual rate of growth in the money supply. People who disagreed asserted that Reagan's kind of hard-nosed monetarism has hardly proved a wild success.

Meanwhile, the so-called structuralists saw an economy without "real" unemployment. A German economist maintained that all of his country's unemployed were either actually working in the underground economy, enjoying leisure and not really looking for work thanks to a too generous social welfare system, or lacking the skills needed to find work in the modern German economy. Critics said that there were in fact people really out of work, and that the German economist's thinking paralleled that of some American economists who were convinced the United States had no "real" unemployment even when the rate peaked at 25 percent during the Great Depression.

Then there was the supply-siders' analysis of the cause and remedy. Governments all over the world had distorted or dampened free-market incentives, and these had to be restored. Moreover, rejuvenating the economy would require more investment and a better-educated and -trained labor force. Critics of the position wondered how this could be true when little correlation exists between the degree of government intervention and economic success—the Japanese economy being the most successful and the one most subject to government intervention, regulation, and manipulation.

A school called "rational expectations" was also represented. Theorists of this persuasion believe that because there is little or nothing that government can do to make the economic situation better (or worse), one shouldn't do anything, but simply endure things until the world economy starts to pick up on its own.

Two other schools had partisans among the economists in Tokyo. The first of these advocated a conception of "satiated wants." Having purchased so many goods and services, these economists asserted, the consumer no longer really wants anything more, and economic growth has stopped due to diminished demand. The solution: learn to adjust to an economic environment that doesn't grow much or doesn't grow at all. Finally, there was economic Darwinism, whose disciples argue that our economic problems are a blessing in disguise. Only hardship weeds out the economically weak and unfit. After the toll is taken, growth and general prosperity will return, thanks to the efficiency that the surviving and fittest economic players can bring to the economy. Until then, the purge must go on.

The current intellectual disarray among economists is matched only by a parallel time of confusion during the early days of the Great Depression. Economists then could not agree on what caused the Depression or what to do to get out of it. Individual economists were supremely confident that their own theory would work, but without a decent consensus within the economics profession, policy makers didn't know how to proceed. So basically they did nothing.

Keynesianism rescued economics from that time of confusion. For the professional economist, confidence in the new theory meant that government could act to prevent economic downturns (something denied in the previously existing conceptions), and for the citizen, the theoretical power to prevent them meant government's practical responsibility to do exactly that.

Fifty years later, you as a citizen are charged with choosing the best economic navigators from among the many hawking their ideas. How are you to know who is right? What are the supposed experts arguing about, and just how do they look at the problems they say they understand so well? Why has the discipline once again become so discordant? Where are the theoretical currents of economics taking the profession, and should the layman care? This book tries to provide some of the answers.

Though my answers here will not solve the country's economic problems, they will, I hope, help us to understand what they are and how they are perceived by professionals. The point is that the convulsions now affecting the discipline of economics do not simply attract academic interest but strongly influence intellectual environment and public climate in which real economic choices are made. A layman cannot right the currents of economics, but it is very important, I feel, that he understand what they are. And if the layman occasionally finds my book tough sledding technically, I ask his forbearance. I want to be as precise as I can without succumbing totally to the language of the trade. But we need some technical precision because many of the assertions confidently made by the economist, which are then translated into policy by our political leaders, are only assertions—unproved. If we are to expose what is unproved and in general try to demystify the language of economists, we must to some extent fight them on their own technical ground, where they seem to hold sway completely. Occupying the high technical ground with a boldness and confidence that to me is not justified, economists have been able to cow the public, press, policy makers and politicians in ways not usually open to academics and technical people. Paradoxically, this happens even while economists are not held in especially high repute.

To my mind, mainstream American economists reflect more an academic need for an internal theoretical consistency and rigor than it reflects observable, measurable realities in the world we all live in. Accordingly, my book is a critique of economics as it is by and large taught and practiced in the

United States. I am convinced that accepting the conventional supply-demand model of the economy is rather like believing that the world is flat, or that the sun revolves around the earth —you can make a rigorous case, on paper, for both propositions, but hard evidence is more than a bit scarce. Moreover, if you choose to act on either belief, you can get into a lot of trouble. Which is where I think the policies of the Reagan Administration have put the economy.

For the professional economist, I would like this book to provide a respite, a chance to get away from the usual intense focus we economists bring to this or that specific dispute in the trade and try to gauge the broader currents at work in our discipline. Which way is our profession headed, and is it going in the right direction?

But any occupation with thousands of practitioners is like an ocean. As you chart the major currents that flow within it, you shouldn't forget that subcurrents and eddies are always present and moving in contrary directions, and a great body of water is always more varied and less settled than the chartmaker's abstractions. Nonetheless, the Gulf Stream does move out of the Caribbean, up the east coast of the United States and heads off toward Europe, along the way very much influencing the climate of both North America and Europe. My book concerns itself only with the major currents at work within American economics. I don't talk about many worthy subcurrents within American economics or about major foreign schools of thought.

In any case, one can safely say that some fifty years ago Keynes and Keynesian analysis effected a fundamental shift in the main currents of economics. By the earlier dominant theory, which was based on a simple equilibrium price-auction view of the economy, a phenomenon like unemployment could not exist—all markets operated strictly according to the principles of competitive supply and demand.

But when the Great Depression produced huge rates of unemployment, Keynesian analysis was devised to explain the existence and persistence of very high levels of joblessness. And in the process Keynesianism created a major new field of economics, macro-economics—the study of economic behavior in the aggregate—which opposed itself to the conceptions of the price-auction economist. The older set of ideas lived on but was relabeled micro-economics, and confined itself to explaining the behavior of individual economic actors—firms and individual people.

But as the problems and anxieties of the Great Depression slipped into history, and inflation developed into a problem of acute public concern, the currents of economic thinking began to shift back toward the price-auction conception to explain both macro- and micro-economic behavior. Monetarism, supply-side economics, and rational expectations—schools of thought this book will examine in detail—all rely on the primacy of the price-auction model. In sum, the classical, price-auction, economics of the 1920s was replaced during the Great Depression by Keynesianism, which was in turn supplanted by the new classical economics of the 1980s. Keynesianism was toppled after fifty years of dominance.

The major purpose of my book is to examine and render comprehensible the re-emergence of the equilibrium price-auction analysis as the prevailing intellectual mode in economics and to ask whether that development improves our understanding and control of the economy itself. I, for one, don't think it will do either.

But beyond a shift in ideas, something else has been at work: the profession, the discipline of economics, is on its way to becoming a guild.[2] Members of a guild, as we know, tend to preserve and advance traditional theories rather than try to develop new ways of thinking and doing things to solve new problems. The equilibrium price-auction view of the world is a traditional view with a history as old as that of economics itself: the individual is asserted to be a maximizing consumer or producer within free supply-demand markets that establish an equilibrium price for any kind of goods or service. This is an economics blessed with an intellectual consistency, and one having implications that extend far beyond the realm of conventional economic theory. It is, in short, also a political philosophy, often becoming something approaching a religion.

Price-auction economics is further blessed because it can assume mathematical form—it can work hand in glove with calculus. Expression in mathematics imparts to the theory a seeming rigor and internal strength. But that rigor easily degenerates into scholarly rigor mortis, as mathematical facility becomes more important to the profession than a substantive understanding of the economy itself. To express an idea mathematically gives it the illusion of unassailable truth and also makes it utterly incomprehensible to anyone untutored in mathematics. Then, too, young scholars aspiring to the profession are required to demonstrate a technical virtuosity in math before they are even considered eligible. By analogy, once the Confucian scholars of ancient China passed a very complicated set of entrance examinations, they used the same examinations to keep others out. Both then and now, all honor is reserved for those who can explain current events in terms of "The Theory," while anyone trying to develop new theories to explain recent developments is regarded with suspicion at best. In economics today, "The Theory" has become an ideology rather than a set of working hypotheses used to understand the behavior of the economy found in the real world. But it is my guess that price-auction theory will still prevail among academic and professional economists long after the Reagan Administration and its chastened (I would presume) economic policy makers have left Washington.

All over the globe, we have recently witnessed a return to religious fundamentalism. In my view, the return to the equilibrium price-auction model in economics represents a parallel development—a desire for psychological certainty in a world that is, in the last instance, uncertain.

Finally, if you criticize a discipline, you can easily sound too negative. A critic tends to see what's wrong, not what's right. In any case, nothing I have to say will deny the fact that in their 200-year history, economists as a group have advanced our understanding of economic behavior. In fact, the problems with economics are no more serious and the disagreements no more prevalent than those in other fields. They are just more visible—being reported on daily; and more important—affecting the immediate economic well-being of everyone. So even as I criticize the economics profession, let me say at the outset that I am myself proud to be called an economist.

DANGEROUS
CURRENTS

CHAPTER 1

Fixed versus Flexible Prices

Fundamental Crosscurrents

If you were to ask the average economist what was wrong with his discipline, he would no doubt tell you that something was really wrong with macro-economics: the profession has lost its ability to understand or control the aggregate economic problems of inflation, unemployment, and low productivity growth. But the same person would probably also say that micro-economics is fundamentally sound, that the profession fully understands the behavior of individual economic actors.[1] He would probably then say that though he wasn't sure exactly how the issues in macro-economic theory should be resolved, the source of the difficulty is clear; namely, that macro-economics is not securely grounded in micro-economic theory— the equilibrium price-auction (supply and demand) view of the world.

The perceptions here are accurate, except for one. Micro-economic theory is *not* fundamentally sound, and the real problems in economics are to be found in a micro-economic theory that is unsatisfactory. Too much of real individual behavior, as I will try to show in this book, is unexplained or explained away by the equilibrium price-auction view of behavior. Macro-problems do exist, but they will not be solved until some fundamental reform occurs in micro-economic theory.

Keynesian analysis as I will also try to show, is currently in trouble because it started with a postulate—rigid wages— which was inconsistent with the price-auction view of the world. The Keynesian revolution ultimately failed to sustain itself because Keynes's disciples confined their interest to macro-economic problems without constructing a micro-economic theory upon which their analysis could rest. Without a consistent micro-economic theory, it was only a matter of time until Keynesian analysis would be intellectually done in. And it was.

A Basic Internal Contradiction

As an academic and professional discipline, economics lives with a fundamental internal contradiction: what is taught in conventional micro-economics is incompatible with what is taught in macro-economics. In the former, every market is a price-auction market that clears based on competitive bidding within a framework of supply and demand. Accordingly, any market is always in equilibrium, having no unsatisfied bidders, and every individual is a maximizer in his decisions to consume and produce. Macro-economics, on the other hand, is basically the study of markets that do not clear and are not in equilibrium. Such contradictions, of course, are not peculiar to economics. Physics uses both particle theory and wave theory to describe electromagnetic phenomena. But the contradictions in economics are perhaps more severe than in other disciplines.

In equilibrium price-auction markets, it is impossible to find over- or under-employed resources. Every factor of production is paid in accordance with its own productivity (marginal product) and every factor of production that wishes to be employed is employed at a wage or price governed by that productivity. In other words, if an unemployed worker really wants to work, he has only to lower his wage request and some employer will hire him, and fire someone already employed if necessary. Eventually the labor market will reach the point where everyone willing to work at or below the equilibrium wage is working, while those who are unemployed are asking for more than the market will bear.

Given markets like this, unemployed resources are obviously impossible. Accordingly, macro-economic policies, monetary or fiscal, designed to raise or lower aggregate demand to eliminate unemployed resources are not only unnecessary but positively harmful. No one should intervene in the market to improve its performance because the results are the best it is possible to get. Interventions of any sort can only hurt, never help.

Similarly, by this conception, inflation either can't exist or doesn't matter. It can't exist because a price increase in any one area (say, the price of energy) will force reductions in demand—less income is available to be spent after paying for energy—and hence offsetting price and wage decreases in other areas. Inflation doesn't matter because the perfectly rational Homo economicus looks only at his real income and relative prices of various goods when making decisions or judging his economic success. Affecting neither real incomes nor relative prices, inflation cannot matter. Replacing barter with the use of money complicates the basic supply-demand model, but does not fundamentally alter the conclusions because money can affect neither real incomes nor relative prices— money is neutral, a mere veil covering real economic activity, or so Homo economicus would reason.

If the equilibrium price-auction market adequately described the real world, every economist would agree on the outcome in the real world. If all markets (over time, across space, and those for insuring risk) existed and functioned perfectly as asserted, then a competitive economy would generate the best economic outcome possible given the real resources and preferences of the population.[2] The economy would be operating at an optimum optimorium. No intervention could improve upon results. There is no unemployment, inflation concerns no one, and growth occurs at the highest possible rate consistent with the preferences of the members of the society. The only interventions that might be called for are those flowing not from economics, but from the ethical principles governing income distribution and initial endowments of resources.

Disputes arise over whether the necessary markets do exist, could exist, and if they existed, the transaction costs it would entail to use them. The real economic world is obviously not a literal auction market. But does it proceed "as if an auction" were occurring? Put another way, does the real world come close enough to the competitive model so that it can be described as in accordance with the model? Skeptics point to the nonexistence of certain markets—namely, those that would allow a person to make trades between the present and the distant future, and the transaction costs of implementing other markets. Many of the markets for selling risk and uncertainty either don't exist or have such substantial transaction costs that few individuals use them. In many markets only a few firms exist, and entry costs are high.

There are also major controversies among economists as to how long it takes markets to adjust. Speedy adjustments are crucial to the price-auction view of the world since the concept of equilibrium is only relevant if markets get there rather rapidly. If adjustments are not rapid, one must build a micro-economic model based upon fixed prices, since the real world always lives in the fixed-price short run and never in the flexi-ble-price long run.

Price-auction true believers, however, see a real world in accordance with the equilibrium price-auction model. Other, less committed but like-minded economists see a world basi-cally in accordance with the model even if they admit there are a few places where it currently diverges.

Conversely, there is also no disagreement as to what would happen if wages and prices were rigid downward, the basic Keynesian assumption, where demand is not self-regulating; where external shocks, such as oil price hikes, lead to inflation and unemployment; and where as a consequence a definite need exists for macro-economic policies. An oil price hike raises the average price level—oil prices go up and other prices fail to go down. This reduces demand for other goods and services—less disposable income is available after paying more for energy. Faced with lower sales, firms outside the energy area lay off workers, unemployment rises, incomes fall, and a reduction in aggregate demand results. Stagflation com-mences, and Keynesians would say to reduce unemployment one must raise aggregate demand. What should be done to curb inflation in an economy of rising unemployment is left unspecified in Keynesian analysis, since it was developed dur-ing the Great Depression, when prices were falling and infla-tion was not a problem.

It is important to understand that there are no theoretical controversies about what happens in a fixed- or flexible-price world. The controversies are empirical ones as to which of the two models better describes the state of the world as it actually is. And because there are smart people on both sides of the dispute, deciding which of the models is most accurate is not easy. If it were, the issue would have been resolved long since.

The preponderant weight of economic opinion now lies on the flexible-price side of the argument. Why? Because almost everyone uses the flexible-price model in his micro-economic analysis. Moreover, in some markets, such as the one for grain, we find that prices clearly do adjust in accordance with the basic axioms of the supply-demand model. The weakness of Keynesian analysis is that it does not have a micro-economic theory to defend its macro-economic assumptions in other markets, such as the one for labor, where wages do not seem to adjust as they should.

There are basically two paths for eliminating the tensions between micro- and macro-economics, and many of the disagreements among economists spring from which is chosen. The rational expectationist school, for example, attempts to eliminate the tensions by denying the existence of macro-economics and asserting that everything is accurately described by the price-auction model. What looks like curable macro-economic problems to less informed economists are really uncontrollable, large random shocks. More about this school later.

The alternative here is to construct a new micro-economics consistent with macro-economic problems, and then to build a new macro-economics upon that foundation. This means a micro-economics that can explain why wages do not fall in the labor market when unemployment rises. But the new theory must also explain unemployment and wage rigidity not as a market imperfection, but as an integral part of the efficient functioning of the labor market. Implicit contracts theories in which workers and managers agree not to let wages fall—so maximizing cooperation and hence productivity over long periods of time (see Chapter 7)—are attempts to move in a new direction.[3]

Depending upon which of the two basic alternatives is chosen, the intellectual currents of economics head in very different directions. All economists are reacting to the same fundamental problem, but unfortunately no line of argument is now compelling enough to command universal assent.

Quantification

Most economic disputes involve not the existence of various real-world economic outcomes, but their size or speed. The price-auction model, however, almost never predicts either the size or speed of different outcomes or effects, but simply allows economists to predict in qualitative terms that various effects will occur. All economists, for example, agree that income taxes produce an income effect positive to work effort (as after-tax incomes fall, individuals work more to achieve some desired standard of living) and a substitution effect adverse to work effort (as taxes rise, take-home income per hour of work falls and leisure becomes relatively more attractive—cheaper). But economists disagree as to the relative size of the two effects, and the speed with which they occur over time. This empirical disagreement, for example, and not any theoretical disagreement, lay behind the controversies as to whether Reagan supply-side economics could have had the large rapid effects predicted by its supporters.

A specialty within economics, econometric analysis, was supposed to answer the question of size and speed, but as we shall see later, econometrics has not proven up to the job. Slight differences in the specification of an econometric equation make large differences in the estimated results; moreover, results are not stable—"robust" in the jargon—even over short periods of time.

In general, economists can't find hard empirical constants, such as the speed of light in physics, because economists are not studying the immutable rules of nature but the mutable generalizations that govern human behavior. When the world changes, the observed behavior of the economic actors follows it. Wage and price behavior, for example, was different before and after the first OPEC oil shock in 1973–74. Before the shock, few contracts explicitly contained cost-of-living escalator clauses. After the shock, cost-of-living escalator clauses were added to most industrial wage or product contracts. And price and wage behavior in an indexed world is quite different from price and wage behavior in an unindexed world, as we will see in Chapter 4.

The economic world also evolves in response to shocks. For many years, for example, a rough empirical relation between GNP and unemployment known as Okun's Law existed.[4] This predicted the changes in unemployment that would correspond to any given growth of GNP. Any such relationship, however, depends upon a steady rate of growth of productivity. If that rate accelerates, more output will be necessary to generate a given number of jobs. Conversely, if the rate decelerates, less output is necessary to generate a given number of jobs.

Consequently, shifts in the long-term trends in productivity growth must induce shifts in the relationship between production (GNP) and labor demands. As America's productivity growth rate fell from more than 3 percent per year before 1965 into the negative range after 1977, Okun's Law gradually became less and less accurate until it was dropped as a tool of analysis entirely.[5] Meanwhile, physical constants, such as the speed of light, have not been known to change in a matter of a few years.

The Market Clearing Mechanism

The controversial question in economics is not, Are markets competitive and do they clear?—all markets clear and most American markets are competitive in the sense that few producers have no competitors. The real question is, Do markets clear based on fluctuations in prices? To have a working equilibrium price-auction market, the market must clear based on changes in prices. With other clearing mechanisms (fluctuations in production, for example) the economy still has competitive markets that clear, but these markets have different characteristics and outcomes.

The observation that wages do not fall in response to unemployment, for example, should not lead you to conclude that labor markets fail to clear. When wages are rigid downward, employers seek to find the best possible employees that can be hired at the existing wage. In other words, the market clears based on the qualifications of the workers—education, skills, age. But if the market is clearing on some basis other than price, the market will have characteristics other than those claimed by supply-demand fundamentalists. Instead of moving to the equilibrium point given by conventional supply-and-demand curves, the market may clear by shifts in the curves themselves. The supply of labor will effectively fall as some workers are rationed out of the market because they do not have the "required" background characteristics. Here workers bid for jobs based on their qualifications rather than on their willingness to work for lower wages. So new potential workers may be willing to work for the current or even a lower wage, but find their bids not accepted. Because of the disruption to teamwork and motivation, employers are not willing to fire existing workers to make room for new workers. It may also take a long time for someone to acquire the demanded qualifications. And some of them, such as the ability to play professional basketball, may not be acquirable at all. In contrast, price bids can be changed instantly. But if workers compete based on their skills rather than willingness to work for lower wages, unemployment becomes possible, something that is impossible if all markets instantly clear based on price alone.

A competitive equilibrium can exist on many levels, but the standard model requires price competition—the easiest, speediest, and lowest-cost form of competition. Since anyone can lower prices quickly and with a minimum of transaction costs, price competition should drive other forms of competition out of business. And since price competition forces everyone to produce and sell at their lowest possible costs, economic efficiency is obtained.

But the real world, which we readily see all around us, is often marked by non-price forms of competition. In fact, you could say that price competition is too easy. Because no one thinks that he can get a comparative advantage by simply cutting prices, a business tries to focus competition on areas (quality, service, product differentiation) where it may be possible to get a non-duplicable edge. Restaurant owners know that customers may be attracted by posh surroundings and good service rather than cheap food.

Technically speaking, non-price forms of competition can always be described as if they conform to the textbook model of strict price competition. Instead of one good, there are now two goods—good X and good X plus posh surroundings—and markets for both are price-competitive. But that semantic redefinition obscures the reality that some goods are being sold in markets where real price competition plays a very limited role. And when price competition plays a limited role, prices are not going to fall as the standard model prescribes and requires. Better service does not show up as a lower rate of inflation. And if that is the case, prices are not going to fall in response to macro-economic policies designed to produce excess capacity, which is what would happen if all markets cleared based on real price changes.

The smooth real-world functioning of the price-auction model also depends on relatively large responses on both the supply and demand sides of the market to changes in prices. Technically, the model can work with any responses, large or small, but reasonably large ones are really required. If the elasticities (responses) are very small, price hikes such as those that recently occurred in oil result in such large real-income changes (people cannot cut their oil bills by buying less) that the public is politically unlikely to let the market work. Small elasticities also mean that public policies, such as lowering demand to induce price cuts, have to be so draconian to induce a decrease in prices that they are unlikely to be adopted.

But econometric studies tend to indicate very low price elasticities of demand whenever anyone attempts to estimate the entire structure of demand elasticities. In the Houthakker-Taylor estimates, only 17 out of 83 products have price elasticities of demand greater than one, which means that a 1 percent cut in price will produce more than a 1 percent increase in sales. Fifty-three products have zero elasticities of demand where a drop in price has no effect on sales. Another eight have elasticities of less than 0.5. These small responses do not totally undermine the price-auction model, but they do severely alter its working characteristics.[6]

Equilibrium versus Disequilibrium

Many of the disagreements among economists spring from the agnosticism of the competitive model with respect to the length of time necessary for markets to clear. Given an existing economic equilibrium, how easy is it to dismantle that world quickly and create a new economic world consistent with a new set of external conditions? How fast, for example, will you be led to buy a new heating system when the price of oil goes up?

The equilibrium price-auction model is often taught in the classroom as if instantaneous adjustments occur, but technically the model is silent as to how long it takes markets to clear. Some products such as housing or copper would seem to take substantial periods of time to move from one equilibrium point to another, simply because it takes a very long time to build the new facilities necessary to alter supplies significantly. If adjustment times are substantial, a whole set of rather difficult questions arises about what happens during the period of adjustment (disequilibrium) and how that period affects the future course of the economy.

Just as the price-auction model is silent about the time necessary for markets to clear, it is just as quiet about what happens during those periods of disequilibrium. But these cannot be ignored. If the period is long enough, the economy is going to generate a flow of what is called "disequilibrium quasi-rents" —a flow of earnings above or below normal for factors of production involved. These new higher or lower factor incomes alter the demands for goods and services, and hence the economy's pattern of demand and production. With different goods being produced, marginal products and earnings change. Some initial shock or change in external conditions starts the economy off from one equilibrium point toward another, but the very process of movement generates income flows that send the economy off toward yet a different equilibrium. As a result, the actual path of the economy always makes an impact on the course of the economy. This may sound excessively technical, but much of the debate swirling about the price-auction model centers on questions of whether markets are, or are not, in equilibrium. And much of the disagreement springs from semantic differences in the definition of equilibrium rather than from real differences in economic analysis. Two economists may view exactly the same phenomena, yet one will see equilibrium and the other disequilibrium. What do I mean?

Suppose, for example, that there is a shortage of hotel rooms in New York City. Rooms can be profitably built and rented for $100 per night but are actually renting for $125 per night. An unexpected surge in demand from foreign tourists, attracted by a cheap dollar, has pushed demand above where it was expected to be. Is the market in equilibrium?

Rents of $125 per night will stimulate the building of a lot of new hotel rooms. So viewed, the market is not in equilibrium. The supply of rooms is increasing and nightly room rates are above long-run equilibrium levels. But new hotels cannot be designed, built, and ready for occupancy in less than four years. So viewed, the market is in equilibrium. There are no short-run opportunities for new entrants to make above-average rates of return, and the rent of $125 per night is a short-run equilibrium rate for allocating the existing supplies.

Suppose that a potential investor analyzes the situation and finds that there are already a sufficient number of rooms under construction, so that if he were to build a new hotel, by the time it was finished he could not rent rooms for more than the equilibrium rate of $100 per night. In that case, the market would then also be in a long-run equilibrium because the $125 per night has potentially brought on line every hotel room that it is going to bring on line. But there are still those disequilibrium quasi-rents of $25 per room per night being earned by those fortunate enough to own hotels already. Someone gets that $25 dollars, it affects their purchases, and hence the production and earnings of the rest of the economy.

Imagine that after the new hotels are constructed, the value of the dollar unexpectedly rises due to high American interest rates. America becomes a very expensive place to vacation and foreign tourists disappear from New York. As a result, when the extra hotel rooms actually are completed they cannot be rented for $100, much less for $125. The nightly rent falls to $75. The $75 per night more than covers marginal costs of existing hotels, so that none of them closes down, but when fixed (capital) costs are considered, owners are losing money. Owners incomes fall, changes occur in their demands for goods and services, and the path of the economy is once again altered.

If equilibrium is defined as "Are there opportunities to make abnormal profits?," the economy is continually in equilibrium.

If equilibrium is defined as "Is there a non-equilibrium flow of factor earnings that will alter the course of the economy?," the economy is in persistent disequilibrium.

Some economists would describe the New York hotel market as being in equilibrium because no short-run or long-run opportunities to make above-average profits exist. Other economists would describe the New York hotel market as being in disequilibrium because disequilibrium quasi-rents (the plus or minus $25) are being earned. Fundamentally it makes no difference how you describe the market as long as everyone realizes that there is a flow of earnings that will alter the nature of the economy. But it certainly appears as if the economics profession knows very little indeed when two economists can look at the same thing and one calls it "equilibrium" and the other "disequilibrium."

Since prevailing economic theories are not dynamic—can't trace out changes over time—economists rely on what is called "comparative statics." This is the analysis of how different initial conditions produce different equilibria without regard to the path by which the economy gets between those two points. The procedure has been followed not because economists are stupid, but because economic dynamics has proven to be too hard to model formally—or at least no one has found a satisfactory way to do it yet. But as we have just seen in the hotel example, comparative statics also often creates misleading results. The path between two equilibrium points always matters if substantial quasi-rents are generated.

"In the long run" is a favorite expression of economists because there is a widespread assumption that in the long run, equilibrium conditions will prevail and the economy will eventually move to a new equilibrium position if the initial conditions of the old equilibrium are perturbed. Given the assumption, perpetual disequilibriums are impossible, and if found, would be labeled "market imperfections or rigidities." Understood that way, disequilibrium, if it exists, can only produce temporary effects. Markets will eventually adjust and the economy will eventually move to a new equilibrium.

While adjustment time rescues the concept of reaching equilibrium, it does nothing to help the concept of reaching the precise equilibrium state predicted from an analysis of comparative statics. Given substantial quasi-rents, the economy moves to a new equilibrium, but it is not the equilibrium previously calculated. The real-world path taken perpetually alters incomes and the position of the economy. And as long as those quasi-rents are accruing, the new equilibrium will verge further and further from what was predicted. In short, the economy does not reach the equilibrium calculated, no matter how much time passes.

If the adjustment period is lengthy, external shocks may also come faster than the adjustments to shocks, meaning that the economy never does move to an equilibrium position. Always reacting to new shocks, the economy can never settle down. As a result, actual analysis of what happens in the world has to focus on disequilibrium conditions, even if economists do not want to call them that. Empirically, econometric models seek to model economic behavior over time, but they are to some extent always unsatisfactory, since they are never based on a theory of dynamics. No such theory exists, yet all economies are dynamic.

To consider a related issue. While the price-auction market method of organization maximizes profits at a point in time, there is no reason to believe that it maximizes production or profits over time. Other forms of social and economic organization may lead to more investment, more research and development, a better motivated labor force, more engineers, or whatever else is required for higher output and profits. Indeed, if the Japanese and American economies were compared, any neutral observer would say that the American economy came closer to being described by the equilibrium price-auction model, but that the Japanese economy performs better. Why? Economists can retreat to vague references about "cultural differences," but that hardly flatters economic theories that are supposed to be applicable across all of human behavior.

Empirical Refutations

In the physical sciences, empirical observations can often be used to confirm or dismiss some particular theoretical hypothesis. If it had not been a fact that light is bent by the gravitational field of the sun, scientists would have dismissed much of Einstein's work. But it is usually impossible to find a definitive experiment where the outcome will prove one group of economists right and the other wrong so conclusively that those who are wrong will recognize that they are in error and recant. And even when definitive empirical experiments can be constructed on paper, it is usually impossible to implement them because no one is willing to let economists experiment with his economy or livelihood. Moreover, since economic reality is always much more complex than any theory, it is always possible to shift to an alternative theory to account for any one puzzling fact. In general, no one fact can beat the equilibrium price-auction model. In economics, only a more persuasive theory can beat the present theory.

Economists can, for example, always retreat to unobservable variables to explain unwelcome facts. The price-auction model, for example, calls for equal wages for those with identical skills, but it is very difficult to find those predicted homogeneous wage groups.[7] No matter how fine the background classifications, the job descriptions, and other explanatory variables, the variance in earnings within each group in the United States is almost as large as the variance in earnings for the population as a whole. But economists can claim that unobservable variables are at work. In this case the most frequently used is the "willingness to take risks." Seemingly equal workers earn different wages because some are more willing to take risks than others. But since no one knows how to measure the "willingness to take risks," this is an explanation that cannot be definitively proven or refuted. Either one believes it or one doesn't.

Or it may be said that identical workers are getting different amounts of psychic income (nonmonetary benefits such as pleasant working conditions) from their jobs.[8] These nonmonetary benefits lead money incomes to differ but leave total incomes, money plus psychic, identical. Here again the explanation may be true, but there is no way to prove it.

Or the observation can be dismissed as a "market imperfection"—something that exists but should be eliminated to bring the real economy into conformity with price-auction theory. Union induced seniority wages might, for example, be preventing homogeneous wages from developing. The solution for those who see a "market imperfection" is to eliminate the problem—unions. If the economic actors are not doing what they are supposed to be doing, something is wrong with either the actors or the market. In short, the theory is always right.

Slight differences in semantic definitions also often become important to economists. Consider again the raging dispute about whether the labor market clears as the standard model says it clears. Specifically, is there such a thing as involuntary unemployment? Everyone agrees that in a simple textbook labor market no involuntary unemployment could exist. Everyone agrees further that government statistical agencies will find people who say that they would like to work but cannot find work.

But what does it really mean to be involuntarily unemployed? Are you involuntarily unemployed if you were laid off while others with identical skills are still working at the wage rate you used to get? Or to be involuntarily unemployed, must you demonstrate that you cannot find any work at any wage rate? Many are involuntarily unemployed in the first sense; fewer in the second sense.

How long must you search before you are classified as involuntarily unemployed? Suppose you are looking for a job which you will eventually find but which it takes several weeks to find. Are you involuntarily unemployed during those weeks or are you simply investing (absorbing necessary search costs) in your human capital?

Suppose you have some particular job skill, and you go to a firm that employs workers in your job category and offer to work for less than those already employed. If the employer refuses your offer, is this evidence of involuntary unemployment? Or is it evidence that your offer was not low enough to cover the transaction costs of hiring you, an unknown new worker, and firing a known old worker? Or is it an example of an isolated market imperfection (a stupid employer) which you just happened to uncover?

Consider the Keynesian observation that real wages did not fall in response to unemployment in the Great Depression. During that time, money wages fell, but prices fell just as fast, so that real wages remained constant despite a 25 percent unemployment.[9] The existence of rigid real wages can be accepted as a fact but seen as a market imperfection springing from the economic collapse of the Great Depression, a peculiar and unique period.

In any case, since World War II, unemployment has not been high enough to reduce money wages. Some economists would explain this by arguing that what is measured as unemployment is "voluntary" unemployment and not real "involuntary" unemployment. So 11 percent of the work force is asserted to be simply spending time looking for jobs they really want. Wages *would* respond to real involuntary unemployment. There just hasn't been any. How is this absence of unemployment known? Wages haven't fallen as they would have if there had really been any involuntary unemployment.

Thus what appears as wage rigidity—no downward movements in response to rising unemployment—is in fact simply a stable wage produced by an equilibrium labor market. It should be noticed, however, that the whole argument has become completely circular. Real unemployment exists only if wages are falling. If wages aren't falling, there is no real unemployment, no matter how "real" it may seem to be to those not initiated into the mysteries of economics.

Economic events are also seen to be produced by two processes. One of them is the deterministic process which economists seek to model, but the other is a stochastic and random process that cannot be modeled. Oil or grain prices are subject to the deterministic rules of economics, but they also get hit by large stochastic and random shocks such as the OPEC price increases of 1973 and 1979, or bad weather. As a result, any one fact can always be seen as a random deviation from the predictions of economic theory. In short, the economic weather is becoming more and more unpredictable for unknown reasons.

So, in general, an economist's prior beliefs about what is true play a very important role in the way he sees economic evidence. Once their beliefs are formed, it is difficult to prove any economist's priors wrong so convincingly that he will change his beliefs about the way the world works. And because of its seemingly comprehensive answers to all economic questions, the price-auction model creates a very strong set of prior beliefs.

A Nonexperimental Science

The public perception that economists do not agree on anything is probably even more disconcerting than the failures of economists to predict or control events. Something happens to the economy, and on the TV screen appear two economists who in the thirty seconds allotted them seem to be giving diametrically opposed economic views. If economists disagree that sharply, how can they possibly know *anything*? But economists disagree among themselves much less than the general public thinks, with most of the disagreements involving the noneconomic aspects of economic problems. The public's perception is not surprising, however, given the nature of economics as a discipline.

Economics is a nonexperimental science, and disagreement is common in any similar area where it is impossible to conduct laboratory experiments wherein tight control is maintained over the secondary variables not being studied. In 1980 there was a great dispute among nutritionists in the United States as to whether Americans should or should not eat butter. No agreement was possible in what, after all, seems like a relatively trivial matter. When it comes to burning more coal to generate electricity, meteorologists cannot agree whether the extra carbon dioxide will cause the earth to warm up, melt the polar icecaps, and flood most of the major cities of the world, or whether it will cause the world to cool off and our major cities to be crushed in another ice age. Before Mt. Saint Helens erupted, the MIT earth sciences department thought something might happen so they placed some remote telemetry instruments in the Pacific Northwest. But they put them on the wrong mountain.

Given such scientific disagreements and failures, the problems we have in economics are not surprising. Scientists can agree only when they are talking about some phenomenon that can be produced and replicated in the laboratory. Very few economic activities are laboratory phenomena, and if you look around, nonlaboratory scientific phenomena are subject to just as much disagreement and controversy as you will find in the economics profession. Economic forecasts are often wrong, but so are scientific ones about what will happen in the real world. Heavenly motion is the one great exception. Here it is possible to understand what goes on so well that the positions of the planets can be predicted millions of years into the future. It is the inspiration of this model that keeps everyone searching for deterministic process when events seem random and stochatic, but what astronomers can do in this instance should not be ascribed to science in general.

Indeed, scientists cannot discern the coming of earthquakes, major floods, and volcanic eruptions, all of which are more unpredictable than economic events. Often the failures compound themselves. If the weather cannot be predicted, economists cannot predict food prices or the demand for heating oil. If the political scientists cannot predict revolutions in Iran and wars in the Middle East or geologists cannot predict future oil supplies, economists cannot predict energy prices. For both economist and physical scientist, forecasts are difficult, because no one—scientist or economist—can predict the large random shocks that regularly occur outside the laboratory.

Consider geology and natural selection, scientific disciplines that do not lend themselves to experiments. Like economics, their ability to control or predict events is limited. But the fact that a lot of dry holes are drilled in the search for oil does not prove the intellectual bankruptcy of geology; more dry holes would be sunk without it. Relying on historical evidence, natural selection is full of missing links and controversies. Since no one has actually ever seen one species evolve into another, it is hard to settle arguments.

Economics is similar as a discipline, but also suffers from the fact that its subjects can learn and change their behavior. To explain economic behavior today does not necessarily mean you can explain it tomorrow. With learning, even the ability to conduct laboratory experiments would not eliminate many of the problems facing economics. If economists are to be charged with any crime, it is not that of knowing too little relative to what they *can* know, but with the crime of being too certain about what they think they do know.

The Best Economic Game

Economics is like other disciplines in that it attempts to deduce theories that allow it to describe and predict reality, but it differs from all other fields because it also has a theory of what "ought" to be. This explains why economists are always recommending the elimination of this or that "market imperfection," like the unions mentioned earlier. In fact, any unpopular regulation is denounced by those not liking it as a market imperfection. In contrast, no astrophysicist recommends the elimination of planets (observations) that he does not like as "market imperfections."

Here the economists' recommendations flow from the peculiar role that the concept of a free market plays in economic theory. The equilibrium price-auction model is not just a tool used by economists to describe and predict events. The particular economic game called free competitive markets is regarded as the *best* economic game. It is assumed to produce the highest possible welfare, and at best, other economic games can only equal its performance. As a result, economists feel at liberty to recommend the "free market" to society and to recommend that actual economic games be made to conform with the free-market game.

Think the academic division between economics departments and business schools. While economics departments work out ever more sophisticated versions of the free-market game and watch for market imperfections imposed by government or monopolies, business schools teach students how to become better maximizers within the constraints of the free market. If economists successfully get their point across in business schools, they guarantee that at least part of their economic theory—the existence of profit maximizing producers—will come into being. No other discipline attempts to make the world act as it thinks the world should act. But of course what Homo sapiens does and what Homo economicus should do are often quite different. That, however, does not make the basic model wrong, as it would in every other discipline. It just means that actions must be taken to bend Homo sapiens into conformity with Homo economicus. So, instead of adjusting theory to reality, reality is adjusted to theory.

What this creates, however, is a lot of confusion both among economists and the public as to whether economists are speaking as predictors or as prescribers. Suppose some economist says that energy price increases cannot cause inflation. Is he saying that higher energy prices do not cause inflation in the real-world economy, or is he saying that higher energy prices would not cause inflation in a perfectly competitive free market where any price increase must be balanced with price decreases somewhere else in the system?

The belief that competitive free markets constitute the best possible economic game also rests on a highly restrictive set of assumptions. The conclusions are technically correct only in a static world of fixed tastes and static technology where the basic economic problem is one of exchange. Every economist knows the dozens of restrictive assumptions (perfect knowledge, ease of entry, exogenous independent preferences) that are necessary to "prove" that a free market is the best possible economic game, but they tend to be forgotten in the play of events.

If tastes are endogenous (created in the process of conducting economic activities), it is not obvious, for example, that a free market leads to the highest possible welfare. If tastes differ depending on what economic game is actually being played, competitive markets with their opportunities for invidious comparisons might make people more unhappy with their standard of living than some other economic game where the "winner" is not the one with the most goods and services. The perverse preference of envy (my welfare goes down when your income goes up), for example, destroys the nice utility maximizing outcome of any free-market economic game where everyone is supposed to look at his own income and only his own income when judging his welfare.

The economic game played by Homo economicus may or may not be the best economic game for Homo sapiens, but it is almost always so advocated by economists.[10]

Different Uses of Economic Models

Many of the disputes among economists stem from a failure to understand the different uses to which economic models can be put.

1. Economic models can be used to describe and organize events or ideas.
2. They can be used to understand what would happen in a controlled environment.
3. They can be used to predict what will happen in the real world.
4. They can be used to design policies to influence and control economic events.
5. They can be used as normative models to indicate how a perfectly rational Homo economicus should act and how his activities should be organized.

Physicists can predict heavenly motion, but they cannot control or influence it. A model of how Homo economicus ought to act does not necessarily let the economist accurately describe how homo sapiens in fact does act. To understand the complex chemical and physical interactions between air, water, and earth in the laboratory does not necessarily allow the meteorologist to predict the weather, but it does tell him what he should look for. Tide tables can be published, even though actual tides will often differ significantly from those published.

Given a clever economist armed with a concept that can't measure anything in the real world, any activity can be described and organized as if it were the outcome of a free-market maximization process. All consumption purchases represent utility maximization; all job choices represent income (psychic plus money) maximization. There is nothing wrong with formulating models with unknown and in principle unknowable variables if everyone is clear that the result is merely a descriptive model that might help us catalogue activities. The capacity to provide such descriptions, however, does not mean that the model is an economic model in any of the other four senses. To be that, the model must be capable of being proved wrong.

Because economists cannot measure nonobservable variables such as psychic income, they cannot make predictions from a model based upon them. And if you don't understand how these unobservable variables are created, you can't understand economic activity in the real world. But without that, influence or control over the economy is impossible. Yet economists often talk as if they can do all of these things simply because they can build a descriptive model.

Economists who hold this view in its most extreme form cling to the following syllogism: (1) The price-auction market is the most efficient economic game that man can play. (2) More efficient economic games drive less efficient economic games out of business. (3) Therefore the real economic game must be an equilibrium price-auction game.

The only remaining problem is to understand how what is not a price-auction in form and what often appears to be out of equilibrium is in fact an equilibrium price-auction, or acts "as if" it were. The assumption here is that markets are as close to perfection as they can be, not because we have proved it, but because we know that it must be so. Other than recommending that government get out of the way (there are even recent tendencies to eliminate this reservation), there is nothing that can be done to ensure maximum efficiency.

As they deal with public policies, economists have not placed enough emphasis on the distinction between control and influence. For the same reason that economic events are not predictable, they are not completely controllable. At any moment will come unpredicted influences and stochastic shocks as well as policy impacts. The 1968 tax increase, for example, influenced the economy—it grew more slowly than it otherwise would have—but other events led it to expand faster than was desired or predicted.[11] Policies exist to influence the economy, but they do not, of course, exist to control the economy.

Value Judgments

Public-policy recommendations are also subject to dispute because of the noneconomic value judgment that has to be made to advocate my policy. The basic problem springs from the fact that there are no public policies so good that everyone's income goes up or so bad that everyone's income goes down. In short, every policy has income-distribution effects. In economic theory it is possible to avoid the problem using the concept of Pareto optimality, in which concept state A is better than state B if the winners in state A could compensate the losers in state B. And since this is always possible as long as the GNP in state A is bigger than the GNP in state B, Pareto optimality is reduced to a simple problem of whether the GNP is or is not larger. In the real world, however, the potential ability to make compensatory payments becomes irrelevant. They only become relevant if they are actually made, and they are almost never made in live economies. Consequently, any economic policy recommendation must contain two major elements.

First, there has to be some hard economic information as to whose income will go up and whose income will go down, and the net result of those gains and losses. Is the GNP in fact larger or smaller? This is the scientific part of every economic problem.

Second, however, there is an ethical value judgment as to whose income "ought" to go up or down, which has nothing to do with technical economics but usually lies at the heart of public-policy differences. For example, everyone agrees that a windfall profit tax on natural gas will reduce the supply of gas below what it otherwise would be. While there are minor disagreements as to how much of a drop in gas supplies will occur, the major disagreement is focused on whether the drop is a price worth paying to prevent shifts in the distribution of income that would occur if natural-gas prices were simply deregulated, with the fruits of higher prices going to the natural-gas firms.

"What should we do about problem X?" (where X may be inflation, productivity, unemployment, or some other public problem) is a question commonly posed and answered by economists, but it is a question designed to produce disagreement. The issue again is only partly technical. Ought America to raise unemployment to stop inflation? Different economists have different answers to the "ought" question, even if they agree on the technical outcome and the distribution of gains and losses.

To find the professional economic disagreements, a different question must be asked. "If we were to adopt policy Y, whose income will go up, whose income will go down, and how much?" In most circumstances this question will produce a substantial amount of agreement. Liberal and conservative economists most frequently disagree on who ought to be hurt and who ought to be helped. Their technical disagreements on who will be hurt and who will be helped are much less frequent. But by the very fact that we can use the words "liberal" and "conservative" when referring to economists, we are saying that the discipline is a peculiar one. No one talks of liberal or conservative chemists, but only of chemists who in their private lives happen to be liberals or conservatives.

No economic dispute better illustrates the problem of ethical value judgments than the perennial controversy over the minimum-wage laws.[12] What is fought over as if it were a dispute about economic facts is really a dispute about the values that society "ought" to follow. The pertinent economic facts are widely accepted by all economists, whether they are for or against the minimum-wage laws.

All agree that the minimum wage will create some unemployment for those whose productivity is below that wage. All agree that it will raise the wages of other intramarginal workers who remain employed and get the new higher minimum wage. All agree that if the elasticity of the demand curve is less than one (a 1 percent increase in wages will lead to a less than one percent reduction in employment), the total income going to those in the low wage group (employed and unemployed) will go up. The elasticity of the demand curve is estimated to be less than one by both liberal and conservative economists.

As a result, all agree that aggregate incomes will go up, but that there will be a group of losers who will be forced into unemployment because of the higher wage rate. And no disagreement exists about who those losers are. The minimum wage raises the income and employment of adults, especially females, while concentrating unemployment among teenagers.

Economists also agree that the minimum-wage laws are only loosely enforced, with minimal penalties for those who are caught violating it. Small businesses regularly violate the law, and millions of workers are simply illegally paid less than the minimum wage. So whatever the theoretical effects, the actual effects are much smaller because of the enforcement problem. Those who must obey the minimum-wage laws are large firms which would be embarrassed to have it publicly revealed that they were deliberately violating the law of the land.

Moreover, there are regulations allowing employers to pay only 75 percent of the minimum wage to full-time students and young people receiving training. The relatively sparse use of these provisions and the failure to enforce the minimum wage indicates that a subminimum wage for teen-agers would have only a minor effect on teen-age employment. It is also agreed that many of the people, especially teen-agers, who do or would benefit from higher minimum wages come from families that are not poor. Thus the income-distribution effects of the minimum wage are not highly favorable to the poor. Most of the redistribution occurs among the women and children of lower-middle-income families.

Given all the agreement, why the enormous disputes about the minimum wage in general and a subminimum for teen-agers in particular? The answer is simple. The minimum-wage dispute is not a quarrel about economic facts, but a political dispute about whether government should or should not intervene in the market to alter incomes. Is the good society a laissez-faire society or one in which government intervenes to produce a "good" distribution of income? It is an important question, but not primarily an economic one.

Economic Imperatives

Economic decisions also seem more controversial and subject to less agreement because of the context in which the decisions are made. Often decisions have to be made and cannot be postponed no matter how great the uncertainty and ignorance. For example, if scientists are uncertain as to whether the space shuttle will work, they will abort or postpone the flight. But if economists are equally uncertain about whether a policy will work, the economic voyage cannot be canceled or postponed. It simply proceeds, and the repairs have to be made while the ship is under way. Moreover, the voyage affects everyone, not just a few who have volunteered to become astronauts. So because repairs have to be made during a voyage that is already under way with everyone on board, it is not possible to be an agnostic about economic alternatives. Everyone is forced to take a position on what must be done, regardless of his ignorance.

Macro-economic decisions seem more controversial than micro-economic ones because the latter can be made on an individual basis. I may make a mistake, but it is my mistake. And when I make a mistake, I seldom advertise the fact. In contrast, macro-economic decisions must be made in a political context under the glare of public scrutiny. Communal mistakes may be no more prevalent than individual mistakes, but they get reported. The misleading statement is often made that public officials are playing with our money while private businessmen are playing with their own. In the case of people who run large corporations, however, the managers are no more playing with their own money than any public official. Still, the glare of publicity is more intense in the public than in the private sector.

Being public, economic advice has to become a form of salesmanship. The public must buy the solution being advocated, and good selling seldom occurs if you draw attention to the defects of the product being sold. No one has ever convinced the public to undertake some action by appearing uncertain about his information or theories. Exaggerating the qualities of the product is more effective and thus more common among economists, as well as others, who seek to alter public decisions. And because much of economics is conducted in a political environment, the claim to absolute certainty is understandable though regrettable.

The present supply-side economics of the Reagan Administration presents a good example of the phenomenon. The predicted positive effects of the Reagan tax cuts were so large that few economists believed them, but their advocates nonetheless predicted them with great certainty. Supply-side economics may be wrong, but it sold very well indeed.

CHAPTER 2

Economic Failures

Typhoons and Tidal Waves

For economists the golden age of the profession encompassed a relatively brief period in the first half of the 1960s. It was then that economists were perceived as having all the right answers—their forecasts were correct and their policy recommendations worked.

Since the economy itself was performing satisfactorily and all appeared under control, there was little change in the ocean currents of economics thought. But with the onset of the economic failures of the 1970s, economists *seemed* to lose control over economic events. One can argue that memories are too short, or that the public expected too much, or that bad luck had supplanted good luck, or that the perception of economic failure was false. But the perception of failure produced a sea change in the basic intellectual currents of economics. In relatively short order, Keynesian analysis and its practitioners went from the front cover of *Time* magazine to being widely condemned as failures.

The Macro-Typhoons

The 1950s witnessed three recessions, with real per capita disposable income growing 19 percent during the decade—not much compared with the 32 percent growth achieved in the 1960s or the 26 percent in the maligned 1970s.[1] In fact, economic discontent was high during the 1950s, hardly a sound basis for the nostalgia that often suffuses that seemingly uneventful decade.

As the late 1950s ended, Americans were worried about their own poor performance, economic and military, vis-à-vis the Russians. Sputnik orbited the earth, our satellites didn't. At the United Nations, Khrushchev banged his shoe on the desk in a temper tantrum and promised the United States, "We'll bury you!" The American people were afraid that he might. There was, after all, a missile gap and a growth gap.

Responding to public discontent, the Kennedy economists designed a set of tax cuts and investment incentives—the investment tax credit, accelerated depreciation—which pushed the economy to a 4.7 percent annual rate of growth from 1960 to 1965 and reduced unemployment to 4 percent by the end of 1965 while keeping the average inflation rate at 1.6 percent.[2] And not only were the results good, they were precisely what had been forecast.

Nothing succeeds like success, and the most visible members of the economic profession—those working on macro-economic policies in Washington—bathed in recognition and esteem. In truth, these economists may have been very lucky, since in the last half of the 1960s they failed as miserably as they had succeeded in the first half. But the public did not care whether they were right because they had been lucky or whether they were right because they had been right. They had succeeded.

This claimed and apparent success established the economics profession as the cause of success or failure in the economy itself. Earlier practitioners received neither the credit for good times nor the blame for bad. Now the success of the profession was linked to the success of the economy with both on the front lines together. This meant that economists literally became the messengers bringing good and bad news. Government economists gave the press briefings in which good or bad economic statistics were released, and they explained their significance to both the media and Congress. Meanwhile, television news teams sought out economists to interpret the economic events of the day. What the profession forgot in its new-found celebrity was that messengers bringing bad news have had a rough time of it for at least two thousand years.

As is usually the case, economic imperialism sets in when a period of vigorous republican growth ends. Reputations often lag behind events and may even be on the rise at precisely the time that new developments are at work to discredit those very reputations.

An Age of Imperialism

This happened to economists and economics. If the early 1960s were the economists' golden age, the late 1960s and early 1970s became the age of economic imperialism.

Economists filled journals with articles on the economics of crime, marriage, suicide, and other social phenomena once regarded as the exclusive preserves of other social sciences.[3] Economists thought they had a better analytical apparatus for studying these phenomena than other social scientists, and what's more, their imperial claims were accepted by many other academics. No self-respecting law school or medical school could exist without its economists, and members of the profession regularly appeared on the rosters of university departments of social work, engineering, and urban and architectural studies, as well as traditional economics departments and business schools. Joint degree programs sprang up almost everywhere with almost every other discipline as graduate students in other departments and schools felt that a substantial part of their course work had to be done in economics. To protect their flanks against the inroads of economists, other academics felt that they had to become more like economists.

Yet at the same time the economy itself was widely perceived as out of control with economists unable to remedy the situation. Without warning, double-digit inflation and unemployment arrived simultaneously. Though the economy did not collapse, the readers of newspaper headlines often felt it had. Meanwhile, economists neither predicted the advent of the problems nor seemed to have solutions for them as traditional economic wisdom became discredited.

The imperial summit was probably reached when the Carter Administration took office in 1976. Five of the sixteen Cabinet members had Ph.D.s in economics, with only four being the lawyers who normally occupied the corridors of public power.

Yet the public esteem of economists had never been lower. Some months earlier, at a League of Women Voters' presidential primary panel on economics, Senator Henry Jackson provoked the only real burst of audience favor when he asserted that it was time to stop listening to economists. Jackson was tapping a well of public animosity that was to become increasingly apparent. With bad times sinking their reputation, Johnny Carson's evening monologues portrayed economists as ludicrous modern witch doctors unable to explain or control the economy's mysterious gyrations.

At the same time, economics was recognized as a science with the establishment of a Nobel Prize. Economic forecasting services such as Data Resources, Chase Econometrics, and Wharton flourished; major antitrust cases came to employ almost as many economists as lawyers; corporations upgraded their internal economics departments. Previously most large corporations had had an economics department, but they resembled the pillars on Scarlett O'Hara's mansion—an imposing façade, but not much real use and never entrusted to provide basic inputs that would be used for actual decision making. Now no self-respecting company could exist without its in-house economic forecasts and without its miniature econometric model of the markets that it faced.

The decline in public esteem for economists had begun with the 1968 tax increase, one that was supposed to stop the inflation engendered by the Vietnam war. By today's standards the inflation during the Johnson Admininstration seems mild (3.3 percent per year from 1965 to 1968), but it was then considered intolerable.[4] The 1968 tax increase, the standard Keynesian remedy for inflation brought on by excessive aggregate demand, was supposed to slow excessive growth in that demand and to stop inflation. But the measure did not work, inflation actually accelerated, and by 1970 was running at 6 percent. For the first time in a decade, economic forecasts were wrong and recommended economic policies did not seem to produce results.

It is easy now to understand why inflation did not abate.[5] Increases in Vietnam defense spending were larger than expected and offset some of the increase in taxes. There was also an unexpected boom in auto sales that carried the rest of the economy with it. Finally, lag times were long and the inflationary momentum more ingrained than expected. But whatever the reasons for the failure or however unfair it was to blame the failure on the economics profession (privately President Johnson's economic advisers warned him of the impending disaster of his Vietnam policies), the fact remained that there was failure. As the Vietnam war escalated, the economics profession was going to be delivering more bad news. Its forecasts were going to be wrong and its policies were not going to work.

In 1969 the Nixon economists took over from the Kennedy-Johnson economists. The Nixon people had a strategy to stop inflation based upon the then widely accepted Phillips curve. The following positions and policies were adopted: the economy would be deliberately stopped with the late acting help of the Johnson tax increase, unemployment would be raised, and inflation would be pushed out of the economy. The economy would then be reflated back to a full employment but not beyond, in time for the 1972 election.[6] As predicted, growth stopped and unemployment rose, but inflation continued apace. In the months just before the imposition of wage and price controls in August 1971, inflation stood at a 6 percent annual rate.

At the same time the dollar was coming under periodic attack as overvalued in currency exchanges. While there is no technical reason why a falling dollar should be perceived as evidence for economic failure, it was so regarded by almost everyone—especially by a people proud of the phrase "as sound as the dollar," and who had not seen a dollar losing value relative to other currencies in living memory. The economy seemed under assault from both without and within, an impression compounded in August 1971 when President Nixon announced that the United States would leave the gold standard and adopt wage and price controls—a policy that he had repeatedly forsworn in the past. Suddenly the rocks upon which the economy was presumably buttressed seemed more like quicksand.

Other unforeseen shocks followed. In 1972 the Russian wheat deal led to an unexpected explosion in grain prices, an explosion that should nonetheless have been predicted. Absent a significant shortfall in Russian wheat production, grain prices had no reason to rise. But given the shortfall and the Russian wheat sale, even the most ignorant economist should have predicted rapidly climbing prices. We simply sold more grain to the Russians than we had to sell at prevailing prices.

While economists were blamed for failing to predict the

skyrocketing food prices that resulted, as far as anyone knows no economists in or out of government were consulted on the inflationary impacts of the sale. The deal was made in secret, and what various Nixon officials knew about it is, and was, a subject of controversy. Some say that the United States was simply outsmarted by the USSR. Centrally planned Communism took advantage of unplanned capitalism to simultaneously place orders and buy a large fraction of available supply without disturbing prices. When Americans discovered what had happened, prices soared. Others see it as a conspiracy organized by the big American grain-trading companies to increase their profits by using inside information obtained from various assistant secretaries of Agriculture. Still others see it as part of a Kissinger deal to extract American troops from Vietnam. Everyone now agrees that economists played no role in the initial decision to sell grain to the Russians. But economists were still blamed for the food inflation produced by the deal; they brought the bad news to the public; bad news that could have been avoided, it was presumed, had economists been properly advising policy makers.

Food prices are especially sensitive politically, since people buy food several times a week, watch prices closely, and know when they are up. Durable-goods inflation is much less sensitive, since consumers do not buy the products regularly, do not remember what they last paid, and do not know how much of any hike in prices is due to an improvement in quality rather than to general inflation.

In any case, the lifting of wage and price controls and the jump in food prices quickly redeposited the inflation rate at 6 percent in 1973. This should have been entirely expected given an overheated economy facing grain shortages, but the inflation rate served to discredit wage and price controls as a policy instrument. The "liberal remedy" had been tried by a conservative President and found "wanting." Here again one could argue that wage and price controls had not been given a fair test, but fairness was irrelevant. Controls were imposed and for whatever reason they had failed.

In late 1973 the first OPEC oil shock struck, as oil prices quadrupled and the general inflation indexes shot up to 11 percent. More important, gasoline lines appeared. Waiting in line to buy a basic commodity like gasoline is something that no American had ever experienced. Shock and irritation were high, but those lines were like the first small heart attack—an indication of mortality. Maybe the American economy was growing old and becoming vulnerable. Maybe the American economic dream of an ever rising standard of living was over. Small may be beautiful, but if that phrase meant a lower standard of living, then the average American considered it a nightmare.[7]

The Nixon-Ford Administration responded with oil and gas price controls. As a vehicle for holding down prices, controls were bound to fail. For one thing, world prices would have to be paid on that part of consumption imported from abroad; for another, controls make it too easy for oil companies to hold oil in the ground or not to look for new supplies oil until prices rose. When controls did fail, the public's feeling that the federal government and its economists were incapable of managing anything efficiently was further reinforced.

What was worse, economists could pose no solution to the energy problem. Influential professionals, such as Milton Friedman, predicted that the oil cartel would quickly fall apart. It didn't. Other economists recommended that prices be allowed to climb to world levels, but that wasn't a solution to the problem faced by the average American. Higher prices would force him to change his life style. He might respond to higher prices with smaller cars and colder houses as economists predicted, but he liked doing neither and he could vote. No one considered a forced change in life style a solution.

Once again, falling back on the principle that higher unemployment would produce lower inflation, monetary authorities tightened the rate of growth of the money supply in an effort to slow the economy, raise unemployment, and push inflation out of the economy. This time the policies produced a credit crunch. For six months in late 1974 and early 1975 the GNP fell at the fastest rate ever recorded. Even the rates of decline in the Great Depression had been less precipitous—although of course longer and deeper. Anxieties quickly shifted from an unacceptable inflation rate to an unacceptable unemployment rate, and the term "stagflation" was born.

Stagflation was both a term and an indictment, since econo-

mists had taught that the phenomena—slow growth, rising
unemployment, and rising inflation—could not all exist at the
same time. Yet they did.

To the professional economist analyzing the events after the
fact, the events were eminently explainable. The excess aggregate demand inflation set off by spending for the Vietnam war
was compounded by energy and food price shocks. To coun-
teract the inflationary shocks, the government deliberately
tightened monetary and fiscal policies to slow economic
growth, raise unemployment, and push inflation out of the
economy. Meanwhile the oil price hike both boosted the inflation rate and stopped economic growth. Paying more for oil
was, after all, nothing but a tax increase legislated by foreign
governments. Because the inflation rate lags behind economic
events, the economy slows down and unemployment rises before inflation decelerates. And in fact, inflation fell rather
quickly in response to the 1975 recession. By 1976 the rate was
less than 6 percent per year. But the public expected something better. Compounding these woes, of course, was Watergate, which, among other things, produced the strong
impression that the Nixon Administration was not only in-
competent but crooked.

Although Jimmy Carter recruited many economists to serve
in his Administration, the profession's reputation was on the
skids. Objectively speaking, everything was as bad or worse in
1980 as in 1976. Inflation rose from 5.8 percent in 1976 to 13.5
percent in 1980. Unemployment fell from 7.7 percent to 7.1
percent, but it had reached 5.8 percent in 1979 and was climbing rapidly near the end of Carter's four years. Meanwhile,
economic growth fell from 5.5 percent in 1977 to minus 0.2
percent in 1980.[8] Subjectively speaking, things were worse
than they were objectively. The Administration seemed to
lack an economic rudder. Carter's term of office began with a
$50 dollar tax rebate that was proposed and then quickly with-
drawn, and in his final year he proposed a budget, withdrew
it, and then resubmitted it within a few weeks when it failed
to gain the confidence of the financial markets. In both instances the changes of course were so sudden that they could
not be seen as responses to changing realities, but had to be
regarded as signs of the policy makers' incompetence and in-
decisiveness.

Making Carter's problems still worse was the gradual decline in the rate of productivity growth—the ultimate determinant of a country's standard of living. While the onset of the decline is now dated back to 1965, no one paid much, if any, attention until the last half of the 1970s. By that time productivity growth had slowed from over 3 percent per year to 1 percent and was about to enter the negative range in 1978. The economics profession could with some justification be charged with ignoring the country's major supply-side problem.

With productivity slowing down and finally falling, our standard of living could only grow more slowly and then fall. No one can assert that the economics profession caused productivity to fall, but no one likes such a situation regardless of whose fault it is. Accordingly, the economics profession, the scapegoat as before, should have kept the American standard of living rising. Or like an investment adviser who makes mistakes on behalf of his client, the entire profession should have been fired.

In many ways the early 1980s can be seen as a replay of the early 1960s. After a period of extreme dissatisfaction with American economic performance, a new group of economists took over. In 1981 the Reagan supply-side economists were making predictions that were even more glowing than those made twenty years earlier. If supply-side policies were put in place, the predictions had it, inflation would drop to 4 percent in 1985 and growth would accelerate to 4.5 percent per year in 1982 and stay there.[10] While tight monetary policies would stop inflation, large tax and social welfare cuts combined with large increases in defense spending would trigger economic growth. The standard of living would begin very quickly to climb once more.

If the supply-siders and monetarists succeed because they were right or because they were lucky, they will succeed in enhancing the reputation not only of themselves but of the economics profession—including those that disagree with them. Economists will once again be perceived as messengers delivering good news and as the cause of that good news. The controversies now buffeting economics will cease, and intellectual calm will return. But if the supply-siders and monetarists fail because they were wrong (as seems likely in the winter of

1983) or simply because they encountered bad luck, controversies will intensify and their failure will be seen as the failure of the entire profession.

Micro-Mirror Images of Macro-Failures

While the macro-economic failures of the public policy makers appear in the headlines every day, the micro-economic failures in prediction and control are equally large and just as corrosive to public confidence in the economics profession. In fact, much of what is perceived as a macro-failure is a failure in micro-economics. If success or failure in predicting and controlling events determines whether an economic theory is solid and deserves respect, then micro-theory is in as bad a shape as macro-theory.

Unforeseen and uncontrollable price shocks in energy and grain markets are failures in micro-economic prediction and control—not macro-failures. And micro-economic efforts to control food or energy prices were no more successful than macro-economic efforts to control inflation in general. Those analyzing investment decisions, human and physical, should have foreseen the slowdown in productivity and recommended policies to stop it. If wages are rising faster than productivity and causing inflation, that is a micro-economic phenomenon. If macro-economic failures are shaking the foundations of macro-economic theory, micro-economic failures should be similarly shaking the foundations of micro-economic theory, but the latter failures have no such effect.

Consider the standard economic recommendation of the 1950s and early 1960s for protecting oneself from inflation. Conventional wisdom had it that to preserve wealth, one had merely to invest in corporate stocks. According to the verbal traditions of the staff of the President's Council of Economic Advisers, Paul Samuelson is supposed to have said in the early 1960s that anyone who did not protect himself from inflation by buying corporate equities was so stupid that he deserved to lose his wealth.[11] Prices could rise only if corporations were raising prices, and therefore corporate stocks had to be a hedge against inflation. In fact, corporate equities were the worst possible inflation hedge. From 1968 to August 1982 the real value of common stocks fell 54 percent as measured by the

New York Stock Exchange Index, and 65 percent as measured
by the Dow Jones industrial average.

Economists could come up with many possible after-the-fact
explanations for the poor performance of corporate equities.
Some pointed out that since oil prices were set not by American corporations but by foreign governments, prices could rise
without corresponding increases in American incomes. Others
asserted that because taxes were not indexed, the tax collector
was taking a larger bite of real profits. Still others said that
inflation produced greater variance in prices and hence more
risk and uncertainty that had to be compensated for in the
form of lower prices. With an unhappy electorate, economic
risks were compounded by the political risks of government
interventions designed to hold prices (and hence profits) down.
Both events increase the risk premium used to evaluate future
earnings streams and net present values decline. Another
group pointed out that investors might be discounting future
earnings for the under depreciation of plant and equipment,
but failing to correct their balance sheets to reflect the lower
real value of corporate debt.[12] Future earnings might be discounted with interest rates that reflect inflation, but those
same inflationary expectations might not be embedded in the
estimated future earnings streams as they ought to be. Alternatively, public subsidies for housing might be so large that they
were simply attracting funds out of the equity markets.

All of these explanations were offered. Some or all of them
may even be true. But regardless of the persuasiveness of these
explanations, the fact remains that economists' standard remedy for protecting capital values in a period of inflation failed
—the bottom line being that the best micro-economic wisdom
was no better than its macro-economic counterpart.

Consider also the problem of income inequality, a trouble-
some area where society tried to use micro-economic remedies. In the 1950s and 1960s blacks, women, and the poor all
began to demand a share of the American economic dream.
The standard answer to the problem of income inequality was
education. Economists argued that market earnings could be
raised and made more equal only if the distribution of human
capital were raised and made more equal. Put another way,
when the human capital possessed by blacks caught up with
the human capital possessed by whites, blacks would earn what

whites earned. Pump a more equal distribution of human capital into the economy, and a more equal distribution of earnings had to flow out of it. More human capital would also accelerate our productivity growth rate. The strategy was adopted and followed. It did not work.

The educational attainments of the labor force forged ahead in the 1970s, but productivity stopped growing by the end of the decade. By 1978 there was no educational gap between men and women who work at year-around full-time jobs (both have 12.0 median years of education), but women continue to earn 58 percent of what men earned. Education had become much more equally distributed since World War II, but the earnings of the top quintile rose from 19 times that of the bottom quintile in 1948 to 27 times that of the bottom quintile in 1980. Between 1950 and 1980, 80 percent of the black-white educational gap was eliminated, but only 50 percent of the income gap was eliminated for full-time full-year workers.[13]

One can think of many reasons why education may only have appeared to have failed to promote growth and equality when in fact it has succeeded. The positive effects of education may simply have been swamped by other factors. Among them, changes in the age-sex composition of the labor force have led to a more inexperienced work force, the demand for more part-time jobs has automatically led to more low-earnings workers, and unemployment is now higher than it used to be.

To factor out these alternative explanations one can look at the distribution of education for year-around full-time male workers 25+ years of age from 1968 to 1978. The distribution of education has become much more equal (see Table 1). Whereas the bottom quintile had 10.6 percent of total education in 1968, it had 12.4 percent of total education in 1978. Based on the proportion of total years of education possessed, the gap between the bottom and top quintiles should have been reduced by 20 percent. Moreover, a substantial narrowing of the earnings differential between educational classes has occurred (see Table 2). Over the ten-year period, the earnings of the lowest educational class rose 7 percent relative to that of the top educational class.

Since year-around full-time male workers 25+ years of age

Table 1

Distribution of Education and Income
Year-Around Full-Time Male Earners 25+ Years of Age

Quintiles	*Percent of Total Years of Education*		*Percent of Total Income*	
	1968	1978	1968	1978
Bottom	10.6%	12.4%	7.4%	7.5%
2	17.9	18.7	14.1	13.6
3	21.0	19.1	18.2	18.3
4	21.7	22.9	23.6	23.5
Top	28.7	26.8	36.7	37.0

have experienced both a more equal distribution of education and a compression in their relative wages across educational classes, a substantial reduction in income inequality should have occurred. *But it didn't.*

From 1968 to 1978 the distribution of earnings for year-around full-time male workers 25+ years of age was basically stable (see Table 1). If anything, there was a slight shift toward inequality. The top quintile gained and the second quintile lost. But more important, the large movement (something on the order of 30 percent) toward equality that should have occurred did not.

Most of the obvious factors (female participation rates, unemployment, part-time work) that might have offset growing educational equalities could not, of course, affect the data on employed year-around full-time male workers. Of the possible explanatory factors, only age remains. But on close examination neither can that variable explain what needs explaining. A rising proportion of young (25–34) workers with below-average earnings does, of course, raise income inequality. But this effect is more than offset by the equalizing effects of a falling proportion of elderly (55+) workers with below-average income and a falling proportion of middle aged (35–54) workers with above-average income. If the 1968–78 shift in the age distribution is applied to the 1968 distribution of earnings by age, the age shift should have caused the total variance in earnings to fall by 0.4 percent between 1968 and 1978. Shifts in age distribution deepen the mystery.

The one easy explanation for what happened is also ruled out by the observed changes in relative earnings across educational classes. If the supply of labor was becoming more equal but the demand for labor was becoming more unequal at the same time, then there is no mystery as to why the distribution of earnings failed to respond as forecast. Supply-side effects were working as predicted but were masked by unanticipated-demand side effects. The supply of college educated-labor went up, but the demand for it went up even more. But if demand effects had dominated supply effects, the observed differential in earnings across education classes would have risen. Since educational earnings differentials actually fell (see Table 2), the supply-side effects were demonstrably larger than the demand side effects. Shifts in market demands for educated labor cannot explain what needs to be explained to sustain the conventional price-auction human capital models.

Other explanations could be given for the failure (see Chapter 7), but as far as the public was concerned, the reasons for the failure were irrelevant. Society had a problem. To solve it, massive public and private expenditures were made based upon the recommendations of economists. The recommended solutions did not work. Society wants results, not explanations for failure. The consequences of the economists' failure to predict what would happen are real. Because of this perceived failure, President Reagan could abolish federal manpower and education programs with barely a whimper from the public.

In general, any review of public policies over the past thirty years will show that micro-economic recommendations based upon the equilibrium price-auction model have been as unsuccessful as any based on macro-economic theories.

The Reagan Administration, which proposed that economics be abolished as a field for funding at the National Science Foundation, has been mounting a strenuous attack on the once imperial position of the economist. But the stability of the profession's position—funds were cut but not eliminated—springs finally not from the degree of perceived success but from an understanding that the discipline has a client relationship with society. A few economists (Marx, Keynes, Beveridge) have strongly influenced society's agenda, but economists in

Table 2

Relative Earnings by Educational Attainment
Year-Around Full-Time Male Earners 25+ Years of Age

	Relative Earnings *(Average Earning as % of* *Earnings of High School Graduates)*	
Years of Education	1968	1978
0 to 8	62.9	65.1
8	77.0	78.4
9 to 11	86.5	85.5
12	100.0	100.0
13 to 15	116.9	109.5
16	153.4	139.5
17+	169.6	163.2

SOURCE: U.S. Bureau of the Census, *Current Population Reports.* Series P-60, #123, pp. 213 and 218, and #6, pp. 28 and 123.

general survive by being willing to work on society's agenda —whatever it is. In fact, the profession is willing to change its research interests and focus of attention very rapidly in response to society's perceived needs and funding largess.

In the 1950s the public's interest in economic growth in underdeveloped countries and in staying ahead of the Russians led to an explosion of theoretical models of economic growth and empirical studies into the sources of growth.[14] Although growth had traditionally been explained in terms of expanding capital and labor stocks, analysis indicated that a substantial fraction of the growth of the United States could not be ascribed to the growth of physical inputs. The economy's performance was above what would have been predicted from an analysis of the factors going into the economy. This extra "residual" gradually came to be associated with improvements in the quality, as opposed to the quantity, of capital and labor.

New pieces of equipment were used to perform tasks that could not be undertaken with old pieces of equipment. Laborers learned new skills, and managers learned to organize the same units of capital and labor more efficiently.

Accordingly, the expansion and dissemination of knowledge was seen to be a key ingredient in expanding the economy. Many of the post-Sputnik education programs were in fact based on this conclusion—education was perceived to be the route to economic success for the individual and the society.

Twenty years later, when economic growth slowed dramatically, the same type of analysis—growth accounting—produced large unexplained negative residuals.[15] Growth was less than what would have been expected from an analysis of factor inputs. There is not yet a general agreement on what these negative residuals should be ascribed to, but the profession seems to be moving toward the position that social unrest or a decline in the work ethic is responsible. But what is a satisfactory explanation for good news is not one for bad news. Once again, on the productivity front, the economists did not seem to understand what was happening.

Partly because of the importance of education to economic growth and partly because of society's interest in eliminating poverty and discrimination, the 1960s were marked by studies of the rates of return in educational investments.[16] Economists noted, of course, that many skills were created on the job rather than in formal education and training, but that was considered a mere technicality. Workers merely paid their employer (with wages below what they could otherwise be earning) rather than a school to teach them new skills.

Anomalies were noted. Economists work with models where identical wages are paid for identical skills. Yet the real world did not seem to be marked by equal wages for equal work. For most skills there was a rather wide distribution of wage rates. One consequence of this was that standard economic variables (skills, IQ, hours of work, etc.) could explain only 20 to 30 percent of the variance in individual earnings. But this was more or less ignored when it came to recommending public policies. Yet technically the equations were saying that 70 to 80 percent of earnings were randomly distributed and that only 20 to 30 percent were distributed in accordance with economic models. Twenty years later, when education failed to have the predicted effects on the distribution of income, economists came to recognize that the world was much less deterministic and more random (stochastic) than they had traditionally believed.

The problems and failures of the profession's conception of human capital were not sorted out. Instead the focus of attention shifted from problem to problem, with economists just staying ahead of their most recent failure. As it became obvious in the late 1960s and early 1970s that education and training programs were both expensive and did little to alter the distribution of earnings, public interest shifted. Welfare reform, minimum family incomes, and guaranteed jobs surfaced as headline social and economic issues.

A major part of the frustration here stemmed from the differences between what the public believed, or wanted to believe, and what economic analysis and government officials knew to be the case. Economic self-sufficiency for the poor was obtainable, but only if taxpayers were willing to put a very high price on "earned" as opposed to "transferred" income. Analysis demonstrated that it was often cheaper to give many low-skill individuals a lifetime income than it was to raise their earnings capacities by the same amount.

The conclusion led to the design of two variants of the negative income tax—incumbent President Nixon's family assistance plan and presidential candidate McGovern's demogrant plan. But among other things, the election results of 1972 demonstrated that taxpayers were unwilling to pay the necessary price for self-sufficiency, while at the same time being unwilling to give up the ideal of self-sufficiency. Because the voters were unwilling to make a choice, neither an efficient income-transfer program nor an adequate skill-augmentation program could be designed, proposed, and implemented.

Partly to test the feasibility of the idea and partly to postpone having to make decisions, a number of negative-income-tax experiments were conducted. These showed that the policy produced a small negative-work-effort effect for families with a working head. This was expected, since both the income effect (more income without working) and the substitution effect (higher taxes on income from work) were adverse to work effort. But politically the small negative effect was treated as evidence that the programs would not work.

What the programs were supposed to do was eliminate the high implicit tax rates of the welfare system for those that were on welfare. No longer would recipients face an economic world where a mother with children would find that $1 in earnings led to $0.50 reduction in her basic welfare benefit, a $0.25 increase in her rent paid to public housing authorities, and a $0.30 increase in her bills under Medicaid. Without high implicit taxes, advocates argued, more of the nonworking poor would go to work.

Although the experiments proved that the adverse work effects on the working poor were minimal and that the effects on the nonworking welfare poor were positive, nothing happened after the expenditure of hundreds of millions of dollars.[17] Hard economic information was irrelevant. When the Reagan Administration came to power it ignored a decade of research on benefit formulae. To "save" money, the implicit tax rates on the working poor were promptly increased. Benefits such as Medicaid were reduced more for every dollar earned.

The negative-income-tax programs were conceived during the economic successes of the 1960s and were buried when the atmosphere of economic failure intensified in the late 1970s. What the public was willing to think about had simply changed. Since any welfare-reform measure resulted in some short-run increase in costs (unless benefit levels were reduced substantially in high benefit states) to make it more efficient in the long run, all reforms were opposed. In the end, all of the effort expended in collecting better economic information was wasted. It was not fair to blame what happened on economists any more than it is fair to blame them for the bad macroeconomic policies pursued during the Vietnam war, but economists were nonetheless blamed.

Partly because of frustration with "unsolvable" social problems and partly because of concern with the environment, the public's interest once again shifted in the 1970s and began to focus on the environment and the limits to growth. Economists responded by dusting off the concept of externalities.

Whenever one person's actions have a direct impact on another person's economic welfare, externalities exist. Owners of factories that discharge smoke and force those around them to breathe dirty air are creating negative externalities. Conversely, if I drain my land and make it cheaper for you to drain yours, I am creating positive externalities (disregarding possible environmental considerations). In our technically advanced and highly congested society, one group's actions very often have an immediate impact on another group—airport noise, for example. Our technology has also produced long-standing externalities previously not recognized—the cancer-causing potential of asbestos fibers, for example.

The standard economic solution to the problem of externalities is to compensate the producer of them with charges (positive or negative) on those suffering (enjoying) the external effects. Pollution can, for example, be turned into market problems by imposing "effluent" charges. Individuals and business are charged for their polluting activities until these activities are reduced to the desired level, until the funds raised are adequate to clean up the environment, or until the funds raised are adequate to compensate those who must suffer the effects of pollution. Similarly, many safety problems can be turned into market problems with accident charges that are raised until they produce the desired level of safety or adequately compensate those being hurt. There are circumstances in which market solutions would be difficult to implement (cancer agents, for example, with long time delays), but such solutions can be used in many cases.

Yet despite the supposed influence of economists and our society's professed belief in market solutions, the approach was resisted by almost everyone. Environmentalists thought market solutions would not work or did not like the idea that pollution was for sale. Business did not want to pay for what it now got for nothing. So instead of internalizing externalities with "effluent" charges, society turned to direct regulation. To the public the regulatory approach seems to be direct and certain, while the "effluent" approach appeared indirect and uncertain of achieving the desired objectives.[18]

While the expansion of direct regulation was deplored by equilibrium price-auction economists, the same expansion breathed life into the field of industrial organization, an area of analysis that had been moribund for a number of decades. The types of regulation whose success was mixed when dealing with monopolies would be applied to safety and the environment.

Economists played only a small role in designing the new rules and regulations. Their major role has mostly been rearguard, as they argued that the benefits caused by rules and regulations were too small to justify the costs imposed. As a result, environmentalists have to a great extent come to see economists as enemies. Economists were in favor of a dirty environment—knowing the costs of everything but the value of nothing—though the profession generally was simply against the techniques being employed rather than the ultimate ends. The public perception was reinforced, however, by those particular economists most actively opposing environmental regulations. Often they were not interested in more efficient means of reaching the goals desired by environmentalists, but had other goals, such as restarting economic growth, at the top of their agenda.

.When the unexpected energy crisis hit, energy economics almost instantly jumped from a specialty employing only a handful of people to one that at times seems to be absorbing most of the profession. In a similar manner, the surge in agricultural prices breathed new life into agricultural economics. Stable industries do not interest economists intellectually. And, of course, society has little demand for their talents when prices are stable, output growing on some smooth path, and economic discontent slight.

In both the energy and food, substantial resources have gone into estimating better supply-and-demand relationships. At what prices will supply and demand match, and what supplies are to be expected as prices rise in the future? Both are critical questions. While a lot of good work was being done, none of this work could change the fundamental problem—energy and food prices were going to be erratic. If you feel unfairly treated at the gasoline pump, an understanding that your demand will go down by 10 percent for every 100 percent increase in the price does little to make you feel better. The public wanted a solution for the reductions in its standard of living induced by oil or food prices, not an explanation as to how the market would reduce their standard of living.

Spiraling food and energy prices led to the perception that the economy was out of control, which in turn led the profession to work on stochastic processes and optimal control mod-

els where events were subject to random shocks.[19] But more
work did not produce better economic performance.

For reasons that are not entirely clear, spectacular failures
in micro-economic predictions and control have not led to the
dramatic shifts in intellectual currents caused by the equally
large failures in macro-economics. But it is important to understand that the intellectual confidence in the price-auction
model has not been created by demonstrated success using the
model to make predictions, to control events, or to design
public policies.

It is, however, impossible to understand the prevailing currents of economics without understanding the perception of
macro-economic failure and micro-economic success. The failures have led to major changes in the intellectual currents of
macro-economics. Monetarism, supply-side economics, and rational expectations—all of which we will consider closely later
—have emerged or been strengthened by the macro-economic failures in the world at large. But equally large micro-
economic failures have little effect on the legitimacy of the
equilibrium price-auction model. Keynesian economics finds
itself in turbulent waters, but the price-auction ship sails
smoothly on, seemingly unaffected by the storms that should
be swamping it.

The result is testimony to the strength of the economics
profession's belief in the truth of the price-auction view of the
world. A tidal wave of truly enormous proportions would be
necessary to alter that belief. Yet if the equilibrium price-
auction model were judged as Keynesian macro-economics is
judged, it would be considered a failure.

CHAPTER 3

Inflation

A Psychological Storm

Nothing has upset the public more or done more to alter the currents of economic theory than the economists' inability to predict or control inflation. Yet few people outside the profession know that inflation does not matter in the standard model of economic behavior. Only relative prices—the price of one kind of goods in terms of another—matter. Accordingly, because a general increase in the price level does not affect relative prices in the equilibrium price-auction model, there is no theoretical reason for eschewing inflation. Yet the same price-auction economists are often the foremost proponents of the position that society should undertake drastic action to stop inflation. Since the concern of these economists cannot be derived from the economic theory in which they profess to believe, the concern reveals the profession's behavior when confronted with a discrepancy between economic theory and popular beliefs. In this case, as in most others—such as the importance of balanced budgets—popular beliefs win out.

Because no theoretical arguments lead anyone to believe that inflation is economically harmful, empirical arguments are advanced to justify a fierce fight against it. These assert that inflation slows the rate of economic growth by attracting workers out of productive enterprises and into speculative enterprises, increases the variance in prices and hence the risk or information costs of economic activity, causes the public to economize on the use of a good (money) with zero social costs of production, and alters the distribution of income or wealth in an unfair manner.

As a matter of empirical fact, the first argument is simply wrong. No correlation between inflation and long-run economic success exists. Since World War II some of the countries with the highest inflation rates—Brazil, Japan—have turned in some of the best economic performances.[1] Meanwhile, countries with a relatively good inflation performance—the United States among them—have finished near the bottom in the growth race. One can certainly point to speculative activities which proceed apace with or without inflation, but it is difficult to pinpoint those productive activities abandoned in favor of speculation.

In fact, if anything stops economic growth, it is not the rate of inflation, but the public policies designed to fight inflation with recession. A realization of this has produced a "just-among-us-economists" argument that inflation is bad because the public incorrectly believes that it is bad. The public therefore insists on policies which produce low growth and high unemployment. But of course the correct solution for this state of ignorance is not for the economic admirals to direct the fleet against inflation, but to educate the public as to the genuinely benign nature of inflation.

Theoretically, in the price-auction model no reason exists for a higher absolute price level to lead to more variance in the movement of individual prices. If the variance in prices does go up, the theoretical model needs to be modified in some major way, which hasn't been done. But if there is any increase in the variance of prices during a period of high inflation, the evidence is very weak and the observed increase is very small —so small that no one can really make an argument that the increase is having a significant deleterious effect on economic decisions.[2] And if an increase in the variance of prices or economizing on the use of money has a deleterious effect, it would have produced visibly lower growth rates for those societies with the most inflation—something that has not been observed.

The "unfair" income-distribution argument is a peculiar one. Many other economic factors affect income distributions in an "unfair" manner but are considered noneconomic ethical concerns beyond the competence of economics. But the charge is also untrue. Examination indicates almost no changes in the income distribution (rich versus poor, black versus white, male versus female, the elderly versus the young) of the American economy during the 1970s and certainly none that can be traced to inflation.[3] It is true that any particular price increase transfers income from the consumer of that product to someone on the producer's side of the market, but when indexed pensions are included, almost everyone is both a consumer and an earner of income, and the net effects are negligible. Individuals may be hurt, but people are always being hurt by a myriad of random "unfair" economic events.

The fact is that the American standard of living depends on productivity and not on the rate of inflation. If productivity rises, our collective standard of living will rise regardless of how the storms of inflation may rage. There is simply more output to be divided. If productivity falls, our standard of living goes down regardless of how calm and stable prices may be. There is simply less output to be divided. In the late 1970s and early 1980s the American standard of living stopped growing. The cause of that, however, can be found in stagnant productivity growth and not inflation. None of the economists analyzing the slowdown in American productivity pointed to inflation as a major culprit.

Yet the public wants to treat inflation as if it were a form of cancer. The reasons are not hard to discern, even if they are reasons that the Homo economicus of the equilibrium price-auction model would dismiss out of hand. In the decade of the 1970s the American real per capita disposable income—a measure that corrects for population growth and taxes as well as inflation—rose 26 percent, but money incomes rose 131 percent. Suppose the money man left $131 dollars on your doorstep, but by the time you could get to it only $26 was left. Would you feel objectively $26 better off, or feel that someone had ripped off $105? To ask the question is to answer it.

With no inflation the money man would still have delivered only $26, but you know that $131 was delivered and feel cheated. All of us can see how inflation reduces our standard of living but possess a blind spot toward the price increases that lead to income gains for us. Somehow I find it hard to direct the same kind of moral outrage at MIT tuition increases that lead to salary increases for me that I direct at other price increases that lead to higher incomes for someone else. Money illusion is something not suffered by Homo economicus, but it is endemic among Homo sapiens.

Suffering from money-illusion inflation also seems to speed up the economic game and make it seem imperative that we actively participate. Our wealth seems to have no safe resting place, even though a 12 percent rate of inflation and a 15 percent interest rate are equivalent to a zero inflation rate and a 3 percent interest rate. Withdrawing from the economic game to an absolutely safe resting place is never possible, but in an inflationary world the economic game seems more uncertain even if objectively it is not.

Although inflation is not the economic equivalent of cancer in its ultimate consequences, the analogy has a certain aptness nonetheless. Like cancer, inflation is the number one problem in the mind of the public, as long as unemployment (heart disease?) is not rising too rapidly.[4] Like cancer, inflation is not one disease, but many diseases. Like cancer, some kinds of inflation are controllable—though with a lot of pain and a certain amount of amputation—while other kinds are uncontrollable. And to wish for a cure does not necessarily lead to a cure in either case. In both instances the desire for a cure can lead the public to follow Pied Pipers advocating crackpot solutions. And finally, in both cases the patient often switches doctors and charges his old doctor with incompetence for not having effected a cure.

While attempts by the economics profession to predict or control inflation have met with very limited success, at least two techniques exist to describe inflation. The first breaks inflation down into its various sources, and the second focuses on necessary relationships between monetary variables.

The Sources of Inflation

The sequence of events that led to high inflation begins with a bad judgment that now belongs to the long ago. To avoid making an unpopular war even more unpopular, President Johnson decided to ignore the recommendations of his economic advisers and chose not to raise taxes when they should have been raised in 1965, 1966, and 1967. America was to have a war, but it was going to pay for the war covertly with inflation and not overtly with taxes. When the demand for leather to make military boots increased, there was simply going to be less leather left over for civilian shoes. With fewer civilian shoes made, shoe prices would increase and shoe consumption would fall. The noninflationary economic option of cutting shoe consumption with tax increases was rejected for political reasons.

Since all the indices of capacity utilization were at full employment before the Vietnam war began, it was widely predicted by economists in and out of government that the war would create excess-demand inflation. There simply wasn't any spare production capacity to meet the new military demands. And the economists were right. All across the economy, prices started to rise as demands exceeded production capabilities.

Although the policy mistakes began in late 1965, it is important to remember that inflation only gradually accelerated from 2.2 percent in 1965 to 4.5 percent in 1968. Price and wage pressures gradually spread across the economy, but it took a long time for these pressures to build up, even though the economic mistakes made to finance the Vietnam war were very large. The economy did not respond quickly to inflationary pressures, just as it would not later respond quickly to deflationary pressures.

President Nixon's strategy for coping with the fruits of President Johnson's mistakes was to administer the standard economic medicine. Monetary and fiscal policies were tightened to induce a recession. Idle resources, men and equipment, would result from a falling GNP. As these idle resources attempted to find work they would bid down wage rates and capital costs in accordance with the equilibrium price-auction model. Once prices and wages had stopped rising, the direction of monetary and fiscal policies would be reversed, and the economy returned to full employment in time for the next election.

A mild recession arrived on schedule in 1979 and 1970, but by the summer of 1971 the rate of inflation had not yet begun to fall. Instead it continued to accelerate to an annual rate of 6 percent in the first half of the year—matching the 6 percent unemployment rate.

There are many reasons to believe that if President Nixon

had continued his restrictive policies he could, in time, have stemmed the rate of inflation. But the inflationary momentum of the Vietnam war was so great that it was not going to be stemmed unless the President was willing to incur a much bigger or much longer recession than he was willing to accept. A recession hurts those who are unemployed. Their income falls and the unemployed quite naturally vote against someone forcing them to be the economy's inflation fighters. To those unemployed without income, a stable price level is of little benefit. Those still employed benefit from the sacrifice made by people out of work.

After what was a very mild recession, the public opinion polls showed President Nixon trailing his presumed future Democratic challenger, Senator Edmund Muskie, in the summer of 1971. Not wanting to run for a second term with the electorate preoccupied with high unemployment (which many, including Nixon, blamed for his 1960 defeat) and inflation, the President dramatically changed his economic policies in August 1971.

Despite repeated promises never to use wage and price controls, Nixon did impose them in an effort to stop inflation, while monetary and fiscal policies swung strongly toward stimulating the economy to lower unemployment. Within the economics profession of the time, a large majority was against peacetime wage and price controls. Within the group of conservative economists advising President Nixon, the consensus against controls approached unanimity. The peculiar combination of expansionary fiscal and monetary policies with controls was universally condemned as a technique for creating price pressures that would explode when controls were removed. And no one thought that the controls could work without building a bureaucracy to administer them. Yet President Nixon attempted to run the system with a few agents borrowed from the Internal Revenue Service. In sum, despite the objections of economists, both the controls and expansionary policies were adopted. And when they failed, the economics profession was to take the blame regardless of its earlier opposition or its insistence on adequate enforcement.

The Nixon policies made for a short-run political success but long-run economic failure. When the controls were lifted in 1973, the inflationary pressures that had been corked by the controls in 1971 and 1972 reappeared in an intensified form. In short, the excess demand engendered by overstimulating the economy in 1972 appeared as price increases in 1973. America had been paying an economic price for President Johnson's decision to misfinance the Vietnam war, and it was about to begin paying another price for President Nixon's re-election campaign.

All of this was compounded with more bad luck and poor judgment. Bad weather led to crop failures in Russia. To raise farm incomes and help in his election efforts, President Nixon sold too much wheat to the Russians in the summer of 1972. When Russian sales were subtracted from American supplies, there simply wasn't enough wheat left to meet normal demands at the prevailing prices. So prices rose sharply.

Nevertheless, the Department of Agriculture left acreage controls in place for 1973. After twenty-five years of trying to dispose of surpluses, that federal agency simply could not believe that a period of shortages had arrived. When coupled with the 1973 corn blight, supplies fell even further behind demands. Then anchovies failed to appear off the coast of Peru, forcing European cattle feeders to shift from fish meal to American grain. The net result: a 69 percent rise in agricultural prices from 1971 to 1974.[5] A modest industrial inflation was now joined to a raging agricultural inflation.

The economics profession found none of this mysterious. It was all produced by supply and demand. The Johnson and Nixon economists opposed the macro-economic policy choices made by their respective bosses. One can only argue that those economists should have resigned when their advice was ignored. In any case, inflation cannot be justly blamed on policies poorly designed by economists. As for the Russian wheat sale, economists seem not to have been consulted at all. Once it was announced, the profession knew that agricultural and food prices were going to soar. The flow of Soviet-American relations, the spread of the corn blight, and the disappearance of anchovies off the coast of Peru are outside the domain of even the most imperial of economists.

With a synchronized business cycle, all of the major industrial economies were also growing rapidly in 1972 and 1973. Demands for raw material expanded much more rapidly than it was possible to raise supplies. Shortages arose. Real shortages plus the contagion of the turmoil in world grain markets led to panic and speculative buying that produced even greater price increases than were warranted, given the real shortages. Prices exploded, although a short time later materials prices were to fall back to their old levels.

The final blow was OPEC's price increases and the Arab oil boycott in late 1973. Imported oil prices soared with corresponding price pressures on other energy sources. Since energy prices are an important part of the production and distribution costs of almost everything, significant cost pressures started to work their way through the economy. A cost-push industrial inflation was now incorporated into the remnants of the earlier excess-demand inflation. Given a simple equilibrium price-auction world, however, prices other than those paid for energy should have fallen because of reduced purchasing power, but that did not happen. The net effect was a substantial upward movement in all prices.

Given this sequence of events, the double-digit inflation of 1973 and 1974 is not surprising. In fact, anything else would have been. But the shock of double-digit inflation triggered another sequence of events. Politically something had to be done about inflation. But what? The decisions of Presidents Johnson and Nixon could not be undone. Good weather and crops could not be legislated. American economic policies could not reverse OPEC's pricing decisions. Not knowing what else to do, and in political disarray thanks to Watergate, the Nixon Administration applied a very large dose of the classical medicine—tight monetary and fiscal policies designed to slow growth, raise unemployment, and force wages and prices down.

The medicine worked when it came to slowing the economy. The real GNP stopped growing in the fourth quarter of 1973 and fell gradually throughout the first three quarters of 1974. Every quarter the GNP got smaller, more and more idle men and equipment were created, a reality the rate of inflation did not quickly reflect. In the panic of the Watergate transition from President Nixon to President Ford, monetary policies were tightened further and further until they created the infamous credit crunch in late 1974. High interest rates attracted funds out of the banking system because of regulation Q (the regulation limiting interest rates on normal savings

accounts to 5¼ percent) and with this outflow of funds, banks
had no money to lend. The result was private credit rationing,
so that many potential borrowers found that they could not
borrow at any interest rate. Demand fell rapidly. Home construction fell from 2.1 million units in 1973 to an annual rate
of fewer than 900,000 units in late 1974.[6]

While the real GNP had fallen at an annual rate of 3.4 percent from the fourth quarter of 1973 to the third quarter of
1974, it then began to plunge rapidly—falling 5.5 percent during the fourth quarter of 1974 and 9.6 percent during the first
quarter of 1975. The result was almost 9 percent unemployment. Instead of inflation, America now had stagflation. How
was the country to recover from the sharpest recession since
the Great Depression in an environment of rising prices?
Economists did not have a stock answer.

Regarded as a way to slow down inflation, the 1974–75 recession was a great success. The rate of inflation fell to 5.5 percent
by mid-1975—partly because of the severity of the recessionary shock and partly because the adverse consequences of any
supply shock eventually die out. But the costs, political and
economic, were too high to permit further declines in the
GNP. Government reversed its monetary and fiscal policies
and reinflated the economy. When the GNP stabilized, the
rate of inflation stopped falling despite massive amounts of idle
capacity (30 percent of the country's industrial capacity and
almost 9 percent of its labor force were idle in mid-1975). After
holding in the 5.5 to 6 percent range for more than two years,
inflation started to accelerate once more in 1978.

But the acceleration was no more mysterious than the earlier outbreaks. Under the pressure of inflation and declining
productivity growth, various groups in our society—farmers,
the elderly, the steel industry, low-wage workers—were demanding that the government do something to enhance their
economic security. In response, the government reintroduced
a system of agricultural price supports, raised Social Security
benefits, adopted trigger pricing to protect the American steel
industry, and sharply increased the minimum wage to help
low-wage workers. The net result of these and other actions
was to raise substantially the rate of inflation (See Table 3).

Other exogenous "bad luck" factors were also at work—a
rise in meat prices, a falling dollar—but government caused

Table 3

Sources of Accelerating Inflation in 1978

The Underlying Inflation Rate: 1976–77		5.3%
Actual Changes in Consumer Prices: 1978		7.7
Increase in Inflation Rate		2.4
Accelerating Effects: 1978		
Food Prices		0.7
Policy measures	0.3%	
Livestock	0.4	
Falling Dollar		0.4
Minimum Wage		0.1
Social Security and other policies		0.3
Homeownership (interest rates, etc.)		0.6
Demand and Protection		0.3

SOURCE: Robert Gough and Robin Siegel, "Why Inflation Became Worse." *Data Resources Review* (January 1979), p. 1.16.

more than half of the increase in the inflation rate that occurred from 1977 to 1978. This did not happen because the Carter economists were stupid or because they did not know the effect of their policies. The government was simply trying to raise the incomes of particular groups in our society. But to do so, it must raise prices, cause inflation, and reduce the income share of other groups.

In 1979 the second oil shock hit, with oil prices almost tripling between 1978 and early 1981. Inflation jumped to 13.3 percent in 1979 and 12.4 percent in 1980. Once again not knowing what else to do, the policy makers imposed tight monetary and fiscal policies. As a result, the real GNP was slightly below the level of the first quarter of 1979 four years later (in the fourth quarter of 1982). Unemployment gradually rose, but inflation did not start to subside until late 1981.

Here again there was no mystery in the slowdown. Independent noneconomic events (good weather, slow Russian grain sales, high OPEC oil production) were leading to reductions in the price of oil and grain. Competitive Japanese economic pressure reduced price and wage increases in major industries such as autos. Also, the consumption of housing is overweighted in the American consumer price index. This exaggerates the rate of inflation when housing prices and mortgage interest rates are rising, and the reverse when they are falling.

The sharp 1981–82 recession and rapidly rising unemployment was also having the traditional short-run favorable effect
on slowing prices and wage increases.

There is no problem with the economists' understanding of
the sources of inflationary storms disturbing the economy.
Like the meterologist, he can describe the factors that produced the storm, but as with meteorology, to understand the
causes of the storm does not mean that either meteorologists
or economists can stop the storms they understand.

Perhaps some of the inflationary pressures could have been
avoided if economists' advice had been heeded, but it wasn't.
Other pressures (fight a war, get re-elected) were more important. Economists did not foresee some of the factors that were
to cause inflation (oil, food) but there is no reason to have
expected that they should have foreseen them. And even if
they had, they would have been in no position to prevent
them. Once these events had occurred, there was no easy cure
for inflation.

Monetary Cures for Inflation?

The monetary description of inflation received renewed life as
monetarism (the prevailing economic theory of the 1920s) re-
established itself after the Keynesian revolution.[7] This happened for a number of reasons. The extreme Keynesians—but
not Keynes himself—clearly made ambitious claims that were
going to be deflated. The supply of money is important. Econometric models that left out monetary variables did not work
as well as those that included them. And some sectors of the
economy, such as construction or autos, simply could not be
explained without the use of monetary variables such as interest rates.

In addition, the forced savings—war bonds—of World War
II had built up an enormous excess degree of liquidity that
would eventually disappear. When it did, the supply of credit
would again became an important variable. In any adequate
economic model, the stock of wealth affects the flow of consumption, and the desired composition of wealth in part depends on monetary variables: interest rates and credit
availability.

Debates about the relative role of monetary policy (interest rates and the supply of money) and fiscal policies (aggregate tax and expenditure decisions) are more heated than normal because the debate tends to become polarized along political lines. Those emphasizing the importance of taxes, government expenditures, and interest rates—the Keynesians—tend to be liberal, while the monetarists tend to be conservative. The real political debate revolves around the question of whether government expenditures should grow or contract. But the issue tends to get fought out as monetarism versus Keynesianism because there is always an argument as to whether higher government expenditures will or will not return the economy to full employment in recessionary periods.

But the ascendancy of monetarism as a policy model for fighting inflation reflects not so much its intellectual dominance as the fact that politically no one is willing to apply the equilibrium price-auction fiscal remedy—tax increases and expenditure cuts—for inflation. In real life even liberal Keynesian governments such as those of Presidents Johnson and Carter practiced monetarism.[8] They had to do something. They weren't willing—or perhaps able, given the necessity of getting congressional approval—to raise taxes or cut expenditures. So they tightened the monetary screws.

Monetarism has a great political appeal for another reason. Its advocates still have great faith that if the government will only control one and only one variable—the money supply—inflation will disappear. A short mild recession might occur, but the economy will quickly return to full employment. In contrast, the Keynesians have no simple answer and are not at all confident that a tax increase would stop inflation even if legislated.

The confidence of the monetarists, however, springs from a semantic distinction rather than a demonstrated ability to control inflation. Monetarism redefines inflation as a "sustained" increase in prices rather than an increase in the price level. This rules out the supply shocks coming from oil or grain as sources of inflation, not because they do not cause prices to rise, but because they do not cause a "sustained" rise in prices. A once-and-for-all increase in the price of oil may cause a once-and-for-all increase in the price level, but that, by the monetarists' definition, is not "inflation."[9]

The redefinition of inflation also leaves unspecified how long the price increases must continue before they become "sustained" and are relabeled inflation. Nothing goes on forever, and supply shocks do not lead to instantaneous increases in prices. But where do you draw the line between a sustained price increase and a once-and-for-all price increase? Not being specified or being an elastic line that can be drawn wherever it is convenient strengthens one's debating posture, but not one's understanding of the real world.

If the monetarists' semantic distinction is accepted, inflation is "everywhere and always a monetary phenomenon," as the war cry of the monetarists claims. But even this is not the same as saying that inflation is everywhere and always caused by government. Suppose a supply shock, such as an increase in the price of oil, gets embedded in an economy where all wages and prices are tied to some price index. Indexing causes supply shocks to get converted into an inertial inflation that could continue indefinitely. Wages rise this year because prices rose last year, which leads this year's prices and hence next year's wages to rise. If the government passively validates the inflation—allows the money supply to grow to keep inadequate money supplies from braking the economy and causing the GNP to fall, as slow monetary growth would in a world of 100 percent indexing—government can only be described as the cause of inflation in a very peculiar sense. The failure to rescue a drowning swimmer who cannot be saved except at the cost of one's own life does not mean that one has committed murder. "Cause" implies an active, leading role, which does not here exist.

The Quantity Theory of Money

The basic equation, the quantity theory of money, used in a monetary description of inflation is an identity—true by definition (see Equation 1). No one disagrees with it, because the velocity of money is defined as the money GNP (PT) divided by the money supply (M). To make the quantity theory of money useful, some nontautological hypotheses must be advanced about the determinants of the velocity of money and how any increase in monetary stimulus (MV) is divided among prices (P) and real output (T). This I will explain in what follows.

Equation 1

MV = PT

where M = quantity of money (now defined as cash, plus all accounts upon which checks can be written in official statistics)

V = velocity of money

P = price level (implicit price deflator for the GNP)

T = real GNP (transactions before the days of national income accounting)

and where by definition V = PT/M

Keynesians tend to play down the importance, but not the algebraic validity, of the quantity theory of money in favor of a view that sees interest rates—the price of money—as the key monetary factor governing economic decisions. Since interest rates do not appear in the quantity of money, the Keynesians do not use the quantity of money as a causal equation, but see it instead merely as an accounting identity. Money is important—the supply of it and demand for it determine the interest rate—but the impact of money on the economy is filtered through the effect of interest rates on consumption, investment, and government expenditures. Since Keynesians assume a world where at least some prices (usually wages) are rigid and slow to adjust, interest rates are one of the variables that government can use to raise the demand for labor to the point where real economic activity (T) brings about full employment. If lower interest rates are perceived to be necessary, the central bank raises the money supply and lowers the rates. As a consequence, Keynesians look at the real rate of interest (the rate of interest minus the rate of inflation) to gauge the degree of restrictiveness implicit in monetary policies.

In contrast, monetarists see a direct link between money and inflation (P) or real economic activity (T) without the intermediation of interest rates. Technically the real rate of interest is supposed to remain constant and invariant to changes in the rate of growth of the money supply.[10] According to monetarist theory, a cut in the money supply reduces real economic activity in the short run, but since prices are assumed to be flexible, real economic activity quickly returns to its natural (full employment) level. Therefore a cut in the money supply must necessarily show up as a reduction in prices or the rate of inflation. And if that is true, the rate of growth of the money supply becomes the key variable for controlling inflation. Unemployment or real economic activity take care of themselves.[11]

So in the first quarter of 1982 the monetarists saw easy money policies, whereas Keynesians saw the opposite. Real short-run interest rates were 15 percent, while the money supply was growing at 11 percent.[12] Keynesians saw a world where monetary policies should effect lower interest rates to stimulate economic activity; monetarists, on the other hand, saw a recession that would cure itself if given just a little time and a money supply growing much too rapidly.

Within the quantity theory of money, disputes revolve around the extent to which this descriptive equation allows one to predict, understand, or control inflation. Two basic problems arise.

First, there is a question as to whether the government can in fact control MV. The supply of money (M) is not under the direct control of the government, since it includes demand deposit (checking) accounts under the aegis of the private banking system. While the government can in principle manipulate supply variables (cash and banking regulations) to offset changes in private supplies of money, those private changes must be accurately predicted if they are to be offset. To control the effective money supply (MV), it is necessary to accurately predict shifts in the velocity of money.

Second, a decrease in MV is going to show up as an equivalent decrease in PT, but how much of that decline will show up as a fall in P, less inflation, and how much will show up as a fall in T, less real growth and more unemployment? The quantity theory of money does not say yet that division is the heart of the problem. Monetarists argue that there may be small short-run effects on T, but rather quickly all of the decrease in MV will show up in the form of less inflation, a lower P. Keynesians argue that the initial effects of a decline in MV will be primarily on T, less growth, and only very slowly and after a very long period of time start to show up as less inflation, a lower P.

The Velocity of Money

To be something besides a description, the quantity theory of money must be supplemented with a subsidiary equation accounting for movements in the velocity of money. The critical questions are (1) the extent to which the velocity of money is stable (can be modeled with econometric techniques), (2) depends upon the rate of interest, and (3) is subject to random as opposed to deterministic influences. If a good velocity-of-money equation cannot be found because the random component is too large or because different variables affect the velocity of money under different circumstances, it is not possible for the central bank to control MV, even though it can control M. To control MV it must predict V, and that is impossible. If the velocity of money is highly sensitive to interest rates, then interest rates become an important policy variable— something denied by the monetarists.

With the possible exception of wage and price equations, velocity-of-money equations are, empirically speaking, the poorest in macro-economic modeling. The velocity of money seems to be unstable and very difficult to predict (see Table 4). If one were to have used the quantity theory of money to control the GNP over the past ten years, one would have confronted a velocity of money that varied erratically from 3.2 to 11.2 from one year to the next, and even more from quarter to quarter.

As a result, even monetarists often treat monetarism as a black box. "We know that a bird flies and have some insight into how it is able to do so without having a complete understanding of the aerodynamic theory involved."[13] Monetarists do not understand exactly what is in the box, but they know what will come out of it. Basically the matter comes down to the belief that the velocity of money is not infinitely elastic but ultimately constrained. If the government cuts the money supply (M) long enough and hard enough, it can eventually reduce MV.

It is this monetarist belief that keeps the quantity theory of money alive as a way to control inflation rather than just a

Table 4

Monetary Variables

	Velocity of Money (Change in GNP/ Change in M1)	Change in Money Supplies (M-1)	Change in Prices (Implicit Price) (Deflator)
1972	5.1%	9.3%	4.2%
1973	10.0	5.5	5.7
1974	9.3	4.4	8.7
1975	8.3	5.0	9.3
1976	8.7	6.6	5.2
1977	7.9	8.1	5.8
1978	8.6	8.3	7.3
1979	9.8	7.2	8.5
1980	8.5	6.4	9.0
1981	11.2	6.3	9.1
1982	3.2	8.5	6.0

SOURCE: Council of Economic Advisers, *The Economic Report of the President*, pp. 233, 303, 236.

description of algebraic realities. If the government authorities can control M, and V is not infinitely variable, there is always some change in M that can overwhelm any change in V. While technically true, that fact does not make MV controllable. The quantity of money is forever trying to offset a slippery velocity of money that is not stable enough to be kept under control, assuming it could be offset if you knew where it was going. The government can "fine-tune" M, but it cannot "fine-tune" MV because it cannot estimate V. But not being able to "fine-tune" MV, it has no hope of controlling PT—the nominal GNP.

Few economists would dispute the notion that monetary policies can stop inflation if enough emphasis is put on the "long enough and hard enough" when it comes to controlling the money supply. If the money supply is reduced long enough and hard enough, however, all economic activity, including inflation, stops for periods of time that are not considered the "short run" by either citizens or politicians. As the data in Table 4 show, the relationship between inflation and the growth of the money supply is anything but quick.

Conversely, if the economy is flooded with money, inflation has to start. The controversies arise over what happens between these extremes. Can MV be managed with the necessary degree of "fine tuning" to control inflation without destroying economic growth? Is the short run "short" enough to be politically viable? The practical experience of the 1970s and 1980s would answer no. Most industrial governments—some consistently, some fitfully—fought inflation with monetarism, in the process bringing economic growth to a halt for an extended period of time.

The fact is that no one can predict the velocity of money with enough accuracy to make the quantity of money into a good control variable. To some extent the inaccurate forecasts (poor equations) spring from the ability of the financial markets to invent new monetary instruments. The creation of financial instruments such as money market mutual funds or NOW accounts (interest-bearing checking accounts) can raise the velocity of money, since people economize on the use of old "official" money by moving into the new forms of money. As these new instruments come into widespread use, they require a change in the definition of money and force the central bank to shift its focus of attention to a new and more inclusive definition. As a result, the central bank is essentially forever chasing a slippery money supply that it can never quite succeed in pinning down.[14]

Both the Bank of England and the Federal Reserve Board have failed to control the money supply, even though both have sworn alliegence to monetarism under the Thatcher and Reagan governments. New forms of money and the capacity of the private banking system to expand old forms of money have stopped either from achieving the smooth constant control of the money supply advocated by the monetarists. In the fall of 1982 Paul Volcker, chairman of the Federal Reserve Board, maintained that the financial markets were in such a state of transition that he was giving up on the effort to control the money supply for a while. But the important point is that you cannot practice monetarism without being able to measure and control the money supply.

The velocity of money is also erratic because the world is uncertain and our perceptions of that world are even more uncertain than the world itself. That part of the demand for money used to undertake transactions and carry out commerce is probably reasonably stable, but the demand for money to produce liquidity (the precautionary and speculative demand for money in Keynesian analysis) is highly unstable because of fears and anxieties about the future. If only the transactional demand for money existed, the quantity theory of money might be a reasonable representation of the system, · but the liquidity demands make the relationships highly unstable.[15]

In a perfectly secure world, no one would choose to hold any of his wealth beyond what is necessary for transactions in a liquid money form that yields no return. Yielding no direct return, money is not a good store of wealth unless there is a premium to liquidity, and there is no premium for liquidity unless there is uncertainty. It is this uncertainty, combined with the difficulties of quickly buying or selling other assets, that leads to an erratic demand for money to hold. Thus, the demand for money is always shifting as our perceptions of the uncertain future move in uncertain ways. And as our demands for liquidity shift in response to real or imaginary uncertainties, the velocity of money shifts with that perception of uncertainty. As a result it is highly unlikely that anyone will ever discover that stable velocity-of-money equation which will be necessary to make monetary policies into a good control variable for regulating MV. The random component is simply too large.

If the public suddenly wants liquidity, for whatever reason, the economy confronts a problem. As individuals rush out of real goods and into money, the demand for real goods falls. Supply does not create its own demand, because the income generated in selling goods goes into a demand for liquidity (money) and not a demand for real goods. Although money is liquidity for any individual, there is no liquidity for the economy as a whole. Society's wealth is the real assets that it owns —plants, equipment, land, homes—and paper money does not raise that wealth or make it more liquid. The net result is a decline in the demand for goods, and hence in production, as people attempt to achieve what is in the aggregate impossible —unless the authorities respond by raising the money supply.

There is also every theoretical reason to believe that the use of money rises or falls when the price of money (the interest rate) rises or falls, even though empirically the interest elasticity of the demand for money seems to be low, but not zero, and

highly erratic. If the effective money supply is highly endogenous, expanding when the demand for money expands and
contracting when the demand for money contracts, then the
measured velocity will not seem to be responding to higher (or
lower) interest rates, even though interest rates are having a
large effect on MV. The interest-rate effect leads to the creation of more old forms of money in the private sector and to
the development of new forms of money rather than to a
simple increase in the velocity of a fixed amount of old money.
And to the extent that this happens, the real velocity of money
rises and falls.

If an increase in the interest rate leads to a large increase in
the velocity of money, a decrease in the supply of money
leading to higher interest rates need have little impact on MV
because of the induced effect on the velocity of money. Velocity (V) rises as fast as (M) decreases. In sum, the direction of
causation is reversed. Instead of the effective supply of money
(MV) controlling the economy, the economy (PT) controls the
effective supply of money, and direction of causation is exactly
reversed from that necessary for monetarism to be effective.

When monetarists argue that the velocity of money is not a
function of the interest rate (technically the price elasticity of
the demand for money is zero) and therefore not endogenous
to the system, they are arguing something quite peculiar,
given their views on price elasticities in other markets. Money
is a commodity like any other commodity. It is desired because
it is useful as a medium for transactions and yields a liquidity
premium in an uncertain world. But in any of these uses there
are substitutes and ways to economize. Presumably one uses
less money just as one uses less of anything else as the price of
money rises.

The argument about the interest-rate effect on the velocity
of money has gone on for a long time, since the velocity of
money is statistically so erratic that it is difficult to make a
convincing case that it is empirically related to anything. Neither side can prove the other wrong, since the same correla-
tions obtain whether the money supply controls the economy
or the economy controls the money supply.

In Keynesian analysis, macro-economic policies, monetary
or fiscal, exist because there is a market—the labor market—
where price flexibility does not exist. There is a zero price

elasticity of demand or supply for labor. A zero price elasticity of demand and supply for money, and the assumption that real interest rates are always constant, are effectively the monetarists equivalent of the Keynesian assumption of rigid money wages. Both Keynesian and monetary macro-economics depend upon a fixed price model of some important market. In the former it is the labor market, and in the latter the money market. Both assumptions are equally arbitrary because no theoretical reason exists why either should be true, given the equilibrium price-auction model.

If price is not the clearing mechanism in one market—the market for money—there is no reason why it cannot also be true in another market—the market for labor. Accordingly, a belief in the zero price elasticity of the demand for money and the irrelevance of interest rates should produce at least some skepticism about the validity of the price-auction model, but no monetarists have so far declared any doubts. According to the monetarists, price fluctuations clear every market except the money market.

Empirically the assumption of a constant real interest rate seems to be at variance with the facts. In the early 1980s real interest rates rose to unprecedented levels. Though high long-term interest rates can always be explained away as a constant real interest rate augmented by a very high expected rate of inflation in the future, high real short-run interest rates cannot be so explained. A 14 percent real Federal Funds (overnight loans between banks) rate in the first quarter of 1982 cannot be based on expected inflation.

Monetarists have also tried to blame high real interest rates on "erratic" short-run movements in the money supply. Here again, however, the explanation works only with respect to long-run interest rates. Erratic movements of the money supply might confuse investors as to the future behavior of the Federal Reserve Board and lead them to have high long-run inflationary expectations, but erratic movements of the money supply do not obscure the current inflation performance and lead to high short-run interest rates.

There is also a political question as to the extent to which the supply of money can be treated as a policy variable used to control the system rather than as a dependent variable controlled by the economic system. One can admit that the supply of money is a control variable in the technical sense while still arguing that it is politically controlled by the events in the economy—as some models do.

When price shocks such as those administered by OPEC occur, the monetary authorities could technically hold their part of the money supply constant to attempt to force other prices down, but given the political consequences that would flow from the resulting lower growth and higher unemployment, they in fact raise their part of the money supply to accommodate a shock. So, given the real-world behavior of public officials, there is more illusion than reality to the concept of the money supply as an effective policy-control variable. Rather than dominating economic events, money-supply control is itself dominated by economic events and their political ramifications.

The Phillips Curve[16]

For the quantity theory of money, large problems on the MV side of the equation are dwarfed by the problems on the PT side. A realistic mechanism must exist to show us how changes in the money supply affect prices and and the real GNP. In the simple price-auction model, a decrease in the money demand for goods and services leads first and foremost to a decrease in the price of goods and services, and only secondarily to induced changes in the production of goods and services. In the real world, a decrease in the money demand for goods and services seems to lead first and foremost to a decrease in the production of goods and services, and only much later, if at all, to a reduction in the price of goods and services.

The economic understanding of the problem—how is an increase or decrease in MV allocated across P and T?—has undergone a series of transformations as various propositions have been theoretically postulated and empirically rejected.

Before the Great Depression, economists resolved the dilemma with the belief that the real GNP (T) always attained full employment in the long run, but could deviate from that condition in the short run. If some economic accident produced a downward deviation from full employment (a reduction in T), an increase in monetary stimulus (a rising M) would raise the real GNP and speed its return to full employment. At full employment, a point of discontinuity would be reached, and further stimulus would lead to an increase in the price level (P). Conversely, an upward deviation from full employment would produce inflation (a rising P) that could easily be cured with a reduction in the money supply. Meanwhile, the velocity of money was assumed to be constant in the analysis because GNP statistics had not yet been devised, and at the time no one knew just how unstable the velocity was.

While Keynes did not believe that we would always have full employment—the long run being so long as to be irrelevant— he did accept the hypothesis that an inflationary discontinuity was created at full employment.[17] Prices would not start to rise until fiscal stimulus had pushed the economy to full employment. And prices could be rising only if the economy was above full employment. In such a situation tighter monetary policies or a tax increase had only to be implemented to stop inflation in its tracks. So for Keynes, the equilibrium price-auction market did not exist for wages and employment, but it did exist in the rest of the economy.

Both pre–Great Depression monetary views and Keynesian views came to grief after encountering the inconsistent empirical facts of life. The Depression lasted so long that it simply wasn't tenable to argue that full employment would automatically re-establish itself in the long run. After World War II, inflation broke out long before the economy reached anything that could be called full employment, unless full employment was tautologically redefined to mean that level of unemployment where inflation started to occur. And neither increases in taxes or reductions in the money supply seemed capable of stopping it without first stopping the economy.

These realities led to the birth of the Phillips curve. According to the hypothesis, a stable relationship exists between the quantity of idle resources (as measured by the unemployment rate or unused capital capacity) and the division of PT into price and quantity changes (see Diagram 1). (Technically Phillips himself talked only about wages and unemployment, but the concept was quickly expanded to include idle resources and prices). As idle resources fell, any given stimulus (monetary or fiscal) would lead to larger and larger increases in prices

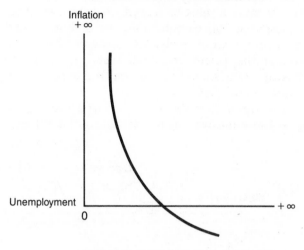

Diagram 1

THEORETICAL PHILLIPS CURVE

NATURAL RATE OF UNEMPLOYMENT

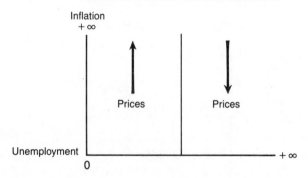

(P) relative to their effect on the real GNP (T). Rather than a sudden shift from real growth to price inflation at full employment, Phillips instead postulated a range of deteriorating trade-offs that involved more and more industries reaching capacity constraints or rising oligopoly power as idle resources shrank. Put another way, as demand approached full employment, capacity queues and shortages developed, leading to larger and larger price increases and smaller and smaller output increases for any given increase in aggregate demand.

The Phillips-curve hypothesis has but one major problem. No one seems to be able to develop good stable price equations using U.S. data for the post WWII period (see Diagram 2). Yet the hypothesis has survived the empirical evidence arrayed against it because it must be true at the extremes. If there are no idle resources, all stimulus must by definition lead to increases in prices. Conversely, idle resources have to reach a level so high that prices would fall. If such notions are true at the extremes, why shouldn't they be true over the range between those extremes?

One can argue that the Phillips curve was theoretically wrong, as those did who were advocating the natural rate of

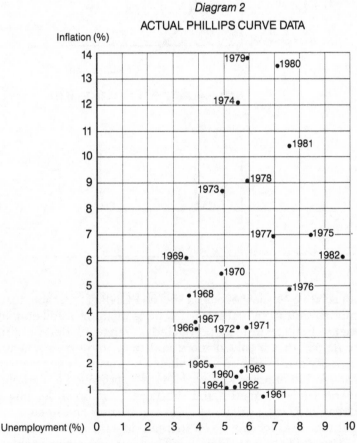

Diagram 2

ACTUAL PHILLIPS CURVE DATA

Source: Council of Economic Advisers, *The Economic Report to the President*, pp. 268, 291.

unemployment hypothesis (see below), or that it was simply overwhelmed by adverse random bad luck that hid the real relationship between idle factors of production and inflation. But it is important to understand that the Phillips curve was not a break with the theory behind the price-auction model. It was, in fact, a direct expression of that theory. If the Phillips curve does not describe or explain economic realities, then something has to be wrong with the basic theory of supply and demand.

The Phillips curve has it that as idle capacity (unemployment in the case of the labor market) goes up, wages will fall. This is a supply-and-demand view of the world, having just two small modifications from the conventional model taught in any introductory-economics class. First, there are time lags. The labor market does not clear instantly—hardly a radical, novel, or controversial assumption. Second, the zero point—the point where wages neither rise nor fall—does not necessarily occur at the point where unemployment, as it is officially measured, is zero. Instead the zero point occurs at some positive level of unemployment. This is easily consistent with the hypothesis that official measures of unemployment contain some quantum of voluntary unemployment—those who don't really want to work or who are exploring the market (searching) to find out what jobs are available.

To repeat, if Phillips-curve principles are faulty, then something must be wrong with the equilibrium price-auction view of markets. Markets are not clearing based on wage changes induced by idle resources—relative supplies and demands. So one can say that the problem with the Phillips curve is not that it is inadequately grounded in micro-economics, but precisely that it is grounded in a price-auction labor market that cannot account for real-world wage behavior.

The Natural Rate of Unemployment

The natural-rate-of-unemployment hypothesis is the currently fashionable theory of how increases in MV are spread across PT.[18] In the concept, we find a return to the idea of a discontinuity or switching point (though not at what would be regarded as full employment in any conventional sense) and a sharp distinction between the short run and the long run. Technically speaking, the natural rate of unemployment is a vertical Phillips curve.

In this view, labor's wage demands are the key component of inflation. Whenever the demand for labor rises above its "natural" full employment level, wages rise, which pushes up costs of production and hence prices. As a result, the entire Phillips curve is not stable but itself rises (moves upward and to the left in Diagram 1) as long as the demand for labor exceeds the "natural" labor supply. Conversely, when the demand for labor is below its "natural" level, wages fall. With falling wages, costs of production fall, generating price reductions and a falling Phillips curve (moves downward and to the right in Diagram 1). The unemployment level below which wages rise and above which wages fall is known as the "natural rate of unemployment." Only at this point will inflation rates be stable—neither rise nor fall. Phillips curves seem to exist, but any attempt to move along them causes them to shift. Hence the observed difficulty in finding stable Phillips curves.

This view represents the simple static price-auction view of the labor market with two modifications. First, wage rates are sluggish and change only gradually in response to excessive or deficient demand, which produces the short-run illusion that there is such a thing as a Phillips curve. Second, instead of postulating that wages rise or fall depending on the official rate of unemployment, some substantial amount of what is measured in official unemployment statistics is according to this theory, not real involuntary unemployment, but "voluntary" unemployment.

Individuals are reported as unemployed, but they are not really so because they are not willing to accept work at their market wage. They have a "reservation" wage which is higher than the one justified by their productivity, and hence cannot find work until they are willing to lower their reservation wage. In short, they exaggerate their own worth and are accordingly unemployed.

This leads to a scaling change. The zero-unemployment–full-employment definition implicit in the simple equilibrium price-auction model is replaced with some positive measured rate of unemployment. But that measured natural rate of unemployment contains zero "involuntary" unemployment.

In short, full employment has been redefined to make the theory true. Full employment is no longer regarded as existing independent of observed wage behavior, but is asserted to be that unemployment level where wages neither rise or fall. So the labor market clears based on prices no matter how much that seems not to be the case. If 40 percent unemployment is the point at which wages start to fall, then 40 percent is full employment no matter how absurd that may seem to other perfectly sane people.

Several other problems arise when the theory is applied to a growing rather than static economy. Since higher wages can and must be paid with higher productivity (marginal products are up), labor does not have a reservation wage below which it will not work, but must have a reservation wage gain below which it will not work. At each level of unemployment, labor demands some real wage increase and asks for some nominal money wage gain that it thinks will generate the desired real gain. At the natural rate of unemployment, labor asks for some nominal money wage increase—which increase may well be greater than the rate of growth of productivity, the only nonin-flationary real wage gain that the economy can pay. If so, inflation occurs at the natural rate of unemployment. Wages are going up faster than productivity, leading to rising costs of production and price increases. But when labor subtracts that rate of inflation for its nominal wage gain, it finds that it has achieved exactly the real wage increase that it desired—and productivity allowed. Being satisfied, labor will ask for the same nominal increase in the next wage round, having no incentive to do otherwise. And since the demanded real wage gain is equal to the economy's rate of growth of productivity, it can be accommodated with no *additional* upward pressure on prices. The resulting rate of inflation may be high or low, but it will be stable.

Inflation will be stable *and* zero only if workers by chance ask for a nominal wage gain equal to the rate of productivity growth. Since there is no economic pressure for this to happen, a zero rate of inflation may or may not occur at the natural rate of unemployment.

If economic policy makers attempt to push the rate of unem-ployment below the natural rate by expanding aggregate de-mand, labor will demand higher real wage gains and ask for higher nominal wage increases. But these nominal gains can only produce more inflation, since real gains are limited by the growth of productivity—no higher rate, as noted, can ever be paid. Consequently the real wage gain, when inflation is subtracted from the nominal gain, will be below what is demanded. Labor responds by demanding an even higher nominal wage increase in the next round. But each higher nominal wage increase is offset by a higher rate of inflation, since real wages are constrained by productivity and cannot rise. Inflation accelerates round after round.

Conversely, if unemployment is above the natural rate, prices fall. Because of higher unemployment, labor reduces its real wage demands below the level determined by productivity gains. With labor productivity growing faster than wages, unit production costs fall leading to price reductions. But with falling prices labor finds that its real wage gain is greater than what it demanded. Not wanting the higher wage gain, labor reduces its nominal wage demands in the next round. Lower wages once again lead to lower prices. Prices fall continuously as long as unemployment is above the natural rate.

In summary, the real GNP is set by the natural rate of unemployment, and policy makers cannot make the real GNP larger or smaller with either monetary or fiscal policies. This is the conclusion that leads monetary economists to oppose using fiscal policies to intervene in the economy.

There is, however, a not very well advertised corollary to the same conclusion: *Inflation does not make any difference to the economy's real GNP.* Because all attempts to push unemployment above or below the natural rate of unemployment eventually show up solely in inflation, and inflation does not change the natural rate of unemployment, inflation does not affect output. The GNP is set instead by that unalterable natural rate of unemployment. Because total output and hence real incomes are unaffected by inflation, there is no reason for public concern about inflation. But if inflation makes no difference, why are the monetary economists so eager to adopt harsh policies for stopping it?

Given the equilibrium price-auction model, the natural-rate-of-unemployment hypothesis presents us with a number of puzzles. Why is the natural rate of unemployment greater than zero? There are only two possible answers. Either some market imperfections lead workers into being involuntarily unemployed or what is perceived as involuntary unemployment is in fact voluntary unemployment. Proponents of the natural-rate-of-unemployment hypothesis are almost forced to argue that the level of unemployment embedded in the natural rate of unemployment is voluntary. If it were not voluntary, proponents would have to account for the persistent market imperfection causing the natural rate of unemployment to be greater than zero when describing the labor market. And if one could alter the natural rate of unemployment by eliminating that "market imperfection" or creating other market imperfections, there simply wouldn't be a natural rate of unemployment.

If what the government measures as unemployment is in fact voluntary unemployment, a different set of problems emerges. Many of those unemployed were laid off. They were not unemployed because they refused to work at prevailing wage rates, because others with similar working credentials are working at those wage rates. Surveys indicate that most of the unemployed would be willing to work at current or even below current wage rates. And many of the unemployed take wage reductions when they go back to work. In what sense, then, are workers "voluntarily" unemployed?

Moreover, how does one explain the cyclical ups and downs of national unemployment? Why were 3 percent voluntarily unemployed in 1969, and almost 10 percent in 1982?

Then, too, if workers possess reservation wages or demanded real wage gains that are too high, why doesn't the economy (their experience) quickly beat down those unrealistic expectations? A high level of "voluntary" unemployment should not last very long.

None of these questions is satisfactorily answered in the theory.

Equilibrium price-auction labor markets may contain some stubborn people who mistakenly have a very high reservation wage because they place a higher value on themselves than the market does. But it is presumed in the theory that the market uses unemployment to knock those unrealistic expectations out of individual workers, who quickly learn what they are "worth," lower their wage demands, and return to work. So why doesn't the market similarly discipline aggregate nominal and real wage demands? In an equilibrium price-auction market, the wage rate can never exceed or fall short of the market clearing price however unreal initial expectations. Wages can get away from market clearing levels only if there is some collective monopoly power or systematic imperfection in the system.

Labor unions can be considered a source of collective power, but unions represent less than 20 percent of the American work force, and even that 20 percent does not bargain as a group.[19] How do you get a collective reservation wage out of the real-world industrial structure? If union wages are set too high, workers are forced out of the union and into the nonunion sector to find work, but this should produce lower wages for nonunion workers—not rigid reservation wages in the aggregate. Aggregate wages are still flexible—all of the flexibility simply has to occur in the nonunion sectors of the economy.

But there is something even more peculiar going on here. Under the dynamic version of the natural-rate-of-unemployment hypothesis, workers have a collective reservation real wage gain below which they will continually ask for higher and higher nominal wage gains. Workers in equilibrium price-auction labor markets have *individual* real reservation-wage *levels* below which each worker will refuse to work, but they do not have a *collective* reservation real wage *gain* below which they will refuse to work. In a competitive market, many reservation wages exist depending on individual needs for income and labor-leisure choices. Why should labor have a collective reservation real wage gain? And with what theory of labor-leisure choice is it consistent?

Taken collectively, are union leaders so stupid that they forever fail to comprehend simple arithmetic? Namely, that labor cannot have a real wage gain greater than the rate of growth of productivity? Higher wages will only lead to higher inflation. Why don't labor union leaders ever learn that the demand for a lower nominal wage gain never reduces their real wage gain, but only the rate of inflation? Why don't they as a result lower their wage demands? Both their own experiences and the clear advice of the economics profession should convince them of the errors of their ways and the truth of the matter.

If the natural rate of unemployment really exists, where do

those mysterious collective real wage demands come from? How are they formed? What factors influence them and cause them to change? Are they stable over time? What is the current collective real reservation-wage gain? What stable rate of inflation is in accordance with it? What is the natural rate of unemployment—6 percent, 10 percent? How high does unemployment have to go before nominal and real wages start to fall —25 percent?

In the natural-rate-of-unemployment hypothesis, none of these questions is answered. Yet if they are not answered, the theory is not really a theory, merely a poorly specified conjecture. The Phillips curve may not exist, but its nonexistence does not demonstrate the existence of the natural rate of unemployment.

Interestingly, the natural-rate model implicitly accepts rigid wages, or to be more precise, a rigid demand for real wage gains. While Keynesianism needs rigid wages to make its macro-economic theories work, the natural-rate-of-unemployment hypothesis depends on rigid reservation wages or rigid real money-wage demands to to make its theory work. But neither has any explanation for why money wages or the demand for real wage gains should be rigid in the first place.

The only difference between the two is that Keynes wanted to use fiscal and monetary policies to shift labor's demand curve so that it intersected with labor's supply curve at the markets exogenously given rigid money wage. In contrast, those advocating the natural-rate-of-unemployment hypothesis want to alter labor's supply curve (letting unemployment rise) so that it intersects with the demand curve at the point where labor's demanded money wage gain will be stable. Both hypotheses have an implicit labor market very different from the one taught in the equilibrium price-auction model of micro-economics.

Stability of Natural Rate of Unemployment

Not surprisingly, the natural-rate-of-unemployment hypothesis, which can be graphed as a vertical Phillips curve, suffers from the same empirical problems as the Phillips curve. The natural rate cannot be found and does not seem to be stable. Most advocates of the hypothesis see a natural rate that has risen over time. This can be seen in the various editions of the *Economic Report of the President*. In the Kennedy Administration, 4 percent was set as an "interim" unemployment target consistent with stable and desired low inflation rates. By the end of the Johnson Administration, unemployment targets had crept up to 4.5 percent. By the end of the Ford Administration, the economic report was defending 5 percent. In the 1979 economic report of President Carter, the unemployment target was 6 percent. In his 1982 confirmation hearings, the chairman of President Reagan's Council of Economic Advisers, Martin Feldstein, saw a 7 percent natural rate of unemployment.

The instability of the natural rate should come as no surprise. Theoretically there is no reason to expect a stable rate.[20] Since the natural rate of unemployment is that rate at which the real wage gain demanded by labor is equal to the economy's ability to generate real wage gains—its rate of growth of productivity —the natural rate of unemployment must vary as the rate of growth of productivity varies. From 1965 to 1980, American productivity fell from a trend increase of 3.2 percent per year to a trend decline of 0.2 percent per year. To accommodate the decline, the natural rate of unemployment would have had to rise enough to force labor to reduce its demand for real wage gains from 3.2 percent to minus 0.2 percent.

Price shocks such as the OPEC oil hike also push up the natural rate. If the share of GNP necessary to buy a fixed quantity of oil rises from 1 to 5 percent, as it did from 1973 to 1980, then real wage gains must decline by a like amount. If productivity rises 4.7 percent (1973–80), but imported oil prices rise to take an extra 4 percent of that extra GNP, then real wage demands must be reduced from 4.7 to 0.7 percent over that same period of time. To bring this about, the natural rate of unemployment must rise to persuade workers to lower their real wage demands.

If a natural rate of unemployment does exist, productivity declines and external shocks have pushed that rate to a much higher level in 1980 than was the case in 1965. So to have used the natural rate of unemployment for policy purposes, it would have been necessary to forecast the jump—since one would have needed to know when the labor market was temporarily out of equilibrium; that is, when unemployment was too low.

To have done this, economists would have had to forecast the decline in productivity growth and the OPEC oil shock—neither of which was foreseen by anyone. The same economists would also have had to specify the speed with which inflation would accelerate in a period when unemployment was below the natural rate because the latter was rising.

Even without the appearance of adverse events, there is every reason to believe that the natural rate of unemployment is unstable. Instead of being exogenous and stable, the labor market works so as to make the natural rate of unemployment endogenous and unstable, thanks to the "filtering" that occurs between the most desired and the least desired workers during periods of high unemployment.

Labor is not a homogeneous commodity. If relative wages do not adjust instantly to bring individual wages and productivity into balance, employers seek to get the best possible employees they can find in the queue of unemployed workers.[21] In times of high unemployment, employers try to replace less preferred workers with the more preferred as the labor force turns over. Consider the changing distribution of unemployment during a recession. Rates initially rise for everyone in the downturn, but when aggregate unemployment stabilizes, unemployment begins to fall for preferred workers and to rise for less preferred workers. Over time this means that unemployment becomes more and more concentrated among the least preferred workers (black teen-agers) and that the unemployment of the preferred groups (prime-age white males) gradually drops, even though the national unemployment rate remains constant.

As the unemployment rate of the most preferred groups drop, their wage demands will as a consequence increase. This confronts the policy makers with a choice: they can further tighten policies to reduce demands to re-establish the level of preferred unemployment needed to contain that group's real and nominal wage demands or they can allow their anti-inflationary policy thrusts to die as the preferred group's unemployment slips below its natural rate of unemployment. If monetary or fiscal policies are tightened to raise unemployment and control the demands of the preferred workers, however, unemployment rises for both the preferred and unpreferred groups. National unemployment climbs and the filtering process starts over again. One can see that the logic requires periodic tightenings and subsequent increases in unemployment in a never-ending cycle to remain consistent with the natural rate of unemployment of the preferred group. As a consequence the national natural rate of unemployment has to grow higher whenever unemployment is above the natural rate.

This would not occur if relative wages were in fact flexible. Groups with low unemployment would be in short supply and their wages would rise. Conversely, groups with high unemployment would be in surplus supply and their wages would fall. Given a shift in relative wages, employers' preferences among workers would disappear and the filtering process would stop. But relative wages seem remarkably invariant to differentials in unemployment rates among groups.

The natural rate of unemployment is also unstable if the real wage gain demanded by labor is unstable. The natural-rate model does not say where this preference comes from or how it is formed. Basically the theory is a psychological theory, but just how the psychological mechanism works is left unspecified. Like utility in consumption theory and psychic income in occupational choice, the natural rate of unemployment depends upon an unspecified, unobservable, unmeasurable variable—the psychologically demanded real wage gain. But whatever is supposed to happen no theoretical reason exists to think that it leads to stable real wage demands.

There is also every reason to conclude that real economic events affect psychological preferences. Homo economicus persumably never suffers from money illusion, but what is one to make of the evidence showing that workers were much more unhappy with their economic progress in the 1970s than hard economic data would warrant? The labor force was clearly dissatisfied, but as noted earlier, its real disposable per capita income went up 26 percent during the decade. This was not much below the 32 percent rise that produced happiness in the 1960s and far above the 19 percent gain of the 1950s. So results that brought satisfaction in one period brought dissatisfaction in another, or workers underestimated their real gains. But if workers think that their income is rising much more slowly than it actually is, they are going to demand higher nominal and real wage gains than they would if they more accurately understood their situation. In either case the natural rate of unemployment becomes unstable.

The theory also leaves unspecified the speed with which prices change on either side of the natural rate of unemployment. If prices rise rapidly when unemployment is below the natural rate but fall slowly when unemployment is above it, the operating characteristics of the system are very different from those that prevail if the reaction times are symmetric. And certainly evidence abounds that wages respond faster to upward price shocks, such as rising energy prices, than they do to downward price shocks, such as falling energy prices. If the relationship is asymmetric and society wants a low, as opposed to just a stable, rate of inflation, the natural-rate hypothesis implies many more months above the natural rate than below it, even if the initial price shocks are equally divided between upward and downward shocks. Combined with asymmetric shocks (more upward than downward price shocks) and a rising natural rate when actual unemployment is above the natural rate, asymmetric time constants create an economy in which unemployment has to be substantially above the natural rate and rising most of the time to keep inflation stable and low.

There is also every reason to believe that the asymmetries have grown. This has occurred because a rising proportion of the economy has privately or publicly indexed itself, meaning that prices and wages automatically rise in junction with some price index. Indexing both speeds up price increases and makes them asymmetric—faster above than below the natural rate of unemployment.

The problem is easily visible if we assume for purposes of discussion a system where government by law indexes all wages and prices. Suppose that everyone bargains in real terms. With a 3 percent gain in productivity, everyone agrees to a 3 percent real wage gain. With the economy indexed, any inflation, once started, is propagated forever forward. So if some initial shock pushes inflation up to 7 percent this year, next year all wages will rise an extra 7 to 10 percent which is bound to produce a 7 percent rate of inflation next year. And so on into the future. Any shock leads to a permanently higher rate of inflation. What starts off as an initial external shock becomes embedded in the the economy as inertial inflation.

With 100 percent indexing only two things can lower inflation: increases in productivity that are for some reason not
reflected in the real wage bargain and negative price shocks
coming from abroad. Indexing means that nominal wage bargains do not decline simply because unemployment is above
the natural rate. No nominal wage bargains can be affected,
since they do not exist. There is only a real wage bargain that
depends entirely upon the rate of growth of productivity. In
this case the asymmetry is complete. Higher unemployment
never leads to lower wage increases called for under the natural-rate hypothesis.

While the American economy is not 100 percent indexed by
law, it is heavily indexed—both by law and informally. And the
greater the indexing, the less wages and hence prices respond
to unemployment, and hence more and more asymmetry. And
with asymmetry, increases in fiscal or monetary stimulus
mostly increase P (create inflation), whereas reductions in
fiscal or monetary stimulus mostly reduce T (create a lower
real GNP and more unemployment).

Although prices and wages are not completely rigid downward (witness recent auto rebates and the reduction in wages
at the Chrysler Corporation), strong asymmetric relationships
do seem to exist (the auto rebates and wage reductions did not
occur until half of the industry was unemployed). Prices and
wages seem to rise easily to clear markets, but they do not
seem to fall to clear markets with the same ease and speed.
Why? The problem is not new. Even the Great Depression
with its 25 percent unemployment rates and ten-year duration
ended up with real wages actually rising. Nominal wages fell
from 1929 to 1933 and then started to rise, but unemployment
was still 17 percent in 1939 with unemployment and idle capacity remaining high until 1941. Why? The question is as
germane now as it was then. Yet the price-auction model has
no answer.

Whatever the cause, an endogenous, unknown, unstable,
and asymmetric natural rate of unemployment just does not
allow policy makers to predict how increases in MV will affect
P and T. As a result they cannot adjust M to produce the
changes in P or T that they want, even if the theory is correct.

Moreover, little difference exists between the hypotheses of
the Phillips curve and the natural rate of unemployment when

it comes to giving advice to policy makers. If society wants to reduce inflation under either, unemployment must rise. The only difference here is the discontinuity postulated in the natural-rate-of-unemployment hypothesis. Below some rate, inflation rises; above some rate, inflation falls. In the Phillips curve there is instead a gradual transition. But since no one knows just where the natural rate's discontinuity is to be found, policy makers must in practice gradually raise unemployment until they find a point where inflation stabilizes or starts to fall. Which is precisely what a policy maker must do if he is working under the assumption of the Phillips curve. Unemployment must be forced up to a point at which society is satisfied with its rate of inflation. Since the two theories lead you to exactly the same practical action, it hardly matters which you believe theoretically.

Trench Warfare versus A-Bomb Monetarists

Although most money-supply monetarists accept the natural-rate-of-unemployment hypothesis, they can be further divided into trench-warfare and atomic-bomb varieties depending on their strategy to affect the natural rate of unemployment. One group believes that we can best stop inflation slowly; the other, suddenly.

Trench-warfare monetarists would increase unemployment gradually until they found a point slightly (one or two percentage points) above the natural rate. They would then sit there until inflation retreated to an acceptable level. They admit that our experience and data show that inflation responds to higher unemployment only very slowly. Some argue, however, that if government reaches the desired level of unemployment and then makes it "perfectly clear" that it will not retreat from that level regardless of the political consequences (something that ranges from difficult to impossible in a democracy), the adjustment process will speed up and inflation will fall faster than present econometric evidence would lead us to believe.

Expectations will change; inflation will fall. This has to be taken on faith since there are no recent historical analogues to which anyone can point. Behavioral theories as to how actual events affect economic expectations are conspicuous by their absence. The idea, however, is to frighten labor into lowering its demanded real wage gain. No one knows, however, how much unemployment it takes to engender fear.

There are a number of problems with trench-warfare monetarism. If the economy is being hit with adverse price shocks such as oil or food, the feedback control mechanisms may simply be inadequate to control the system. The policies adopted to offset the adverse shocks may take a long time to work, while the shocks work very rapidly. Inflation gets further and further ahead of the policies designed to control it. But if the policies adopted are harsh enough to control inflation in the short run, they are likely to overshoot their targets in the long run and produce a slowdown in growth that is politically and economically unacceptable. This means policies are reversed before they can achieve their anti-inflationary objectives, as events during the 1975 recession show.

Moreover, with the labor-market filtering mechanism at work, the natural rate also drifts up with the actual rate. What seems like a moderate policy of increasing unemployment slightly leads to the policy maker finally having to create large increases in unemployment to get desired results. Along the way, the structure of the economy itself is damaged. Once the natural rate rises in response to a period of high unemployment, it is not at all clear how the policy maker gets it back down.

But even if higher unemployment causes expectations to shift eventually and so eases inflation, is the voting public willing to put up with the strategy? Will results come quickly enough to persuade the public that the costs are worth enduring? In truth, the enormous costs in terms of lost output will be incurred to cure a psychological problem which should not even be a problem in the equilibrium price-auction model.

A-bomb monetarists, meanwhile, look for ways to speed up the development of favorable changes in expectations. One way is to increase unemployment dramatically and scare the labor force into changing their expectations with a vision of the Great Depression. To some extent the problem is similar to our bombing policy in the Vietnam war. Our military attempted to intimidate the North Vietnamese by gradually increasing the intensity of the bombing, but the approach only made them increasingly immune to bombing as it went along. In the end, American forces dropped enormous tonnage with little effect. The same amount dropped all at once at the beginning might have had a very different effect. The same with higher unemployment. To say that a dramatic sudden rise to some level, let's say 20 percent, would stop inflation is not to say that a gradual escalation to 20 percent over a number of years would do the same thing.

The problem is: How do you make credible a threat to drop the atomic bomb on yourself and everyone else if everyone else doesn't behave the way you want them to? No such threat really ever works. The voters would simply throw out the incumbent politicians. Among current officeholders Mrs. Thatcher comes the closest to being an A-bomb monetarist. She dropped some mini-economic nuclear devices, which knocked 13 percent off the index of British industrial production and raised unemployment to 16 percent in the spring of 1983. She may in the end get what she expected, but in 1982, inflation had just succeeded in getting back to a 9 percent rate, which is where it was when she took office.

As a result some economists have gone out looking for the philosopher's stone, to turn base metal into gold. The economic equivalent here of the philosopher's stone is gold—or more precisely, indexing the money supply to gold. The basic idea is to make an institutional change—use the supply of gold to control the printing of money—that will make credible government's promise to behave and control the rate of growth of the money supply.[22] If this can be done, according to the gold bugs, we may not need the recession called for by both the trench-warfare and A-bomb monetarists.

The case for gold begins with the observation that the German and other central European hyperinflations of the 1920s ended very suddenly when governmental arrangements were changed—usually a new rule that governments must borrow rather than print money to finance their deficits—even though governments did not change their behavior either toward their deficits or their printing of money.[23] In the case of Germany, the money supply grew rapidly the year after inflation stopped. This has led some rational expectationists to believe that only expectations, and not even the rate of growth of the money supply, matter.

According to the argument here, if governments would go back to the gold standard, everyone would understand that the money supply was under control and inflation would stop. Money could only be printed if the supply of gold increased. Accordingly, the public would have confidence in their money because the government was essentially out of the business of determining how much of it should be created. Less inflation would result either because the money supply was growing more slowly or because a favorable change in expectations occurred.

Technically, no reason exists to suppose that the supply of gold would grow at a rate consistent with the real rate of growth of output and the income elasticity of demand for money—the two economic factors that determine the noninflationary rate of growth of the money supply. Depending upon the vagaries of gold mining or the policies of the largest gold miners (Russia and South Africa), gold supplies could be growing above or below the desired rate. And during the time the gold standard existed, prices were not stable. They went up and down substantially, though ending up in 1932 approximately where they began in 1870.

But more important, most of the world's governments left the gold standard in the early 1930s because they found that they could not live with it. What is to stop them from once again leaving it, even if they promise never to do it. How do you make a government promise credible? The truth is, it is only credible if you trust the promisers, and they come and go with the political winds.

Supply-Side Inflation Theories

All the inflation theories examined so far are similar in that they believe that inflation can be controlled by manipulating the demand side of the market. The monetarists have always been convinced that inflation is "always and everywhere" a monetary phenomenon that could be controlled by cutting the rate of growth of the money supply and the money demand for goods and services. At least until recently, the fiscalists believed that inflation could be controlled by cutting aggregate demand with tax and expenditure policies. Both are demand-side techniques that differ only on whether demand is best kept under control with monetary or fiscal policies. Neither focuses on the supply side of the market.

Inflation theories do not focus on the supply-side variables, because supply-side factors can never cause inflation when inflation is defined as a "sustained" rise in prices. But to do that is to redefine inflation in such a way as to eliminate much of what is measured as inflation and very often to miss the real "instigating" factors.

Those who say that supply-induced inflations exist do not deny the validity of the basic model where price shocks (oil price hikes, for example) are balanced by induced price decreases (lower after-oil incomes leading to less demand for other goods and hence price declines) in the rest of the economy. But essentially such theorists argue that the equilibrium price-auction model of inflation takes so long to work that a supply-side solution for inflation becomes necessary.[24]

The problem can be compared to dropping a feather from a tall building. What can we predict will happen to it, based on the law of gravity? The feather will eventually hit the ground. But if the wind is blowing, the feather may go up and not down; it may not hit the ground for a very long time; and it may be a long way from the bottom of the building when it does. None of these possibilities repeals the law of gravity, but they point up factors other than that law which must be taken into account if one wants to predict the feather's rate of descent.

In many ways the law of gravity is similar to the quantity theory of money. Few deny that controlling the money supply will eventually bring inflation down. But that is not the whole picture. One needs to know other things in order to predict what direction inflation will take, to stop it from rising, and to speed up its descent.

Suppose, for example, there was a country where the growth of the money supply (M1) had trended downward at 8.2 percent, 7.4 percent, and 6.5 percent, and 5 percent over a four-year period. What would any good monetarists predict about the rate of inflation? It should be falling, right?

But that sequence of money-supply growth rates was ours from 1978 through 1981. At the same time, however, our inflation trend was up—7.6 percent in 1978, 11.3 percent in 1979, and 13.5 percent in 1980, then falling to 9.1 percent in 1981 (figures using the GNP deflator). If inflation is supposed to respond to a slowdown in the rate of growth of the money supply, that response has been very erratic and slow. In 1982 inflation fell into the 5 percent range, but the costs were high —no net economic growth after the first quarter of 1979, and unemployment approaching 11 percent.

Some monetarists respond by saying that inflation persists because the Federal Reserve Board followed an erratic course, even though its year-to-year growth rates have been consistently down with very little variance. If the 1980 6.5 percent rate of growth of the money supply is analyzed, monetarists note that there was little growth in the money supply from December to May, a 16 percent rate of growth of the money supply (at annual rate) from May to October, and once again no growth in the money supply from October to December. In sum, the short-term movements in the money supply have been too erratic to allow monetary policies to have had the desired effect.

This raises the issue of "fine tuning." Back in the late 1960s the Keynesians were accused of being hopelessly naïve in thinking that they could "fine-tune" fiscal policies. But here the monetarists are being equally naïve in thinking that they can "fine-tune" the money supply adroitly enough to make the system work. Moreover, there is no theoretical reason why short-run fluctuations in the rate of growth of the money supply should overwhelm a consistent long-run slowdown. And until monetary policies failed to work, the importance of short-run erratic movements in the money supply was never mentioned by the monetarists.

In early 1981 President Reagan's chairman of the Council of Economic Advisers, Murray Weidenbaum, was asked how much time was needed for monetary policies to be effective. Did the Fed have to be on target yearly, quarterly, monthly, weekly, or daily?[25] Weidenbaum wasn't willing to specify the time period. If the Fed has to be on target every day, week, month, or quarter for monetary policies to work, the central bank has to exercise a virtually impossible degree of "fine tuning." If the Fed only has to be on target on a yearly basis, it has in fact been on target, and inflation should have decelerated in the late 1970s. Alternatively one can argue that the Fed's monetary policies, like gravity, were working, but that the wind was simultaneously blowing very hard. Oil prices almost tripled from 1978 to early 1981, while wages were rising at a 10 percent rate as productivity was falling. However, such an assertion undercuts the contention that inflation is "everywhere and always" a monetary phenomenon.

In a world where wages and prices are either rigid downward or simply much slower to adjust down than up, there is a clear case to be made for a supply-side anti-inflation policy. This case is strengthened if the operating institutional characteristics of the system (in this instance indexing) can translate a one-time shock into permanent upward price pressures—inertial inflation.

Indexing, basically an insurance policy against inflation, is an example of economic events producing institutional changes that feed back upon economic events. Every rational person, as an individual, wants an insurance policy to protect himself from inflation, but collectively such policies may change the operating characteristics of the system in a perverse manner; namely, inflation becomes less responsive to unemployment, and an external shock, once absorbed, can lead to an unending upward wage-price spiral.

To sum it all up: If employers agree to give their employees wage gains equal to the rate of growth of productivity, plus the rate of inflation, both fiscal and monetary policies lose their capacity to stop inflation. The closer the actual economy is to 100 percent indexing, the less the effects. In terms of the quantity theory of money, whatever the division of a change on MV on P and T prior to indexing, more of the effects will fall on P and less on T after indexing. To get a given fall in wages, unemployment will have to be higher, since indexed wages won't fall and other wages will have to fall that much more to make up for the failure of the indexed sector to decline. The natural rate of unemployment may remain the same, but the payoff from moving to levels above the natural rate will be slower, and a longer divergence between actual and natural rates will be necessary to get a given positive effect on inflation.

Wages are also such a large fraction of the costs of production that it is difficult to get prices to fall unless wages fall simultaneously. In fact, any parade to lower rates of inflation is unlikely unless wage reductions lead the way. But this is exactly what is not going to happen in an indexed system where wages lag behind prices.

Moreover, supply-side shocks in an indexed economy lead to inertial inflation, which, once started, keeps going and along the way is difficult to manage.[26] The inertial component is compounded by another institutional reality: the American labor market is characterized by three-year overlapping contracts. Such contracts make it almost impossible politically for union leaders to cooperate to keep wage increases in line with the rate of productivity growth, even though the leaders themselves know that any wage increase in excess of productivity growth can only produce inflation.

Suppose the elected head of the Machinists Union is negotiating a contract for the next three years. He and his membership know that last year the Electrical Workers signed a three-year contract for an annual 10 percent wage hike. His people often labor alongside the electricians. If the leader is to be re-elected, he must sign a comparable contract. But when the Electrical Workers enter new negotiations, they will find themselves in exactly the same situation. The Machinists got a 10 percent wage hike, and the head of the Electrical Workers must get a like amount to survive politically.

An attenuated version of the same phenomenon also occurs among nonunion employees. A firm that attempts to lower the prevailing wage increase finds that its skilled workers tend to move to the firms that have accepted the standard pattern. It would also find a tendency among its workers to unionize to get the prevailing scales.

The problem is further compounded by the seniority system of hiring and firing. Workers know that a wage demand that is too high will lead to unemployment and inflation, but they also know if *they* run any risk of being fired, since with seniority firing, the new worker, the person with the least seniority, will be fired. But a union leader needs 51 percent of the votes, and 51 percent of the voters (those still employed) are almost always sure that they will not be the people hurt if wage settlements are too large, given the capacity of the economy to pay them.

Indexing and multi-year overlapping contracts with seniority firing produce much of what can be called inertial inflation. Supply shocks get inflation started; inertial inflation keeps it propagated once it is started. This leaves the central bank with little choice but to accommodate inflation, because to refuse will create very large reductions in GNP with very small improvements in the price performance of the economy.

Since the equilibrium price-auction model teaches us that institutions don't matter (they are a reflection of economic reality—always evolving to the most efficient form—rather than a determinant of it), economists are reluctant to argue that institutions must be reformed to solve an economic problem. But two other industrial countries, Germany and Japan, have a better inflation record than we in recent years, and both countries possess economies composed of very different institutional settings.

In Germany, cost-of-living escalator clauses are illegal in wage contracts. Although wages may still rise in response to exogenous shocks such as those administered by OPEC, they do not rise automatically. Given the time necessary to negotiate a new contract, German wages at least rise more slowly. And since any wage increase has to be independently negotiated, it is at least possible for various leaders to put forward the idea that a society cannot index itself against external price shocks without creating an explosive upward price spiral. This has to help slow inertial inflation. The Germans do, however, pay a potential price, since no one is going to sign three-year contracts without the protection of a cost-of-living clause. With more bargaining, more strikes are always a possibility.

In Japan, by tradition all contracts run out on the same day. This produces a period of simultaneous de facto national wage bargaining—the "spring offensive." The result is a period when society can have a national discussion as to what constitutes noninflationary wage behavior in the interests of all. If that behavior calls for a phase-down in wage increases, everyone can accept the burden at the same time. But more important, the "spring offensive" gives every worker time to be educated as to what the real options are. That education does not mean that he will make the right choices, but it does mean he can at least be better informed as to what those choices are. The Japanese also build flexibility into their wage structure with a system of bonuses that account for about one third of earnings. Wages cannot fall in hard times, but bonuses can.

If we were to adopt German and Japanese practices, our inflation performance might be improved. But a change in the system is not a change in the inputs to the old system. Accordingly, the former is regarded as outside the bounds of economics as defined by the equilibrium price-auction market. If the profession were to admit that institutions are important to the economy, it would require a substantial change in the dominant intellectual theory of economics. Techniques other than monetary or fiscal policies would then be admitted to the pantheon of possible policy prescriptions to fight inflation.

The Existence of Price Flexibility

From a supply-side perspective, it is also important to establish whether prices in general are rigid or whether the only problems with the standard model are found in rigid wages. If prices are independently rigid, a supply-side inflationary policy has to affect much, much more than the labor market; namely, product markets as well as labor markets.

It is hard to determine whether prices are independently rigid. If wages are rigid downward, only a limited amount of observed price flexibility is possible. Wages are simply such a large fraction of value added (68 percent in the nonfinancial corporate sector) that prices could be completely flexible within the constraints set by wages, without much observed price flexibility showing through.

Are prices flexible within the limits set by wages? The answer is "yes" according to economists who accept the natural-rate-of-unemployment hypothesis. But to a great extent the correct answer depends on the sector under consideration. Agricultural and most raw-material prices certainly seem flexible if one observes their price behavior, given basic supplies and demands. But what about industrial prices that do not seem to move much?

Historically, periods of inflation are not uncommon, with many having occurred in the past 150 years of industrial history. But times of inflation have always been followed by periods of falling prices, which is something we have not seen since the Great Depression. Why?

One possible answer is a shift in the proportions of the economy that fall within the flexible and rigid price sectors. Suppose that agricultural prices are flexible and that an economy is 50 percent agricultural and 50 percent industrial. Such an economy will seem a lot more flexible than one that is 3 percent agricultural and 97 percent industrial (the American proportions), even though the two sectors may behave identically within the two economies.

Beyond agriculture, larger and larger fractions of the GNP are also being produced in sectors (medicine, government) that are clearly not comprised of simple profit-maximizing firms. What are the pricing rules in these sectors? Government action may also be changing private behavior without changing the formal structure of the economy. Since falling prices mean falling incomes for producers, each of us organizes publicly and privately to ensure that we are not the ones who will experience falling prices and incomes. But if each of us is successful, inflation will be the inevitable result. Upward price shocks will occur which will not be offset by price declines elsewhere in the economy because government will intervene to prevent any negative shocks from lowering anyone's income.

If Japanese competition has begun to force down the price of steel, textiles, and electronic goods, our producers run to Washington for protection to prevent their prices and incomes from falling. Sectors that experience fluctuating free-market prices (like agriculture) demand and get government intervention that stops prices from falling. Meanwhile, minimum wages and prevailing rates on government construction contracts place floors under wages for workers.

Government policies also, of course, affect decisions made by large companies. Large oligopolistic firms know that they have more to lose from cutting prices than from cutting output in markets with only a few firms. And as long as cutbacks in production are modest and of short duration, such firms can informally coordinate them with their industrial competitors. A government guarantee that recessions will be infrequent and short may make price rigidities possible where they would otherwise not be. But market power is not absolute. Prices do not respond to moderate amounts of excess capacity, but they might fall if demand fell enough or if government changed its approach toward recessions.

Economics has a supply-and-demand theory of price determination for competitive markets and complete monopolies, but it has no theory of price determination for oligopolies—the most prevalent form of industrial organization. Many producers have just a few competitors, with the GNP having become increasingly concentrated among the largest firms in the last two decades. Most companies simply cannot be described as a large number of atomistic competitors making a homogenous product that is then auctioned to the highest bidder. If one looks at the few large firms that are increasingly dominating American industry, they just cannot axiomatically fall into the equilibrium price-auction framework, one having many competitors and ease of entry. The number of competitors is too few and the entry costs too high. Although such firms may act exactly "as if" the price-auction framework existed, their behavior has to be established with careful observation rather than simply assumed.

This means that economics needs an empirically useful theory of oligopolistic behavior. How do very large firms, unions, and nonprofit agencies act in the real world when they have few competitors or when they are not simple profit or income maximizers? What moves them to change their prices? How do they decide what constitutes the right mix of price competition and competition on other dimensions—product differentiation and service, among other things? The issue is not "Are oligopolies competitive?" Of course they are competitive. The issue is when, where, and to what extent they are *price*-competitive. If economics does not have a theory of price determination in oligopolistic situations or if prices are indeterminate in such situations, then the profession does not have a useful theory of inflation.

When economists looked at oligopolies, realistic sets of assumptions always seemed to lead to indeterminate results with many possible outcomes. Deterministic solutions required counterfactual sets of assumptions. The world is not, for example, a two-person zero-sum game, and no oligopolist expects competitors to hold their prices or quantities fixed in response to his moves. Yet these were the assumptions required to produce deterministic results.[27]

In general, without an empirically valid micro-economic theory of oligopolistic behavior, it is impossible to predict, understand, or influence oligopolistic behavior or even to build a normative model of how oligopolists should act. They can be described as long-run profit, wage, or sales maximizers, but such descriptions have no operational significance. They may engage in price markups, but how are the magnitudes of the various markups determined? When does an oligopolist introduce a new heterogeneous product and how is the price of that product determined? The development and pricing of new products has yet to be developed as far as economic theory is concerned, yet it is central to a dynamic economy.

Empirical studies would seem to show that problems arise if researchers treat product markets as if they were simple price-auction markets. Different prices seem to exist for the same product even within very limited markets. In one study of homogeneous products in the Boston area there was at least a 2-to-1 difference between the highest and lowest prices quoted for a product in seventeen out of thirty-nine cases.[28] Even competing supermarkets don't charge the same price for the same product, and often a product sells at two different prices (lower near the checkout counter) within the same store. Equilibrium prices are hard to find.

One solution would be to create the competitive markets that economists do understand. But for a variety of reasons, economists' interest in creating competitive markets has waned. Those who believe the earlier syllogism about the dominance of such markets believe that markets are in fact much more competitive than they appear to be. Using antitrust laws to enlarge the number of oligopolistic competitors slightly does not seem worth the effort. Regulating oligopolies is popular with the public, but tends to be seen by the economics profession as producing more inefficiency than it eliminates; and in any case, regulation does not lead to flexible competitive prices. If one does not understand oligopolistic behavior, how can one know that the benefits of eliminating oligopolies exceed the costs? As it is, wide variance in prices seems to exist in what look like classically competitive markets.

As Galbraith has argued, and many other economists implicitly believe, oligopolies may lead to types of de facto planning which the entire economy needs in order to be dynamically efficient.[29] Through their R&D expenditures large firms may also cause or result in the acceptance of more technical change than would otherwise be the case. Their very existence may simply express the reality of and the need for large economies of scale in most industries.

In sum, economics needs a theory of oligopolistic behavior

and especially a theory of oligopolistic price determination. Some economists deny the meaningful existence of oligopolies; some glorify their usefulness; some blame them for almost everything. But no economist understands their pricing be- havior.

Incomes Policies

Supply-side inflation inevitably takes the profession into the question of incomes policies. Incomes policies, like the Phillips curve, have at least nine lives. Whatever the real experience with them, they keep coming back. The inflation-unemploy- ment link lives on because it must be true at extremes of unemployment. Incomes policies live on because they offer the vision of a perfectly consistent painless way to stop inflation and because they may be the only game in town for stopping inflation without stopping the economy.

Imagine an indexed economy with an 8 percent rate of infla- tion. If everyone agreed to raise his wages or prices by only 5 percent, instead of the specified 8 percent, no one would be worse off or better off and the inflation rate would be reduced to 5 percent. The result: a painless cure.

How to accomplish this, however, is not clear. Every individ- ual economic actor has an incentive to raise his wages or prices by the full 8 percent, since he will have increased his real income by 3 percent if everybody else accepts a 5 percent gain and he doesn't. Conversely, if he cooperates with the incomes policy and goes down to a 5 percent gain while everyone else stays at 8 percent, he will have suffered a 3 percent income loss. Thus there is no such thing as a voluntary incomes policy; the incentives not to cooperate are simply too great.

The problem is similar to one found at a football game. Suppose an exciting play begins to develop. To get a better view, individual spectators stand up; but if everyone stands up, no one gets a better view and everyone is uncomfortable, since everyone would rather sit than stand. But the first one to stand up gets a better view until everyone else stands up. Only collective action can keep everyone seated; individual decision making here means everyone will stand. But what about the process of sitting down? The first person to sit down gets the worst view, and the last person to sit down gets the best one.

Everyone wants to be the last one standing and everyone remains standing.

So in the inflation game, the first person to raise his prices and the last person to stop raising his prices are the winners. Everyone wants to win, and no one wants to lose. To take one group, farmers can at the same time scream about inflation yet demand agricultural supports to raise farm prices. Everyone wants to inflate his own wages and prices and deflate everyone else's.

Incomes policies also present problems beyond those of non-cooperation. Whenever controls are imposed, some groups will be ahead of other groups. An even phase-down of inflation will leave those that started the inflationary process permanently ahead. Technically it is easy to specify a set of rules that will fairly and efficiently stop inflation from starting, but it is not easy to specify a set of rules for a phase-down. Areas will exist where basic supplies and demands call for raising prices. But for every price that continues to rise, some other prices and incomes must fall by a greater amount to hold the price level stable.

Areas will also exist where supply and demand call for prices to fall, but the political pressure to do something will be much less acute here than in areas where prices are rising. One lives with surpluses more easily than with shortages. Exemptions from the controls will be needed and they will be given. But every exemption leads those who are not exempted to wonder why they and not others are conscripted inflation fighters for the U.S. of A. If some of the inflation is due to the price of imported oil, controls must lower the incomes of some Americans to pay foreign energy producers. Whose incomes should controls lower? No one wants it to be his.

The currently fashionable form of incomes-policy discussion revolves around "tax-based incomes policies." Employers and workers would be given a series of tax incentives or penalties, depending on whether they did or did not live up to some enunciated standard of noninflationary behavior. The strategy would be to have government set a target annual wage increase that would gradually fall over time to the rate of growth of productivity. Advocates of tax-based incomes policies tend to fall into the camp that believes that the real problem is wages, and that if that were brought under control, the inflation problem would disappear. But for the political purpose of demonstrating equity between capital and labor, prices would not be allowed to rise to cover anything but the specified wage increases and fluctuations in commodity prices. (The latter are allowed to fluctuate, since they are bought and sold in markets that everyone recognizes as price-competitive.) Firms that live up to the prescribed behavior pay lower taxes. Workers who work for these firms also pay lower taxes.

A tax-based incomes policy is, however, equivalent to a set of wage and price controls with a predetermined set of financial penalties for violators. Catching the violators and enforcing the rules is no less difficult or expensive. The system is more flexible (if you want to violate the rules, you can pay your penalty and violate the rules), but it is every bit as complex and expensive to administer. Detailed norms must be written and then enforced. In the previous instance when wage and price controls were imposed, in the Korean War, 18,000 inspectors were necessary to administer the system. There have been advances made in computation techniques, but the economy is now much larger than it was in the early 1950s.

Problems of actual and perceived equity are substantial. What about the employee who got no wage increase but worked for an employer who violated the rules? That person is assigned higher taxes, although he does not think of himself as contributing to inflationary pressures. Compare that person to an employee who got a very large wage increase but who worked for an employer who was living up to the wage guidelines. The second would get a tax cut; the first a tax increase.

Any system depends on voluntary cooperation. Laws can only tell us what society wants and force a small minority who do not accept that judgment to conform to society's norms. The system cannot force the majority or even a large minority to conform. Where does the necessary political support come from? How is it sustained?

But the problem is not really administrative costs or the difficulties of achieving equity or securing support in a democracy. The real economic problem is writing a set of rules and regulations with which the economy can live for a substantial period of time. Somebody has to develop some set of rules for allowing wages and prices to change over time. Given the complexity of the economic system, almost no economist thinks that he has the ability to write such rules. Shortages would emerge because some of the rules would not hold water. This would lead prices to drift upward as exceptions were allowed. The pressure to cut prices where they were inadvertently too high would not be as great. But with an upward drift in prices above the targeted levels, workers would become less and less satisfied with their specified wage increases. Political pressures for a change in the rules would inevitably arise.

Conclusions

All current macro-economic theories of inflation and unemployment depend on a fixed price model of behavior. Inflation either cannot exist or does not matter in a world of complete price flexibility. Keynes assumed that money wages did not easily fall. The natural-rate-of-unemployment hypothesis of the monetarists assumes an unalterable demand for real wage gains. No macro-economist systematically adheres to the price-auction view of the world because macro-economic problems cannot and do not exist in that theoretical world.

But adherence to one theory or another does not change the fact that the public wants a solution to what it perceives as a problem. If the economics profession does not have an answer, it is seen as intellectually bankrupt. But the very fact that the public, made up of real human beings, wants a solution to inflation indicates that something is wrong with the price-auction model of economic behavior. In the world of Homo economicus such a thing as painful inflation cannot exist; in the long run, money is neutral and has no effect on relative prices. Since, as the natural-rate-of-unemployment hypothesis maintains, the real GNP is unaffected by the rate of inflation, Homo economicus should not as a rational being worry about the rate of inflation—whatever it is. Yet real citizens are worried. Why? The prevailing economic theories have no answer.

CHAPTER 4

Econometrics

An Icebreaker Caught in the Ice

In the 1950s, when econometrics first emerged, the discipline was seen in America as an icebreaker that would lead the economics profession through the ice pack of conflicting theories. Econometric techniques would, it was presumed, conclusively prove or disprove economic hypotheses, accurately quantify economic relationships, and successfully predict the economic future. Unfortunately, the icebreaker failed to work and the econometric passage to utopia has not been found. The expectations might have been excessively optimistic, but the failures of econometric techniques were to have a profound impact on the discipline of economics.

The problem began with the inability of macro-economic models to predict the adverse events—soaring inflation, steadily climbing unemployment, and the cessation of productivity growth—that were about to hit us in the 1970s.[1] That failure to predict led to a breakdown in both the economics profession's confidence in econometric results and the public's confidence in economists.

Because econometrics did not fulfill predictions made for it, the door was open for both supply-side economics and rational expectations—the concerns of the next two chapters. Supply-side economists argue that the incentive effects of cuts in taxes on work and saving behavior are larger than any empirical econometric evidence would warrant. The supply-siders are able to make the argument despite the econometric "evidence" because the "evidence" is tainted—it has been wrong just often enough, so that no one can "prove" that the supply-side assumptions are wrong so "conclusively" that the claims in the public debate can be dismissed as a silly exaggeration. Rational expectations, in turn, are to some extent an attempt to explain why econometric equations do not work. Because random economic shocks have a much larger impact than previously thought and because economic decision makers change their behavior discontinuously, their decisions cannot be represented by stable statistical representations.

Large-scale econometric models illustrate both the ubiquitousness of econometric models and the problems with them. Nearly all economists use econometrics to provide evidence for and against various economic hypotheses. Econometric models have become, if not big business, very profitable business, with big business interested in both the resulting forecasts and in acquiring the firms that do the modeling. Nevertheless, econometrics has not proven capable of providing either accurate forecasts or conclusively settling economic disputes. Key variables such as the velocity of money or the division of any increase in the GNP between higher prices and a larger output (the Phillips curve problem) don't seem susceptible to econometric modeling. In many areas, the stable equations that economic theory depends on don't seem to exist. Economic evidence is often contradictory, and even where it is consistent, the conclusions have been wrong so many times that the credibility of even consistent results is suspect and can be ignored by those who want to.

But whatever the problem, mathematical models and their empirical analogue—econometric models—have now become the standard tools of economics. From their beginnings in macro-economic modeling, they have spread out to encompass everything. No branch of economics, including economic history, is now free of their use.[2] Fundamentally, modeling gives us the only way to establish the values of parameters which cannot be deduced from economic theory. Theory tells us that higher gasoline prices will lead to less gasoline usage, but exactly how much less? Only econometric studies can provide an answer. As a result, econometric estimation is here to stay regardless of its weaknesses or failures, real or imagined.

A Reversal of the Winds

In the revolution wrought by Paul Samuelson, mathematical models were devices for laying bare economic assumptions and checking the internal consistency of the conclusions that sprang from those assumptions.[3] But mathematical modeling gradually took on a life of its own as assumptions came to be made because they were mathematically tractable rather than because they were realistic. Probably the strongest thing going for the equilibrium price-auction model intellectually is the fact that it is mathematically tractable. Alternative economic formulations just don't seem to fit as neatly with calculus.

Because the mathematical formulations of economic theory are very attractive and because original hopes for econometric testing were dashed, the relationship between theory and data has gradually been inverted. Econometric models were at first supposed to test whether rigorous mathematical specifications of economic theories could be statistically verified. Was the theory supported by the data? Did the data prove the theory wrong?

In the end, econometric testing did not prove up to the assigned task. Equations and coefficients were not stable—robust. In other words, equations that were good at tracking historical experience proved to be poor predictors of the future; equations did not stand up over time; and changes in parameter values were frequent and dramatic. In commercial macro-econometric models, equations had to be re-estimated quarterly with each new set of data.

The reasons for the problem are as clear as the solutions are murky. Economic theory almost never specifies what secondary variables (other than the primary ones under investigation) should be held constant in order to isolate the primary effects. For example, when we look at the relationship between interest rates and investment, what other variables should be held constant: changes in the GNP, the level of unemployment, technology, foreign competition? When we look at the impact of education on individual earnings, what else should be held constant: IQ, work effort, occupational choice, family background? Economic theory does not say. Yet the coefficients of the primary variables almost always depend on precisely what other variables are entered in the equation to "hold everything else constant."

Even more often, the variables that are specified by economic theory are not part of the available data set, and inferior proxies have to be used. So when studying the impact of education on earnings, one would like to examine the relationship between acquired knowledge and earnings, but most studies have to use years of education as their actual explanatory variable. When studying productivity, one would like accurate data on actual hours of work, but data exist only for paid hours of work. Coffee breaks and leisure on the job get counted as if they were hours actually worked.

Economic theory also does not specify the exact functional relationships that should exist between primary variables or between the primary variables and the secondary variables. Interest rates should have a negative effect on plant and equipment investment, but what is the time lag between changes in interest rates and changes in investment? If the relationship must be corrected for the amount of unused capital capacity in the economy, what is the precise nature of the correction? Does education affect earnings in an additive manner having a separate effect on earnings independent of other variables, such as IQ, or does education affect earnings in a multiplicative manner, having a different impact on earnings depending on IQ? Economic theory does not say. Yet the coefficients of the equation almost always depend upon the precise functional forms that are used in estimating the relationships.

Because of these problems, the standard statistical measures (standard errors, t-statistics) used to gauge equation accuracy tend to give misleading estimates of the confidence that one can place in econometric equations. Not knowing exactly what secondary variables should be included in the relationships and not knowing the exact functional forms that should be used, equations are usually estimated many times. By simple random search, the analyst looks for the set of secondary variables and functional forms that give the "best" equations.

In this context the "best" equation is going to depend heavily upon the prior beliefs of the analyst. If the analyst believes that interest rates do not affect the velocity of money, he finds a "best" equation that validates his particular prior belief. If the analyst believes that interest rates do affect the velocity of money, he finds a "best" equation that validates this prior belief. Given the possibility of finding "best" equations from both points of view, neither "best" equation is capable of persuading the other side that *its* "best" equation is wrong.[4]

But when many attempts are made to find the "best" equation, the resulting equation is also not as good as its statistical measures would seem to indicate. In any equation the degrees of freedom (the number of empirical observations minus the number of explanatory variables) are supposed to indicate the degree to which a hypothesis has been tested. Since three observations can always be explained by an equation with three explanatory variables, an equation is only being tested to the extent that it has more than three observations. But with many attempts at finding the best equation, the degrees of freedom (free observations) are essentially exhausted and lose their significance as a test of the equation under consideration. At first glance, impressive equations seem to exist, but on closer analysis they are about as impressive as saying that any two random points can be defined by an equation for a straight line. And because the equations look much more imposing than they really are, everyone is disappointed when they fail to explain other data sets, or predict the future course of the same data sets.

Part of the problem is also due to dynamics. Most economic models are static, but all economies are dynamic, which is to say they change over time. Accordingly, macro-econometric models have to be dynamic. But how long are the lags and what shape do they take? How do periods of disequilibrium affect the equilibrium conditions to which the economy is headed? Since economic theory does not say, the dynamic properties used in economic modeling tend to have a disturbing ad hoc character.

Macro-economic models also make most important economic variables—the GNP, interest rates, labor supplies—endogenous to the model. But this means that models can only be estimated if it is possible to find good exogenous instrumental variables that allow one to isolate the underlying structural relationships. For example, suppose that one is trying to isolate the supply-and-demand curves for corn. Economists do not observe supply or demand curves, but merely the equilibrium intersections of the two. This yields a set of price and quantity observations, but do those observations trace out the demand curve for corn or the supply curve of corn? Obviously they trace out some mix of movements in both curves. In this case, variations in the weather may be an exogenous instrumental variable that changes enough to allow an analyst to find the demand curve for corn. If the supply curve is moving up and down because of the weather and the demand curve is unaffected by weather, then the observed equilibrium of prices and quantities can be used to trace out the economy's demand curve for corn.

But what is the exogenous instrumental variable, the equivalent of weather, that allows you to trace out the demand curve for money? There is none. Most economic relationships lack the good instrumental variables that allow econometricians to find the underlying structural relations that are being sought. Because nothing causes major movements in either the supply or demand curve without affecting the other, it is impossible to separate or identify either the supply or demand curve.

Given this mushy reality, it becomes possible to build models that are equally good statistically from a number of quite different perspectives. Theories could not be accepted or rejected based on the data because economic history did not happen to generate the data that might allow economists to conclusively choose which theory is right. This inability to find structural equations is especially true in models using time-series data. All time series tend to be highly correlated and usually move together. Consequently, not many independent sources of information exist despite the collection of many data series. Scant information in turn produces a situation where different complicated hypotheses cannot be conclusively accepted or rejected. The necessary information simply isn't there. So even when one theory looks better statistically than another, the proponents of the latter know that they have only to wait and the performance of the adversary's theory will probably deteriorate. At any given moment, econometric models looked solid and precise, but they are in fact quite elastic.

Macro-economic modeling was supposed to lead to a great leap forward in the profession because such modeling was where economists would be forced, it was thought, to integrate micro- and macro-theory. After all, macro-models are nothing but a series of micro-equations that have been statistically programmed to interact with each other and explain the aggregate performance of the economy. But it must be said that if macro-economic modeling has failed, then micro-economic modeling has also failed. The two can simply not be considered apart from one another. Macro-models only look weaker because no one even tries to build micro-models to explain all of micro-economic activity. Moreover, the failures of micro-modeling can only be detected if many articles in many publications are read carefully. The inadequacy of macro-modeling can be found in just three or four places. Finally, of course, the press cover macro-economic failures, while ignoring most of the micro-economic variety.

The failings of macro-models are also often exaggerated. Better than any other forecasting technique—certainly better than what we had before—the models have consistently predicted some variables, and have often produced good overall results.[5] One can wish they were better predictors, but nothing right now can do better and no one can do without them.

Nevertheless, the initial expectations were unrealistically optimistic. Good price and wage equations were, for example, never found. And without good price equations, no one had any reason to expect accurate inflation forecasts. In the 1973 version of the MIT-FRB model, the wage equation explained only 48 percent of the observed movement (variance) in wages.[6] Since prices were made a function of wages in the model's equations, what looked like impressive price equations were statistically quite poor. If a model can accurately predict prices once it knows wages but cannot accurately predict wages, it cannot of course really predict prices, even though it has what look like good price equations.

And even if the model could have accurately predicted wage increases, the 1973 price equations would have proved bad predictors after 1973. The shocks (oil, food) and inertial inflation (indexing) that occurred after that year simply did not exist prior to it. Without being able to predict the weather in Russia and the corn blight in the United States, no one or no econometric model could have forecast grain prices. And without being able to foretell that human aversion to risk would lead to widespread indexing as a response to inflation, no one or no model could have indicated prior to the fact that inertial inflation would become embedded in the American economy.

And finally, without being able to predict the 1973 Arab-Israeli war, no model could have foreseen the path of oil prices. Yet no one really expected or now expects macro-economic models to have predicted any of these events.

All econometric models, however, depend upon such exogenous variables, which have to be accurately forecast to get a decent forecast of the endogenous variables. Typically, the exogenous variables are left as just that because they are too hard or impossible to forecast or because they are too much influenced by factors outside the purview of economists; that is, they cannot be predicted by variables used by economists. The weather, OPEC, decisions of the Federal Reserve Board toward the money supplies, taxes and expenditures decisions, demography, and a host of other variables have to be accurately specified to get accurate econometric results. During model construction such variables are known, since models are built to fit historical data. But in forecasts based on the models the same variables are unknown and unpredictable. The result: we get predictions that look much worse than statistical tests of model accuracy would lead one to believe.

Technically speaking, statistical modeling also depends on the assumption of independent, normally distributed errors with zero mean value. This means that a shock in one period is not supposed to be related to nor should influence a shock in any other period, that a plot of the errors (deviations from what was expected to occur) would yield a normal distribution, and that the average value of those errors is zero. Of course, none of these assumptions accurately describes economic events in the real world.

In fact, economic data are collected based on the arbitary divisions of the calendar and not the rhythm of economic events. Shocks are unlikely to come on a quarterly basis and thus are likely to affect more than one quarter's data. Shocks are also unlikely to either be randomly distributed or have an average value of zero. For example, consider the economic effects of weather. One day of bad weather, a severe freeze, can destroy a whole crop. One day of good weather cannot produce a good crop or offset a freeze. If meteorologists are to be believed, weather patterns may also be determined by sunspot cycles that vary but last over several years, which means that weather patterns are not random on an annual basis. The result is a pattern of crop yields from year to year that are not independent of one another. Weather is a random shock, but not a shock with the characteristics assumed in econometric modeling.

Similar examples can be found in most areas of economics. If gasoline prices rise outside the bounds of previous experience, Americans may shift their consumer preferences toward small cars, change the rate at which they turn over the stock of cars, and reduce the amount of gasoline consumed. But the process may take ten years to complete, and during that time gasoline consumption does not have the necessary independence from year to year or quarter to quarter to lend itself to good statistical modeling.

Techniques have been developed for dealing with some of these problems, such as serial correlated error terms where the error observed this quarter is related to those around it, but they are generally not capable of eliminating the problems. To use the techniques to purge equations of the misleading influence of serially correlated errors, one needs to know the precise structure of the process generating the serially correlated shocks—how the errors are related to one another—but it is precisely the structure of these shocks that is unknown, unknowable, and variable. There is no reason to believe, for example, that the relationships between errors are always ones of simple decay (this quarter's error is some specified fraction of last quarter's error)—the standard econometric technique for dealing with serially correlated error terms.

Econometrics has always paid lip service to the idea of stochastic error, but it is only with the breakdown in the economists' ability to predict or control the economy that the size of these shocks has been recognized. Unfortunately, the random component in economic events is much larger relative to the deterministic component than most confident economists thought earlier. But having a large random component, no econometric function can be a good predictor. And without good predictions it becomes difficult to operate the economic controls—taxes, expenditures, money supplies, and interest rates—to obtain the economic results desired by the public.

The problem can be clearly seen in the human-capital equations used to explain individual earnings and justify investments in education. Even with very large numbers of explanatory variables and after thousands of attempts, these human-capital equations can explain only 20 to 30 percent of the variance in earnings in a random sample of the population. Technically, the equations are saying that the world is 20–30 percent deterministic and 70–80 percent random luck.[7]

The source of the problem lies in the wide dispersion of wages within occupational categories. The equilibrium price-auction model calls for homogeneous wages for homogeneous skills, but such wages just do not seem to exist (see Table 5). A natural tendency exists, however, to concentrate on the 20–30 percent of the results that are deterministic results (in particular the coefficients linking education with earnings) and ignore that 70–80 percent of unexplained variance. For some reason everyone then expresses surprise when the results do not accord with what was predicted based on the 20–30 percent of the system that is deterministic. Technically, no reason exists why results should accord with what was predicted. The random component is so large that it can easily mask the deterministic compoent.

In econometric models explaining the behavior of economic events over time, one often finds equations with R^2s of .99. Technically, this asserts that deterministic factors explain 99 percent of the variance in the data and that stochastic disturbance terms account for only 1 percent of the variance. If errors are serially correlated (move together over time), however, it is difficult to tell the difference statistically between random errors and the systematic workings of the economy. The result is econometric equations that tend to explain random disturbance terms rather than ignoring them. Analysts work on their models until they find equations that can explain the maximum amount of variance, but in the process they incorporate the effect of the serially correlated errors in the values of the parameters and variables which they include in their model.

Which is to say that the resulting models explain the past with what looks like a high degree of accuracy, and also look like they can be used to predict the future much better than they can. The world is in reality more random than the models statistically indicate. Parameter values are misestimated, variables are included that should not be, and both are incorporated into the equations to explain the random disturbance

Table 5

Distribution of Earnings

Earnings in 1969	Full-Time Male Physician 45 to 54	Full-Time Male Auto Mechanic 34 to 44
$0 to $1,999	1.1%	2.4%
$2,000 to $3,999	1.0	5.1
$4,000 to $5,999	1.2	16.0
$6,000 to $6,999	0.6	11.4
$7,000 to $7,999	0.8	14.5
$8,000 to $9,999	1.5	23.7
$10,000 to $14,999	6.2	22.2
$15,000 and up	87.5	4.7
Median	$25,000	$8,050

SOURCE: U.S. Bureau of the Census, Census 1970, 1972, Vol PC(2-7A), Occupational Characteristics.

terms. With the resulting high R^2s and other good statistical properties, everyone expects the models to function much better than they realistically can be expected to do. Again the result is disillusionment—often so extreme that observers jump to the conclusion that econometric functions are of no value whatsoever.

Econometrics has also had to rely on historical data for its laboratory experiments. Unfortunately, history has not provided the econometrician with a very wide range of experiments, and when conditions develop to throw the economy outside the range of historical experience, no one knows what will happen.

Consider the problem of forecasting the expenditures of state and local governments. Econometric equations estimated on data generated in the 1950s and 1960s found that the number of school-age (5–22) children was one of the most significant variables determining such expenditures.[8] Because more than half of state and local government expenditures went to education, the importance of the variable was hardly surprising. And over a long period of time, the equations were very accurate both for their statistical properties and their predictive power. But in the 1970s the number of school-age children leveled off, and in the 1980s it will decline. What is to be expected? Will state and local expenditures fall relative to school enrollments in the same manner as they rose? Technically the models say "yes," but they are based on no observations of what actually happens when school enrollments decline. Perhaps expenditures will drop as rapidly as they rose, but it is easy to imagine that the two circumstances are very different. Politically it would seem much easier to raise expenditures than reduce them, a view early results certainly seems to confirm.

Since the discipline of economics tries to make order out of millions upon millions of individual human decisions, human beings must have stable preferences if econometricians are to find stable equations explaining those human decisions. All of prevailing economic theory is based on the idea of stable preferences, but no such stable preferences may exist. Human beings are learning animals who change over time. Which is to say that human experiences—economic, social, political—alter economic preferences. So after peeling away the layers of the onion in an attempt to find that store of stable preferences, the diligent researcher may find nothing. Accordingly, econometric functions cannot be regarded as solid and permanent because individual preferences are not solid and permanent. As preferences gradually change, econometric functions also have to change gradually.

Consider savings behavior. In the 1950s and 1960s savings rates rose when people became uncertain about the future because of either rising unemployment or rising inflation. These people still remembered the Great Depression and wanted to save more to carry themselves across what they thought would be the coming bad times. But during the 1970s the uncertainties of rising unemployment or inflation seemed to lead to falling savings rates. The working man had learned in the meantime that the government was not going to let unemployment get completely out of control; that social welfare payments would cushion the shock if he did become unemployed; that women, minorities, and young people would bear most of the brunt of higher unemployment; and that extra savings just meant more capital losses from inflation. The learning process changed his beliefs, preferences, and behavior.

Price and wage behavior also underwent a change when indexing was widely adopted after the 1973–74 experience of double-digit inflation. Whatever the responses prior to that time, idle capacity and unemployment retarded wage and price increases less after 1973–74 than before. Prior to the watershed years, oil shocks did not automatically get built into wages and could affect them only when the next round of negotiations arrived; after that time, oil shocks were' quickly and automatically built into union wage increases.

Given such changes in human behavior, no one can expect econometric functions to have the lasting power of scientific relationships found in physics. This should intensify the econometrician's humility about the long-term validity of his models, but it need not completely undermine the usefulness of models.

Many econometric models and all macro-economic models contain time trends designed to reflect gradual changes in the economy. A time trend is basically an unexplained variable in the model by which the analyst assumes that something will continue to change regularly with the passage of time. Often such an assumption is perfectly correct. For approximately a hundred years, from 1865 to 1965, it was entirely acceptable to assume an American productivity growth trend of about 3 percent a year. But begining in 1965, for reasons that are still to some extent unknown, and certainly controversial, the economy's trend rate of growth of productivity started to slow down, and by 1978 the trend had become negative. Productivity time trends, as a result, had to be continually adjusted downward. Not being able to explain or forecast the decline means, however, that the model will always lag behind reality and lead to an ever expanding circle of errors. The downward readjustments in the model will always have to be made after productivity growth has already in fact fallen in the real world.

In any case, unless the earlier models captured the decline in productivity growth (they couldn't, almost by definition), they were not going to predict the extent which inflation was to climb. With a lower rate of growth of productivity any given wage increase is going to have a larger impact on production costs and so create more price pressures than previously would have been the case. Inaccurate productivity estimates also generate inaccurate employment estimates. The old models used to predict that in the year to follow a certain number of workers would be needed to raise the GNP by a specified amount, but because productivity rose more slowly than was expected, employment had to climb faster than expected to reach the predicted GNP. The point here is that given one error, a whole chain of error reverberates throughout the system encompassed by the model.

Econometric functions are often based on data for a cross section of individuals existing at some moment in time. Cross-sectional snapshots, however, won't yield an accurate picture unless you believe that the economy exists in a state of long-run unchanging equilibrium. But the economy does not so exist. Consider the following. In the 1960s, rates of return on educational investments were calculated to yield a 10 percent rate of return in the 1960s, while interest rates averaged 5.7 percent.[9] Clearly, education looked to be a good financial investment. But anyone who compared the two rates and decided to invest in education found that by the 1970s, rates of return in education had fallen to 7 percent, while interest rates had risen to 9.3 percent.[10] So what looked like a very good investment relative to interest rates in the 1960s proved to be a very bad investment relative to interest rates in the 1970s.[11] And as rates of return in education continued to fall and interest rates continued to rise in the 1980s, the former investment became increasingly less desireable. The world changed so rapidly in this instance that estimates, even if true when made, were of little use in planning one's economic life.

A Shifting Focus

Given failures to live up to expectations, econometrics shifted from being a tool for testing theories to being a showcase for exhibiting theories. Statistical models were built to show that particular theories were consistent with the data. But other theories were also consistent with the same data, and only occasionally could a theory be rejected because of the data. As a result, good economic theorizing became more important than any data—at least in the minds of economists—and theory came to be imposed on the data. So what started out being a technique for elevating data relative to theory ended up doing exactly the opposite. No set of data could ever upset a theory, since it was always possible to construct an econometric model congruent with both the theory and the data.

In short, untestable and unprovable theoretical models of reality became even more dominant than they were before econometrics was developed. This was bound to reinforce the position of the price-auction model, since that model of the world dominates both the learning and teaching of economists. Because there were no other models to fall back on, consistency with the price-auction model became the only virtue.

Plant and equipment investment functions are probably the best example of the dominance of theoretical beliefs over empirical data.[12] In theory, rising interest rates must produce less investment, and falling interest rates more. Much to the shock of early researchers, econometric equations found the exact opposite to be true; investment rose as interest rates rose. Econometricians immediately went back to their computers to find an investment function where interest rates would be statistically significant and appear with the right—negative— sign. At first all such efforts failed.

As it became obvious, however, that econometric equations were not as robust as first believed and could not really be used to discredit economic theories, another solution to the problem became intellectually respectable. Econometric equations were designed in such a way that interest rates were mathematically forced to have the right sign. A rental cost of capital variable was constructed in which the interest rate was only one of many components, along with others, such as taxes and the expansion of the GNP. If these other variables were related to investment in the "correct" manner, then mathematically interest rates also had to be related in the "correct" manner. The resulting equations did not test the theory, but they described what the world would look like if the theory was correct.

The theory of labor supply furnishes us with another illustration of the same sort. In economic theory an individual is subject to income and substitution effects as he makes trade-offs between income (work) and leisure. If wages go up, the individual is being offered a larger bribe to undergo the disutility of work and will work more (the substitution effect). But as his income goes up, the marginal value of income will also fall relative to that of leisure and the individual will work less (the income effect). Because of these simultaneous but opposing effects, economic theory cannot predict whether an increase in the wage rate will lead to more or less work. But policy makers need to know the empirical size of the income and substitution effects. Precisely this dispute plays a key role in the supply-side controversy: whether a large tax cut will or will not stimulate very great amounts of extra work, savings and investment.

Meanwhile, econometric efforts to measure and identify income and substitution effects have led to a morass. Because every wage change embodies both an income and a substitution effect, the problem is to estimate independently either the income or substitution effect and then find the other by subtraction from the aggregate impact of wage changes on observed work behavior. Because individuals have nonwork sources of income, the standard procedure is to estimate how these independent sources of income (often a wife's or husband's income) affect work behavior and then to find the substitution effect by subtraction. The only problem is that independent sources of income seem to have different effects on men and women. The effects on the latter are as expected, but the effects on males are perverse. A male's work effort goes up as his nonwork (wife's) income goes up.[13]

Given the estimating procedure, an income effect of the wrong sign will, if it is large enough, automatically lead to a substitution effect of the wrong sign. The smaller the bribe that people are offered to give up leisure, the more leisure they are willing give up. None of this makes any sense within the price-auction model.

Other theories might, however, provide perfectly good explanations for why men work more when their wives earn more. Male pride and a feeling of competitiveness may lead males to feel that they must work harder and earn more than their wives. In short, husband and wife are not the joint family maximizers assumed by the standard model.

Such alternative possibilities are ignored, however, as models are constructed that force income and substitution effects to be congruent with what is theoretically believed to be true. So instead of starting with labor-supply models derived from empirical real-world estimation, models now start from mathematical representations of personal choice—so-called utility functions—where work and leisure stand in the "correct" relationship to each other and where the mathematics imposes a "correct" income and substitution effect.[14] These models are then used to predict the impact of some public policy, such as an increase in welfare payments, on labor supply. The irony is that the models are used in the real world, but have no basis in that world.

There may be nothing wrong with elevating theory over data as long as everyone realizes that this is going on. Everyone can then be very cautious when using the results to predict empirical effects, although such prudence is hard to come by. But the practice of elevating theory over data also tends to retard the development of both better economic theorizing and better econometric techniques. Economists' prior theories, such as joint household income maximization, are never challenged by the data and therefore never have to be rethought. New theories don't have to be developed, neither do new statistical techniques to improve the data or the use of it. Problems can be dismissed rather than solved.

For example, no empirical real-world observation of what appears to be a fixed price can challenge the flexible-price theory, because the observations of fixed prices can always be statistically bent to look like flexible prices. This is not to say that the dominant theory is wrong or has not produced useful and valid insights, but it is to say that the world may be much more complicated than the simple price-auction economist ever wants to admit.

For another example, economic theory has always treated work—the giving up of leisure time—as an unpleasant disutility that one must be bribed to accept. All enjoyment—utility—is assumed to spring from consumption rather than production. Economists have always recognized that there were positive psychic income benefits associated with work, but these had to be smaller than the disutilities flowing from it. If it weren't for the net disutility of a job, no reason would exist to pay anyone wages in the standard model. To the economists, man is not a beaver who loves to work but a grasshopper who will work only if privation looms.

It is only now with demands for job enrichment here and the success of the Japanese in getting workers to raise productivity that the possibility of a net positive utility flowing from work has begun to be taken seriously. Power, prestige, friendships, and feelings of accomplishment may all prove to be important aspects of the reward system previously neglected by economists. And as we become more affluent and the nature of work changes, working may become more enjoyable than leisure, even if the opposite were once true.

If taken seriously, such changes can generate fundamental alterations in standard economic conclusions. Although it is true, for example, that one can show that free trade maximizes consumption, free trade does not necessarily maximize producer's utility. If the French love to be farmers or see farmers, it may be rational to protect French farmers with tariffs and quotas. What is lost in terms of extra consumption utility is more than gained in extra producer's utility.[15]

The problem with econometric relationships does not mean that econometrics should be abandoned, but the emphasis should be put on "robustness." Econometric results should not be given great weight unless similar results are produced by different economists using different techniques, different control variables, different models, and different data sets over an extended period of time. There are such results. The price elasticity of the demand for oil has been estimated to be around 0.1 for as long as I can remember. Users of econometric results should demand similar evidence of robustness, and producers of econometric results should make it their number one objective.[16]

If this were done, the pronouncements of economists would have to become much more humble because it is not possible to deliver robustness in many areas where society wants answers. But in the long run everyone and everything, including the reputation of economists, would be better off.

The End of Newtonian Economics

Because of the instability in both the economy and economic models, there is within the profession a growth industry looking at risk and uncertainty, the nature of random stochastic processes, and their optimum control. The initial work on the random walk in financial markets has blossomed into a more general, rational, expectational view of the world that has come to encompass both micro- and macro-economics (see Chapter 6). For the rational expectationists, the economy may seem controllable, but it is in fact not. The deterministic ele-

ments of the economy, according to this school, are not controllable, and the swings in observed variables are produced by
large random shocks. The economy is not where we would like
it to be, but saying that is literally no different from saying that
the planet Mars is not where we would like it to be. The
observation may be true and regrettable, but it is not something anybody can do anything about.

Randomness can come into economic relationships at many
levels and in many ways. Functions may be well behaved, but
the random errors affecting a given economic relationship may
simply be very large compared to that which is deterministic.
Energy supply-and-demand estimates, for example, may be
very accurate, but subject to large random disturbances from
OPEC's production decisions. Or in a more complex world, the
parameters of econometric functions can themselves be subject to random disturbances. Good or bad weather may alter
the relationships between economic inputs—fertilizer—and
economic outputs—yields. Still worse, there are "thick-tailed"
errors wherein the probability of an error's occurrence does
not grow smaller as the size of the error gets larger. Worst of
all, there can be chaos where no one is able to find a stable
functional relationship.

In all of these cases, the problem is not the existence of
randomness but its size relative to deterministic relationships.
Controllability must also be distinguished from randomness;
heavenly motion is not random, it is predictable, but that does
not make it controllable. Conversely, price behavior may not
be predictable, but it is controllable, using the price and wage
controls of World War II.

Any discipline moves away from a deterministic view of the
world with great reluctance. The deterministic nature of heavenly motion was a great scientific breakthrough that set the
example for modern science to emulate. So no matter how
complex and confusing events appear to be, they are assumed
to be deterministic. It is only a matter of discovering the right
way to see things. Forsaking the deterministic ideal is always
risky because it gives one a seemingly easy way out. What
appears to be stochastic may in fact be deterministic if one
only works harder and finds the right perspective and analytical framework.

In any case, economics, along with much of modern science,

is being drawn in a direction wherein events are perceived to be much more stochastic and much less deterministic than had previously been thought. In the economics profession an extreme expression of the trend can be found in rational expectations where any and all straying from the path prescribed by the equilibrium price-auction model is by definition mere random deviation.

The problem is how much and what kind of evidence is necessary before one accepts the conclusion that a given event is dominated by random shocks. One can argue "never" on the grounds that one should always keep searching for the deterministic perspective, and that too often what first seem like random events are shown to be deterministic, if understood properly.

CHAPTER 5

Supply-Side Economics
An Aberrant Current or the Economic Mainstream?

With Reaganomics seemingly having sunk into disrepute and failure in 1982, the economics profession sought to disassociate itself from supply-side economics. In the words of Herb Stein, chairman of the Council of Economic Advisers under President Nixon, the chief Reagan supply-siders were practicing a "punk" form of supply-side economics, where punk was defined as "extreme to the point of being bizarre." The President's "favorite" supply-side economist, George Gilder, had, after all, no formal training in economics.[1]

In the economics profession it was comforting to note that among mainstream Ph.D. economists, few believed in the extreme version of supply-side economics. Sensible professional economists favored enhancing incentives by cutting taxes, but no real economist could believe that the economy's response to supply-side incentives would be so large that a cut in tax rates would quickly produce an increase in tax revenues—the central proposition in the Laffer-Kemp-Roth-Reagan interpretation of supply-side economics. Work effort and savings behavior would respond to the incentives of lower marginal tax rates, but would not come anywhere near offsetting the loss in tax revenue from lower tax rates.

Given the intellectual currents of economics, however, supply-side economics cannot be dismissed as if it were just an aberrant current. After all, the someone professing a belief in the extreme version of supply-side economics was not a "Moonie," but the President of the United States. Public policies were being designed and enacted into law based on supply-side propositions. And if the belief was outside the currents of acceptable economics, how did a political party imbibing supply-side ideas manage to capture the White House? What is there about the discipline of economics that lets "punk" beliefs capture the central economic-policy-making apparatus of the United States?

While Professor Stein is certainly correct in saying that few economists accepted the extreme version of the Laffer curve (see below), Professor Laffer could count on some surprising illustrious fellow enthusiasts. In April 1982 Milton Friedman wrote: "There is ample evidence that the amount reported as taxable income would go up by more than enough to make up for the arithmetic loss from the lower (a maximum of 25 percent) top rate."[2] Arthur Laffer can perhaps be dismissed by the profession as a "punk" economist. Milton Friedman cannot!

The version of supply-side economics recommended by Arthur Laffer, endorsed by Milton Friedman, and practiced by President Reagan may be extreme (I believe it to be extreme), but it naturally flows out of the equilibrium price-auction view of the world. In that model, supply problems take care of themselves. As they go about maximizing their income, individual decision makers automatically provide the "right" amount of capital and labor inputs. Hence, economic growth automatically occurs at the maximum rate consistent with individual preferences about labor-leisure choices and the distribution of consumption between today and tomorrow. According to the model, competition will, if left alone, push the economy toward perfect efficiency, in the sense that there are no alterations that could make everyone better off without making someone worse off. The supply side of the economy is automatically as efficient as it can be.

Hence the supply-siders' inescapable conclusion: if the economy is performing poorly, then something must be interfering with the well-oiled mechanisms of the market economy. Given the price-auction model, private-market imperfections are unlikely to be that "something." A competitive private market can, after all, invent around any private-market imperfection unless someone in the private market has intrinsic monopoly powers. And that isn't likely unless government is supporting the private monopolist. Genuine private-monopoly powers are few and far between, if they exist at all.

Thus, if private monopolies are rare, supply-siders reason, government must be spoiling the smooth and precise workings of the price-auction market economy. Government alone has the power of law and cannot be "invented around." This proposition is not something that has to be demonstrated; a believer in free markets knows that it must be true axiomatically if the economy is performing poorly. Unfettered market economies just can't and don't perform poorly.

To remedy the situation, government must be taken "off the backs of the people and out of the economy." If that were done, the argument goes, the automatic efficiency of the price-auction economy would quickly restore stability and rapid economic growth. The economy can be compared, according to this view, to a coiled spring held down by the great weight of government. Once that weight is removed, the spring will instantly uncoil and assume its normal state.

As the economy springs back, supply-siders have predicted and continue to predict, there will be a spurt of growth and a sharp movement of economic activity from the illegal to the legal sector before the economy settles into its normal long-term upward trend. Meanwhile, the spurt will generate a large increase in the GNP and in government revenues. The changes may well be so large, or so the supply-siders argue, that government revenues go up when tax rates go down.[3]

The supply-side argument may not be valid, but you can see that it does flow naturally out of the mainstream intellectual currents of economics. So supply-side economics cannot be dismissed as a "punk" aberrant current unconnected with mainstream currents of the profession. It represents instead a return to economic fundamentalism in which the basic tenets of the price-auction model are accepted without reservation or sophistication.

The Genesis of Supply-Side Economics

Since World War II we have had two periods when the interest in supply-side economics was high: the Reagan period at the beginning of the 1980s and the Kennedy period at the beginning of the 1960s.

The earlier interest in supply-side economics stemmed from Cold War economic and military competition with the Soviet

Union. During the 1950s, the Russian growth rate was much higher than ours. If the two growth rates were plotted, the Russian economy surpassed the American economy in 1984— a year with a certain literary significance.

The 1960 election campaign was dominated by the missile and growth gaps. To cure the growth gap, the Kennedy economists invented a number of supply-side incentives. Investment expenditures would be accelerated with an investment tax credit and accelerated depreciation. The investment tax credit, as first proposed, would have been a marginal affair applying only to investment over and above what the firm had previously been spending. To ensure that the extra depreciation allowances were actually invested, a provision in the law specified that any funds not invested within a certain period of time would have to be returned to the U.S. Treasury. Forfeited if not invested, the extra depreciation allowances were sure to be invested. In the end Congress refused to listen to the Kennedy economists and passed an average, rather than a marginal, investment tax credit. The depreciation recapture provisions were passed, never enforced, and quietly dropped a few years later.[4]

In the Kennedy version of supply-side economics, the problems encompassed much more than simply trying to stimulate more physical investment. Many of the manpower and education programs that later came to be identified with the civil rights and antipoverty movements were first begun in the late 1950s and early 1960s as ways to enhance growth and beat the Russians. The National Defense Education Act, for example, was designed to enhance foreign-language and scientific skills to help us compete against the Soviets, but also to help eliminate the growth gap. Even the Kennedy policies that focused on the poor, such as the Appalachian programs, were adopted not as charitable antipoverty measures but to bring workers up to their productive potential so that they could raise rather than burden the GNP. Because the Kennedy supply-side programs had a strong component of human as well as a physical capital enhancement, the Kennedy people could legitimately claim that theirs were much more comprehensive programs than the later Reagan supply-side policies that cut human-capital investments.

With the enactment of a large across-the-board tax cut in

1964–65, the Johnson Administration abandoned supply-side measures as a way to invigorate the economy. While it was certainly trumpeted at the time that the tax cut would have positive effects on savings, investment, and work effort, an across-the-board cut was not considered a supply-side device. It represented, instead, a large demand-side policy with small supply-side effects.

And it was so regarded when enacted, even though Arthur Laffer, the current guru of supply-side economics, is fond of quoting the 1963 congressional testimony of Walter Heller, chairman of President Kennedy's Council of Economic Advisers, when Laffer is called upon to defend supply-side economics. At the time, Heller sounded just as optimistic about supply-side effects as Professor Laffer would later.[5]

Paradoxically, a large across-the-board tax cut is no longer just the heart of Keynesian demand-side management, but has become the heart of Reagan supply-side economics, in the process having undergone no change. Whether you are a pure Keynesian demand manager or a pure Reagan supply-sider, you have the same solution for slow growth—a large across-the-board tax cut. That the public is now confused about who is practicing demand- or supply-side economics is hardly surprising. Indeed, the Reagan Administration itself assumed that the 1982 tax cut would be heavily saved (supply-side) as it advocated tax reductions in 1981, but argued that the same cut would be heavily spent (demand-side) when it issued its optimistic 1982 forecasts.

As the New Frontier, the Cold War and the need to get the country moving again faded, the civil rights movement and President Johnson's Great Society programs moved center stage. Emphasizing human-capital development and de-emphasizing private plant-and-equipment investment, the Great Society was the mirror image of Reagan supply-side economics. The prime focus of the Johnson programs was to enhance personal earnings, but it was also asserted that if the programs raised incomes of minorities and women, they would perforce raise the aggregate GNP. If people were educated and trained, the Great Society assumed that their productivity would rise, producing both self-sufficient individuals and an economy that would grow more rapidly than otherwise would have been the case, leading them to become self-sufficient and the economy to grow more rapidly.

While the Kennedy-Johnson programs sprang from the Cold War and the civil rights movement, the Reagan programs spring from America's productivity problems. As productivity growth gradually slowed after 1965 and started falling after 1977, it is not surprising that the economic spotlight swung to focus on supply-side problems. Falling productivity means falling standards of living—both absolutely and relative to the rest of the world. And no genius is required to discern that the American people are going to see a falling standard of living as a problem that needs a solution. More interesting was their willingness to buy an extreme solution to the problem.

Reagan Supply-Side Economics

Reaganomics has five components—a large across-the-board tax cut, a cut in social welfare spending, a larger increase in defense spending, less government regulation, and a restricted rate of growth of the money supply.

The large tax cuts are designed to increase the take-home income of workers and capitalists so that they will work harder and save and invest more. Cuts in the social safety net are supposed to encourage individuals to work harder and save more to provide for their own old age, their own illnesses, their own unemployment, their own standard of living. The increases in defense spending were not designed for economic reasons, but they have produced a federal budget where total expenditures are rising very rapidly because the increases in defense spending are much larger than the cuts in civilian spending. Along with reducing regulations that the Reagan Administration feels have hamstrung private industry, these supply-side policies were supposed to restore vigorous economic growth.

Meanwhile, a slow rate of growth of the money supply was supposed to stop inflation. In itself there was nothing extreme in this last idea, but it was quite novel to suggest that if tight money policies were yoked to strong supply-side policies, the tight money would stop inflation without at the same time stopping the economy.

Reaganomics is often seen as something new and radical, but as its defenders like to point out, it is undeniably and thoroughly grounded in equilibrium price-auction theory. If consistency with that model is the measure of whether one is in the mainstream, the Reagan supply-siders are in the mainstream.

As we have seen, if all markets are auction markets clearing on price changes induced by supply and demand, it is not possible to have unemployed resources. The economy is always at full employment, and the supply side of the economy (the T in the quantity theory of money) takes care of itself. According to the theory, macro-economic government intervention cannot make the real GNP larger or smaller. Tight money, as a result, only reduces inflation.

While no macro-economic government intervention can improve the performance of the free-market economy, microeconomic government intervention can deteriorate the performance of the economy. With high tax rates individuals work, save, and invest less than they would if left alone. And if government insurance policies protect them from the vicissitudes of life, individuals work, save, and invest less than they would if left alone. And if industry is overregulated, it is strangled and produces less than it would if left alone.

In the words of former Reagan Undersecretary of the Treasury for Tax and Economic Affairs Norman B. Ture, "supplyside economics is merely the application of price theory in analyzing problems concerning economic aggregates."[6] "Only price (incentive) effects exist and any income effects (deviations from full employment) are simply the function of 'institutional rigidities' and lead to temporizing rather than long-term or permanent adjustments."[7] In other words, positive incentive effects overcome the negative aggregate demand effects of tight monetary policies.

If Ture is right, monetary policies can be rigorously tightened to stop prices (P) from rising, because such policies will have no long-run effect on the real GNP (T) or unemployment. Once again in the words of the Undersecretary, "Supply-siders and monetarists are in perfect accord that in the long run, monetary magnitudes do not determine real output and income."[8] Consequently, the Reaganauts felt that they could step on the monetary brakes and fiscal accelerator simultaneously without damaging the economy or producing, as they see things, legitimate charges of inconsistency.

The only difference between this view and the one held by the monetarists is that the short-run recession that would be predicted by the monetarists became in the views of the supply-siders so short as not to exist. The predicted speed of reaction may be different for the two schools of economists, but the theory is identical.

Supply-side economics can be understood as a literal and fundamentalist interpretation of the price-auction model, working precisely as it is taught in any introductory class in micro-economics: markets will quickly adapt to new conditions, individuals must be forced to adjust to market circumstances, each individual is an income maximizer responsible for his own standard of living. And left alone, a price-auction market will generate the highest possible level of welfare.

As noted, if any deviation exists here from the main currents of economics, it is the supply-sider's belief about the speed of market adjustments and the size of the incentive effects. But even in this it would be hard to say that supply-side economics is outside the bounds of the mainstream of the discipline. Other schools of economics, such as rational expectationists, believe in instantaneous adjustments, and a famous economist, Milton Friedman, stated publicly his belief that large rapid supply-side effects did exist. Even the supply-side rejection of econometric evidence that showed modest supply-side effects is well within the mainstream of economics.

There are of course many economists who are not Keynesians who disagree with the supply-siders. Some monetarists think that a substantial period of time is required if monetary policies are to control inflation, and that during that time the economy must be pushed above its natural rate of unemployment.[9] In other words, a period of economic pain with negative growth must be incurred to push inflation out of the system. But the monetarist conception here depends on the real-world existence of time lags and a model of fixed short-run prices and flexible long-run prices. Unless an economist is willing to argue that there is some market where prices are fixed or some period of time when prices are fixed, the supply-siders are correct. But if prices are fixed either in some market or for some nontrivial period of time, a fixed price model has to assume importance in economic theory, meaning in turn that the price-auction model only explains part of what needs to be explained. In sum, a theory of fixed prices becomes necessary even if only to explain behavior in the short run.

The belief that the real GNP takes care of itself in a competi- tive economy was undermined, or so everyone thought, in the Great Depression. The economy deviated very substantially from what anyone believed was full employment (25 percent in 1933), stayed away for a long time (17 percent in 1939), and gave no evidence that it was curing itself. A recession within the Great Depression occurred in 1937 and there was no hint of an end to the very bad times until the outbreak of World War II. Without the war, there is every reason to believe that the Great Depression would have continued. But that time in our national life now evokes memories so distant that some economists can develop and advance theories that deny its reality without being regarded as complete fools.

The empirical problem with flexible-price models was evi- dent not only in the nightmare of the Great Depression. Since World War II, unemployment has varied between 3 and 11 percent in the United States. Why? And why have tight mone- tary policies produced an 11 percent unemployment rate in the European Common Market and a 16 percent unemployment rate in Great Britain? In fact, in many European countries, unemployment has been very high for years and they have seen no evidence whatever of the market adjustments that are supposed to reabsorb "temporarily" jobless workers.

Meanwhile, unemployment cannot exist in an equilibrium price-auction market. Yet unemployment does exist. Why is it ignored? The answer is simple. No alternative theory was de- veloped to challenge the price-auction model's explanation of individual economic behavior. So it was almost inevitable that the dominant view of the 1920s would reassert itself when immediate memories of the suffering produced by the Great Depression passed. Today's measured unemployment is defined away as "voluntary" unemployment, and therefore not "real" unemployment.

The supply-siders do, however, have an explanation for the phenomenon. Although fiscal policy—taxes and expenditures —has no macro-economic income effects, it does have effects on relative prices: it distorts them. Since the economic actors in the system are extremely sensitive to relative price effects, a program that cuts taxes and reduces transfer payments can reduce distortions and have a dramatic effect on the willingness of individuals to work as well as save and invest. With lower taxes and transfer payments, labor's reservation wage falls. The GNP rises and unemployment falls, supply-siders say, not because of the macro-economic effects of Reagan's fiscal or monetary policies but because of the micro-economic incentive effects. Everyone suddenly becomes willing to save and work more.

In the words of the President's favorite economist, George Gilder: "Labor and resources, for example are enormously elastic. The average worker exerts himself at about half of capacity and the average executive is vastly less productive than the best ones. Modern economics are filled with fat, grease, and underused or much abused manpower and industry, above ground and below. In an overtaxed system the statistics of economic limits and capacity are mostly mush."[10] In short, the economy is fouled up, but can be immediately cleansed if incentives are restored.

The Laffer Curve

The Laffer-curve idea has been around a lot longer than Arthur Laffer himself, but it got its name from him, since he has made it the centerpiece of supply-side economics and its conception of incentive effects.[11] Like the quantity theory of money, the curve is a truism disputed by no one. If government levies no taxes, it collects no revenue. If government levies taxes at a 100 percent rate, it collects no revenue—no one would work or invest if he knew that government was going to take everything. But governments do collect tax revenue. As a result, the curve relating tax rates and tax revenue must first rise with rising tax rates and then fall with rising tax rates (see Diagram 3). This no one disputes.

The controversial part of the Laffer curve is not its intersection with the vertical axis at 0 and 100 and its backward-bending segment where tax revenue rises (falls) as tax rates fall (rise), but the precise empirical point where in the real world

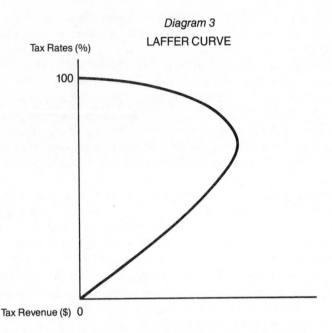

Diagram 3
LAFFER CURVE

Tax Rates (%)

100

Tax Revenue ($) 0

the increase in the tax rate is first offset by an induced decline in work and investment large enough to reduce tax revenue.

As they campaigned for the original 30 percent across-the-board Kemp-Roth tax cut, Laffer and his political allies, among them Reagan, asserted that budget expenditures would not need to be cut because tax revenue would rise, not fall, as a result of the cut. To put the argument to a test, it is possible to work out arithmetically how much extra income would have to be generated either from greater work effort or from a willingness to move already existing activities out of the illegal untaxed economy and into the legal taxed economy. Suppose someone earned $100 a week and was paying taxes at a 10 percent rate. The government would collect $10 in tax revenue. If taxes were cut 30 percent, to 7 percent, earnings would have to rise to $143 per week to generate the same $10 in tax revenue ($0.07 \times \$143 = \$10$). On average, every worker or investor would have to earn 43 percent more to offset a 30 percent tax-rate cut. If some people were unable to earn this much more, others would obviously have to raise their earnings by even more than 43 percent.

Econometric studies show that lower taxes lead to more work effort but by much smaller amounts (see below). Simple introspection about whether a person could raise his own income 43 percent in response to a 30 percent tax cut, however, suggests that the Kemp-Roth proposals are unlikely to have the effects claimed for them.

Laffer himself has never attempted to specify empirically where the breaking point occurs, although he usually draws his curve with the breaking point at the 50 percent tax rate. Those who have actually tried to estimate where the point might be put it at somewhere around the 80 percent tax bracket.[12] But whether the breaking point is at 50 or 80 percent, very few people in the United States are above the necessary percentage, which is to say, would find themselves on the backward-sloping part of the curve. The average American tax rate (federal, state, and local combined) was 32 percent in 1980, and the average marginal tax rate was only slightly higher at 34 percent.[13] As a result, to get the required 43 percent increase in productive effort, the small number of people above the breaking point and so subject to the strong supply-side effects have to experience a phenomenal increase in their income.

Supply-siders argue that some of the large positive effects occur not because of an increase in aggregate productive effort, but because existing work effort will be drawn away from the underground economy and existing investment will be drawn away from nonproductive tax shelters. Neither argument makes sense when looked at closely.

The underground economy now pays indirect taxes—sales, property—when its membership spends money. Only direct taxes would increase when activities emerged from the underground, because those in the underground economy are now getting away with paying none at all. Accordingly, direct taxes would have to be made very low indeed to entice much of the underground activity above ground. Moreover, much underground activity is also illegal not because its participants want to evade taxes, but because society at large wants to put an end to the activity whether people pay their taxes or not. Those in drugs and prostitution will never voluntarily pay taxes because to pay them is to become subject to arrest.

The tax-shelter argument is even more dubious because

most American tax shelters were not designed by some clever tax lawyer who found a subtle unintended nonproductive loophole, but by a Congress convinced that some certain forms of economic activity were so highly productive that they ought to be given special tax advantages to encourage investors to engage in them. Percentage depletion was designed, for example, to encourage investment in drilling for oil. So if Congress was initially right in its position that some kinds of economic activity should be encouraged, aggregate productivity would decrease, not increase, as lower tax rates eliminated the attractiveness of tax shelters. But whatever the truth, tax shelters are not inefficient simply because they are tax shelters. Their inefficiency has to be demonstrated. It cannot be assumed, which is all the supply-siders feel they have to do.

After the supply-side tax reductions were enacted and revenue fell, the major economists of the Reagan Administration, though not Laffer himself, began to argue that they never expected tax revenue to rise when tax rates were cut. They do, however, still expect very rapid, large, positive incentive effects. Secretary of the Treasury Donald T. Regan maintains that Americans will save 60 percent of their tax cut. Michael Evan, an economic consultant and prominent Reagan supply-side sympathizer, estimates that they will save 80 percent.

The weight of economic evidence is against such assertions. Usually but not always, tax-rate incentive effects pull things in the right direction—savings, investment, and work effort go up when taxes are cut—but the magnitude of the effects is almost always small. For one thing, higher after-tax rates of return have a very small effect on personal savings. Moreover, labor-supply analysts typically find vertical or even backward-bending (workers work less as taxes fall and incomes rise) labor-supply curves. Income effects (lower income leading to more work) equal or dominate substitution effects (lower take-home wage rates leading to more leisure and less work) and produce small or nonexistent supply-side effects.

The largest work-effort effect yet found was discovered by Professor Jerry A. Hausman of MIT. According to Hausman, if a proportional income tax replaced current progressive federal income tax, hours of work would increase by 8 percent.[14] To get this, however, the maximum tax rate would have to be cut from 70 to 12 percent—which is far more than a 30 percent cut envisioned by Kemp-Roth. The Hausman study also wanted to estimate what is called "an income compensated labor supply curve." This means a labor-supply curve where workers are held at the same income level while their marginal tax rates are allowed to vary. To get the 8 percent positive work-effort effect, everyone has to be forced to make lump-sum payments to the Treasury large enough to keep their take-home income constant under the old and new tax structures. Unless such compensation is paid, Hausman finds the standard results: income effects approximately equal substitution effects, and work-effort effects are very small when taxes are cut. No one, and certainly not the Reagan Administration, has yet proposed an income-compensated tax cut.

Because of the failure of econometrics, supply-siders could nevertheless argue that all of the existing empirical work was wrong or might be wrong without being generally dismissed as "punk" economists! The Kemp-Roth episode exemplifies the point that economic evidence is too soft to make much difference in practical affairs. If the policy makers want to believe something, they will always find an economist who will confirm their beliefs.

Market Imperfections

Reagan economists believe in free markets and do not in any way want to appear as interventionists trying to force the market to produce a nonmarket result. Accordingly, Reagan economists have approached both tax and expenditure cuts as if they were market imperfections. In other words, the less revenue diverted through government, the more efficiently markets work because fewer distortions will be produced in the economy. Similarly, social welfare programs are seen as insurance policies (market imperfections) with adverse incentive effects. When government collectively agrees to insure its citizens against old age, illness, unemployment, poverty, and personal handicaps, government undercuts personal incentives to save and work to provide for one's own old age, illness, unemployment, poverty, and personal handicaps. Individuals treat these programs as personal savings reducing their own private savings, but because the programs are not savings in the aggregate they result in too little savings relative to what could be produced if preferences were undistorted.

According to Reagan economists, social insurance also creates free-riders: knowing that others will work to provide the resources necessary to insure you against the hazards of life, you reduce your work effort and let others carry the load. But when everyone makes what is individually a rational decision to work less, the result is a collective irrationality—an economy with too little work and output.

An extreme form of this contention is advanced by George Gilder, who argues that both welfare payments and working wives sap male initiative. "The man's earnings, unlike the woman's, will determine not only his standard of living but also his possibilities for marriage and children—whether he can be a sexual man. The man's work thus finds its deepest source in love."[15] "Under guaranteed-income plans . . . marriages dissolve not because the rules dictate it but because the benefit levels destroy the father's key role and authority. He can no longer feel manly in his own home."[16] "When the wives earn less, the men tend to work more and are far more likely to reach the pinnacles of achievement."[17] "Material progress is ineluctably elitists: It makes the rich richer and increases their numbers, exalting the few extraordinary men who can produce wealth over the democratic masses who consume it."[18]

Many economists want to dismiss such statements as pop sociology written by a man who, after all, does not have a Ph.D. in economics. The President may have given Gilder's book, to his Cabinet at the beginning of his Administration, but Gilder, it is asserted by the profession, isn't a real economist. Perhaps not, but one has to ask why he is taken seriously by the President of the United States and the Republican Party.

On the savings and investment side, one finds a similar lack of hard evidence as to large supply-side effects. The only study purporting to find large negative effects from government intervention was one done by Martin Feldstein, now chairman of President Reagan's Council of Economic Advisers, showing that Social Security had a large adverse impact on savings.[19] The study, however, had to be withdrawn because the results were caused by a "computer error." When the analysis was done correctly, the Social Security system had a small positive effect on savings. But this has not stopped attacks on Social Security under the guise of increasing investment.

Savings effects, however, differ substantially from work-effort effects. No substitute exists for individual work, but substitutes do exist for individual savings. Institutions can save. In the United States only 25 percent of our aggregate savings come from individual savings. The other 75 percent come from institutional savings such as corporate retained earnings and depreciation allowances.[20]

This means that even if social welfare programs have an adverse effect on personal savings there are legitimate ways, other than abolishing social welfare systems, to increase total savings in the economy. Government could, for example, increase savings by running a surplus in its budget. Consumer credit could be restricted to produce higher personal savings rates. As a society we could choose to abolish our social welfare systems and retain our system of easy credit and tax deductibility for personal interest payments, but that is an ethical decision and not one forced upon us by harsh economic imperatives.

The supply-side arguments about savings merely demonstrate the principle that value judgments often run under the cover of economic analysis. Economic arguments are advanced—taxes or social welfare programs must be cut to raise savings—to achieve an objective that the advocates want to achieve—less welfare spending—and some generally agreed-upon objective such as more investment is held out as the necessity. The same thing can be seen in the accelerated depreciation schedules proposed by the Reagan Administration. These were not designed to remove government tax-imposed market imperfections, but to create a market imperfection—in this case one desired by those in the Reagan Administration.

To avoid distorting investment decisions, all capital plant and equipment should be depreciated over their actual useful economic lifetimes. If the inflation rate is such that replacement costs rise above historic acquisition costs, then the correct theoretical solution is to index depreciation or allow replacement rather than historic cost depreciation. When we adopt a set of depreciation lifetimes (once known as 10, 5, 3 and now known as 15, 10, 5, 3 for the number of years over which various kinds of assets can be depreciated) that are much faster than actual lifetimes, and, relative to actual lifetimes, much more generous for long-lived plant and equipment than for short-lived plant and equipment, significant distortions are created in the capital markets. Investment will be shifted toward assets such as steel mills and away from assets such as manufacturing equipment in electronics. Capital-intensive firms will find themselves with unusable depreciation allowances, since their depreciation allowances, investment tax credits, and interest deductions will often exceed gross income. Labor-intensive firms not similarly placed will have taxable income. The net result will be a strong incentive to merge the two types of firms to get the benefit of a poorly designed tax law. And nothing could be more contrary to the spirit of competition undistorted by poor government regulations. The merger incentive can be mitigated by the buying and selling of depreciation allowances (lease-backs), but this merely means that efficient labor-intensive firms now pay taxes to inefficient capital-intensive firms. Yet not a word was said against the distortions by the free-enterprise Reagan economists. Here again, what you want to do politically is more important than being consistent with expressed free-market principles.

Conclusions

According to Reagan's version of supply-side economics, if the economy is not working, something must be wrong with government's place in the economy. This has not been proved by empirical analysis but is known so because a priori it is impossible for an undisturbed free-market competive economy to perform badly. If the economy is performing badly, government, the great distorter in a free-market economy, has to be the culprit.

Whatever the validity of the supply-side argument, there is no question that it is a logical product of an equilibrium price-auction view of the world. The supply-siders merely make explicit what is implicit in that model. Mainstream economists may say that supply-siders exaggerate the "truth" to be found in the model, but it is the "truth" nonetheless.

In any case, supply-side economics represents the triumph of literal and unqualified equilibrium price-auction economics. Supply-siders are to that model what religious fundamentalists are to biblical interpretation. No deviations from the revealed truth are possible or allowed.

CHAPTER 6

Rational Expectations

A Nonexistent North-West Passage

If supply-side economics with its primitive view of the price-auction model is the emotional "gut" response to the economic failures of the 1970s, the school of rational expectations is a sophisticated intellectual response to the same failures. Whereas the supply-siders' beliefs are so strong that they are blind to all contrary evidence, the rational expectionists define the world tautologically, permitting no contrary evidence to exist because it can't exist. Here the conflict between micro-economic theory and macro-economic problems is resolved by asserting that macro-economic problems by definition do not exist. Thus, rational expectations are sometimes referred to as the new "classical" economics.[1]

This school of thinking is both very similar to and very different from supply-side economics. Both take the price-auction model literally and believe that markets clear very rapidly based on price fluctuations. Both believe that little can be done to improve the performance of a price-auction economy. Both believe that economic actors are rational in that they do not make systematic mistakes. (Technically speaking, the anticipated value for any variable is its mathematical expectation conditional upon all available information.)

But they part company on how much is known. The supply-siders in practice come close to believing in perfect information. Left to its own devices, a market economy would perform very well indeed. But for rational expectationists the economic actors may be very ignorant of what they should know as compared to the perfect information assumed by the simple equilibrium price-auction model. Perfect information is re-defined to mean that the economic actors know everything that it is *possible* to know, but there may be much that they should know that they do not know.

Rational expectationists also differ from the supply-siders and the monetarists in that they believe that monetary policies have little impact on inflation and that it is not possible to induce the dramatic changes in work and savings behavior that the supply-side economists count on.[2] Like the supply-siders, rational expectationists (such as Lucas and Sargent) believe that government cannot improve the workings of the equilib-rium price-auction market, but unlike supply-siders they also believe that government cannot systematically damage the performance of the market. As a consequence, rational expec-tationists don't believe that economic performance can be sys-tematically improved by removing government interference.

Besides the basic price-auction understanding, rational ex-pectationists see an economy hit by large random shocks or mistakes that cannot be avoided or controlled. These random shocks or mistakes in information can knock the economy off its normal path for substantial periods of time. Unemployment and the business cycle are, for example, caused by mistakes in information.[3] But since the shocks are unavoidable and the information is as good as it is possible to get, government can obviously do nothing about a poor economic performance. A free-market economy may perform very poorly in practice, even as it is performing as well as it is possible for it to perform.

Starting from the same belief in perfect markets, the supply-side path leads one to be very optimistic about our ability to improve the performance of the economy. One need only get the government out of the way. In contrast the rational-expec-tationist path leads us to be extremely pessimistic about our ability to do anything. For the latter school, government inter-vention might be desired because society would like to allevi-ate economic pain, but intervention is not useful, since it cannot cure the pain even if implemented. In other words, there are real economic problems, but there are no economic solutions. The government cannot do anything to help the economy because the economy is already doing as well as it

can. Resign yourself to the fact that the best possible performance may be a rather poor performance.[4]

One of the little known and least emphasized conclusions of
rational expectations is that whatever is wrong with the economy could not have been caused by government. Government
neither helps nor hurts. Controls on foreign-exchange markets, for example, don't matter because their imposition was
foreseen by the market and because the market is capable of
finding ways around them. As a result, rational expectations
can be seen as a sophisticated form of nihilism where "nothing
affects nothing."

The equilibrium price-auction model reigns supreme, just as
it did before Keynes and the Great Depression, but with a
difference. Rational expectations have junked the concept of
controllable market imperfections (market imperfections may
lead to a poor economic performance, but none of these imperfections can be eliminated) and developed the concept of
large random shocks. These adverse shocks and misinformation may produce real results that differ substantially from
those predicted by the theoretical model. But the market is as
perfect as it is possible for the market to be. Economic debates
about this conclusion tend to focus on macro-economic problems, but for the rational expectationist, the results are equally
applicable to micro- and macro-problems.

No controversial conclusions, however, flow from either the
concept of rationality (no systematic mistakes) or the concept
of expectations (economic actors look to the future when making decisions). They all flow, instead, from the theory of an
equilibrium price-auction model augmented by the concept of
random shocks and unsystematic misinformation.[5]

The Origin of Rational Expectations: Random-Walk Theories

The rational-expectations hypothesis marries the theoretical
perfection of the price-auction model to the "random walk"
theory of financial market behavior.[6] The latter contributes
the conception of random shocks and incomplete information.

In a perfectly competitive free market, capital markets are
in equilibrium and each investment yields some common rate
of return. But to understand the real world as the random walk
does, it is necessary to think of at least two different capital

markets. The first is the market for real investments, in which firms and individuals make real investments in plant and machinery. The second is the financial market, in which individuals buy financial instruments without directly managing real assets. Stocks, bonds, and real estate trusts are examples of the latter; factories, stamping presses, and robots are examples of the former.

The basic characteristic of the real capital markets is disequilibrium—not because there are extra profits to be made by any new entrant into the market, but because ex post firms earn very different rates of return. (Remember the New York hotel example given earlier.) Both over time and at any one point in time there is a wide variance in rates of return, which variance exists both among and within industries. Table 6 indicates the after-tax annual rate of return on stockholders equity by industry for 1960 and 1980. There is a wide *persistent* variance in both years. The drug industry for example, was at the head of the list in 1960 (16.8 percent) and third (27.9 percent) in 1980. For twenty years, drug companies have made a return on equity far above average. Of those industries with above-average returns in 1960, only two were below average in 1980. Printing moved from slightly above to slightly below average, with only motor vehicles altering its position significantly. The same pattern of consistency in position but dispersion in results can be seen in *Fortune*'s list of the 500 largest industrial firms. While riskiness can explain high returns in any one year, it cannot explain high returns every year.

Within a single industry the dispersion in rates of return on investment are just as large. Table 7 shows the rates of return for the four major American automobile manufacturers. Although returns rise and fall with the auto market, large persistent differences are observed. In every year for more than twenty-five years, General Motors has outearned Ford. Ford's earnings, on the other hand, have been substantially above those of Chrysler. American Motors is consistent in its inconsistency, earning large returns in some years and small returns in others.

Data on real-capital markets indicate little, if any, tendency for real-capital markets to approach equilibrium as they should if the conventional price-auction model accurately explained their behavior. Returns vary substantially over long periods of

Table 6

Annual Rates of Profit on Stockholders' Equity by Industry
(Percent)

	1960	1980
Industry		
All Manufacturing	9.2%	21.9%
Durable goods	8.6	18.1
Transportation equipment	11.7	1.4
Motor Vehicles	13.5	−10.8
Aircraft	7.4	25.2
Electrical Machinery	9.5	25.1
Metalworking Machinery	5.3	
Other Machinery	7.6	23.0
Fabricated Metal Products	5.6	22.3
Primary metal industries	7.2	16.5
Primary Iron and Steel	7.2	16.5
Primary nonferrous metals	7.1	22.4
Stone Clay and Glass	9.9	16.8
Furniture and Fixtures	6.5	
Lumber and Wood Products	3.6	19.2
Miscellaneous and ordnance	9.2	
Nondurables	9.9	25.3
Food	8.7	23.3
Tobacco	13.4	23.3
Textile mill products	5.9	16.1
Paper	10.2	17.4
Printing	10.6	28.7
Chemicals	12.2	22.6
Drugs	16.8	27.9
Petroleum	10.1	30.7
Rubber and Plastics	9.1	10.7

SOURCE: Federal Trade Commission; Securities and Exchange Commission, *Quarterl₁ Financial Reports for Manufacturing Corporations.* Government Printing Office, Washington, First quarter 1961, p. 10, and First quarter 1981, p. 14.

time. The reasons behind the fundamental disequilibrium are many and varied, but most of them spring from a basic characteristic of the real-capital market at variance with the assumptions of the price-auction model. Namely, large flows of savings are not generated in the household sector and then allocated across firms and industries to equalize real rates of return on physical investments.

In the United States in 1980 and 1981 the household sector

Table 7

Automobile Rate of Return On Stockholder Equity
(percent)

	General Motors	Ford	Chrysler	American Motors
1956–59	16.2%	11.7%	6.3%	19.5%
1960–64	19.7	13.6	10.0	13.8
1965–69	19.7	10.7	11.0	11.1
1970–74	13.9	11.2	4.1	15.4
1975	9.6	5.1	−10.8	−7.6
1976	20.2	13.8	15.0	−14.8
1977	21.2	19.8	5.6	2.6
1978	20.0	16.4	− 7.0	10.3
1979	15.1	11.2	−68.3	19.0
1980	−4.3	−18.0	*	−45.4
1981	−1.9	−14.4	*	−46.5

Source: *Fortune* magazine. *"Fortune* 500," May 1961 and May 1981.

* No positive equity.

provided no net savings to the business sector and kept all of its own savings to finance its residential investment. Accordingly, American businesses are self-financing, often providing savings for the rest of the economy as they did in 1980 and 1981. In 1981 business savings exceeded business investment and government was borrowing business savings to finance its deficit. Even more important, however, each individual business is essentially self-financing when it comes to long-term investment. Firms do most of the savings necessary to finance their own plant and equipment, and funds do *not* flow evenly among businesses on a long-term basis.

In the price-auction model, corporate managers are presumed to be surrogate capitalists, but in the real world their motives are not those of a strict capitalist. Managers who save rather than pay out dividends typically want to invest in their own operations, which is a pattern of investments that brings them, not the stockholders, greater rewards in the form of job opportunities, income, power, and prestige. If they generate extra savings over and above what are immediately needed, the funds will be lent short-term to other businesses, but almost never are they lent long-term. As a result, those who direct most of the economy's savings and investments are not the simple profit-maximizing investors assumed in the standard model. Managers are interested in maximizing profits, but only profits from operations that they themselves manage.

If an average stockholder thinks that one firm is going to be more profitable than another in a world of managerial capitalism, his only practical recourse is to sell, buy, and alter his financial portfolio (a subject to which we shall return). The costs of trying to force a change in management and making his present investment more profitable are simply too high in most cases. Takeover bids certainly exist, but they are more often triggered by a temporary disequilibrium in the financial markets (undervalued natural-resource companies in 1981) than by genuine efforts to improve management and raise rates of return on real-capital investments.

If we ask why managers with large internal savings do not start subsidiaries in high-profit industries rather than reinvest in their own lower-profit industries, we come face to face with the entire structure of restricted competition in the United States. Barriers to entry are often high, and individual managers often do not have the specialized knowledge necessary to make money in another industry. The existence of high profits in the cosmetics industry, for example, does not mean that iron and steel executives could earn the same high profits. To move into cosmetics, the steel company would have to fire its existing managers and hire new managers. But the existing managers are not about to fire themselves, and they are wise enough to know that they could not run a cosmetics firm successfully. As a result, they stay in the steel industry and reinvest their internal funds in steel or closely allied fields almost without regard to relative rates of return. Only after decades of very low rates of return is the American steel industry beginning to diversify.

Conglomerates have been formed in an attempt to take care of the problem, but they have generally failed when they tried to put together a portfolio of companies in very different industries. Good management requires specialized knowledge that keeps them from running a widely diversified group of companies and then allocating investment funds across those companies in a manner similar to that prescribed by the price-auction model.

The existence of large pools of internal savings also tends to distort the flows of the few investment funds that do move through real-capital markets. In fact, lenders face risk and uncertainties about the return of their capital. Borrowers may default. But if lenders put money into firms with large internal flows of savings, they can have great confidence that the borrowers are going to repay them regardless of the success or failure of the specific project for which the funds were lent. Accordingly, because the risk of default is low, funds are attracted to those firms with large internal-savings flows, even though they may not be earning the highest rates of return on their marginal investments. Since World War II, America's iron and steel industry has always been able to borrow substantial sums of money despite a. generally low return on investment.

The net result is a flow of market investments that does not serve to equalize rates of return on physical investments across the economy. The drug industry has, as noted, yielded a rate of return substantially above the national average ever since World War II. Over an almost forty years' period of time, the real-capital market did not drive the rates of return down in the drug industry to the market average, which is what should have happened in a perfect capital market.

Such a consistent pattern of performance cannot be explained by the standard explanation for variance in single year's rates of return—risk. If risk were the answer, a firm might have a high rate of return in any one year, but high returns in one year would be offset by low returns in some other year to give an average rate of return over a long period of time. If a firm or industry shows consistently high rates of return, it is not in a risky business.

Real-capital markets are thus marked by substantial differences in long-run rates of return. And if returns equalize, they equalize only very gradually. In a dynamic changing economy, investment opportunities offering new above-average rates of return will also appear periodically. Thus the economy is never in equilibrium in its real-capital markets. Disequilibrium exists and persists.

This disequilibrium or dispersion in rates of return in real-capital markets, however, provides a role for financial markets. If firms are earning different rates of return, they are not of course equally valuable per dollar of invested capital. Different prices (values) must be placed on different firms so that the financial returns are equalized. Financial markets so perceived serve not to generate and direct real capital to high rate of return investment opportunities, but to capitalize away the differences in real rates of return.

Consider a new real investment opportunity costing $10 million and earning a 30 percent rate of return, or $3 million. With a market rate of interest of 10 percent, this investment would be valued at $30 million ($3,000,000/0.10). If the investment is something that can be repeated so that additional real capital can be invested and also earn 30 percent rates of return, the market may capitalize current investments at very high multiples (think of Genentech and the multiples on other new recombinant DNA firms) because of the prospect of future real investments at above-average rates of return. In this case, current investments are not the appropriate base for capitalization, since prospects exist for earning 30 percent rates of return on a much larger capital base. But the very existence of those high multiples means that investors think that for some reason (perhaps a limited supply of biologists with the necessary skills) capital is not going to be able to flow into the industry to equalize rates of return on real plant and equipment investments very quickly.

Instead, based on current and future expected earnings, shareholders shift their financial portfolios from low real rate of return firms to high real rate of return firms. In the process of course they lower the stock-market value of the low-rate-of-return firms and raise the stock-market value of the high-rate-of-return firms. But shareholders have not changed the underlying rates of return on real assets. When enough shareholders have shifted their investments, the financial rates of return, adjusted for risk, will be equal regardless of the underlying disequilibrium in rates of return on current and future real-capital investments. Instead of allocating real-capital flows, financial markets capitalize real-investment disequilibria into financial equilibria.

Those financial equilibria are not quite, however, what is described in the simple price-auction model. So several hypotheses are advanced about the nature of the financial equilibria found in the "random walk" hypothesis.

First, the expected rate of return on any financial investment is equal to the expected rate of return on any other financial investment in the same risk class. Financial markets are like the economists' vision of perfect capital markets in that they equalize rates of return but only *expected* ex ante rates of return are equalized. In other words, before the fact all bettors have an equal chance of winning. *Actual* ex post returns will differ, since returns are generated by a random (stochastic) process. Some bettors will lose.

Second, once the appropriate adjustment is made for the risk class of the investment, the expected rate of return on any investment will be equal to the average rate of return on all investments (the market average). The financial market is a perfect capital market in that every investment earns the same rate of return but only based on expectations. Future expected returns are equal, but actual returns are not.

Third, the expected rate of return on a financial investment, given no information about that investment (except its risk class), is equal to the expected rate of return on an investment, given all of the legally available public information. Since all information is quickly capitalized into the price of an asset, information has a zero value and it is not worth spending money to get.

It is from this principle that the name "random walk" springs. If information is already capitalized into the price of an asset, knowing it does nothing to make you a better investor. Throwing darts at the financial pages of the *New York Times* is as good an investment strategy as trying to accumulate all of the information available about any stock. Dart throwing is in fact a better investment strategy, since it costs nothing, whereas collecting information is expensive.

Fourth, within each risk class there is a nonnormal random lottery in which individuals place bets on individual investments with equal expected values (an equal chance of winning) but in which investments yield very different returns ex post.[7] As in any lottery, there is an expected average rate of return for any invested dollar, but also, as in any lottery, someone will win and someone will lose. Moreover, the big winners will not be balanced by equally big losers.

Here the argument parallels one advanced in quantum mechanics. Although it is possible to predict the center of mass of

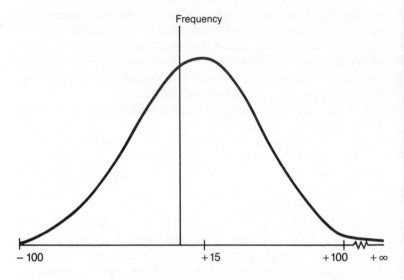

Diagram 4

A NONNORMAL RANDOM LOTTERY

a distribution of a group of electrons (all stocks), it is not possible to predict the movement of any particular electron (a specific stock). More precisely, the lottery within each risk class is thought to be a nonnormal random lottery. There is a long upper tail (see Diagram 4), which postulates that a significant probability exists of making a very large return on an investment because a small number of investments will be capitalized at very high multiples. But there is no equivalent lower tail, because losses are inherently limited. It is of course not possible to lose more than you invest (bet) and no investor can lose more than he has.

For example, in the 1930s you might have invested in a risk class of firms that included IBM. At that time, all of the firms in the class would have looked alike and all would have had an equal expected rate of return. Ex post, some firms went broke, most earned the market rate of return, some earned more than the market rate of return, and a few, perhaps one, earned a rate of return like IBM's. Those who owned such shares became wealthy. They won the lottery. The same process may now be going on with the recombinant DNA firms. In the end some may be big winners, which is the reason large bets are now being placed.

The random walk is a process that will generate a highly skewed distribution of wealth (another one of the empirical facts not consistent with the simple equilibrium price-auction model but which is characteristic of the American economy) regardless of the normal distribution of personal abilities.[8] The distribution of outputs is not a simple function of the distribution of inputs. The negative tail of the distribution of returns has a very different shape than the positive tail, and large fortunes, once created, can be and usually are diversified across many investments. No equalizing principle exists in the random-walk hypothesis, and inequalities, once created, are likely to persist.

What evidence supports the random-walk hypothesis? First, an examination of large financial firms (such as mutual funds) and investment advisory services indicates that none of them (with the recently discovered possible exception of *Value Line*) is able to outperform the market averages consistently. Professional financial managers able to make large investments in obtaining market information cannot beat a random drawing of stocks. Second, no one has been able to design a set of decision rules (when to buy and sell) that yields a greater than average rate of return. Third, tests indicate that stock prices quickly adjust to changes in information (announcements of stock splits, dividend increases). Fourth, there is no serial correlation between changes in stock prices over time. The price at any moment in time or over time cannot be used to predict future prices. Considered together, these findings form an impressive body of evidence—although not impressive enough to convert everyone into random walkers.

If information is quickly capitalized into prices, it is easy to explain why decision rules cannot be found for buying and selling stocks and earning above-average rates of return. If such a rule were found and followed, those following it would invalidate it by incorporating whatever information the rule contained in the price of stocks. Once the information was incorporated in the price of stocks, the rule would cease to work, not because it was wrong, but because it had been mined of its informational value until rendered exhausted and worthless.

Suppose some equation or decision rule predicted that a stock now selling at $50 would sell at $100 one year from now. With a market rate of interest of 10 percent, the value of the stock would quickly be bid up to $90.91 (the net present value of a promise to pay $100 one year from now with a 10 percent rate of interest). During the next year, the market price would gradually rise from $90.91 to $100 in keeping with dictates of compound interest. But once the stock price reached its equilibrium value ($90.91)—something that would happen almost instantly if the prediction were believed—the equation would cease to be valuable. All of the information incorporated in the equation would have been used, and the equation would have ceased to be a good predictor of future movements in stock prices. For this reason it is impossible to build econometric equations that allow investors to predict the value of stocks. Any equation that is correct would quickly make itself incorrect.

All economic modeling is a victim of this conclusion, if the random walk can be generalized to other markets of the economy. Functions become unstable, and bad predictors because whatever information they first contain is continually being built into economic decisions. As this happens, the equations essentially evaporate—making them poor predictors of what will occur.

The same line of reasoning, random walkers assert, makes it impossible for government to intervene to alter market results. Suppose the government enters the market to increase or decrease the value of a particular stock. In a price-auction market, private investors have determined a market price for the stock that fairly represents its expected earnings opportunities and gives them the equilibrium-market rate of return. If the government were to buy shares, the market price would for a moment be pushed above its equilibrium value and the rate of return below its equilibrium value. Investors would see an overvalued stock earning a below-average rate of return, would thereupon sell their shares to get what they would regard as a disequilibrium capital gain and to avoid a below-average rate of return. In the process of selling, investors would push the price back to the status quo ante. Similarly, if the government were to sell shares, the market price would temporarily be pushed below its equilibrium value and the rate of return above its market value. Investors would see an undervalued stock with an above-average rate of return. Given the potential capital gains and high income stream to be earned, they would buy shares until they had pushed the price back to its original position. As a result, the government could not affect share prices as long as shares still lay in the hands of private investors.

This represents the dramatic nihilistic conclusion for which rational expectations are known (nothing affects nothing), but it is important to note that the conclusion does not flow from the introduction of rational expectations into economic analysis. The conclusion is an intrinsic feature of the equilibrium price-auction model.

Does the equilibrium price-auction model adequately describe every market in the economy? The rational expectationists answer "yes." Others, including me, answer "no."

The Macro-Economics of Rational Expectations

There are two solutions to the evident inconsistency between the existence of macro-economic problems and the equilibrium price-auction model. One is to alter the theoretical model of micro-economic behavior so that it becomes consistent with macro-economic theory. The other is to throw out macro-economics as an illegitimate enterprise and to make the equilibrium price-auction model all-encompassing. Rational expectationists choose to follow the latter alternative.

As we have already seen, if all markets clear perfectly, based on changes in prices, no unemployed resources and no meaningful inflation problem can exist. As people optimally allocate their resources over their lifetime, resources are invested or saved. Whatever growth is consistent with these investment decisions is society's correct rate of growth and occurs automatically without macro-economic intervention.

But rational expectationists differ from simple advocates of the equilibrium price-auction model in that they do not necessarily claim that all markets function perfectly. As noted, they believe that all markets function as well as they possibly can but that may be very imperfect indeed thanks to intrinsic deficiencies in information, unavoidable and often substantial transaction costs, and large stochastic shocks.

Rational expectationists also assume that individual decision makers learn rationally rather than adaptively. This means that they do not gradually change their behavior in response to new pieces of information or different circumstances but quickly and discontinuously adopt new decision rules. People are also assumed to look to the future, their expectations, rather than to the past, their experience, in making decisions.

The emphasis on rational, as opposed to adaptive, behavior makes the valid point that man, being a thinking animal, tries to learn from his past and not repeat his mistakes. Behavior is sometimes going to change quickly and discontinuously. Accordingly, any theory which assumes only gradual changes in behavior, adaptive expectations, is obviously wrong. The rapid adoption of indexed contracts after 1974 is just one example of sudden changes in behavior. At the same time it is a mistake to think that man lives by economic theory alone and that experience or habit plays no role. Habit gives a person a way to economize his use of time. Because expectations about the future are also heavily conditioned by our experience, the real question becomes the extent to which our behavior is rational and the extent to which it is adaptive.

Psychologists who have worked on learning theory give us no evidence that human beings instantly arrive at correctly specified rational decisions.[9] Psychologists have found instead that people often make systematic mistakes, that they take time to move from one mode of behavior to another. For example, shoppers often misjudge relative supermarket prices by basing them on store characteristics rather than on actual prices.[10]

Rational expectationists come in strong and weak forms, though the same person can often be both strong and weak depending on the forum he is addressing. The weak-form economist is, essentially, agnostic: though he completely accepts the rational-expectations critique of conventional monetary and fiscal economics, he's not sure anything will be found to replace what is patently incorrect. There may be a way to improve economic performance, but no economist knows what it is. (Given the real problems that exist, the plea for more caution and less confidence in economic "fixes" is something to which everyone should subscribe even if he otherwise disagrees with rational expectationists.)

Strong-form rational expectationists, on the other hand, are a more certain group and argue that they absolutely know that no government policies can possibly affect economic performance. The public has been taught that economists can solve the economic pains caused by markets that are not where the public would like them to be, but the public must be retaught that no economist of any school can solve any of the economy's problems. In short, no systematic improvements can be made in the economy's random course.

But it must be pointed out that rational expectationists believe that no systematic opportunities exist to improve economic performance, not because of empirical studies that show all of the economy's markets function under random-walk principles, but because of the a priori contention that if systematic opportunities did exist, private decision makers would already have acted upon them and eliminated them. Private decision makers know as much as public decision makers and, by definition, no opportunities exist for new market entrants to make above-average rates of return. And if such opportunities do not exist, no one can improve upon existing economic performance. The economy so understood, rational expectationists are the ultimate believers in the perfection of equilibrium price-auction markets. Markets, like the mind of God, are as perfect as they can be no matter how imperfect they may appear to be, not because anyone has proved it empirically, but because it has to be so by definition.

So the problems that macro-economics deals with are non-problems, which rational expectationists define away semantically. All observations must be consistent with the theory. For some unspecified and unknown reason, a particular market may not operate as the simple equilibrium price-auction model would have it—real unemployment might exist—but no market imperfections are possible because they are by definition opportunities to make above-average rates of return. And by the very nature of competitive markets we know that any such opportunities would be very quickly taken advantage of and eliminated by shrewd market players.

Consequently, rational expectationists are not interested in empirically exploring the apparent anomalies and deviations from the simple price-auction model. As they see it, if one were to understand precisely why some phenomenon exists, such as persistent differences in rates of return on real investment, one would not have learned anything useful because no one can improve the existing results. If internal business savings and managerial capitalism dominate America's real-capital markets and produce differential rates of return, they do so because they are the most efficient way to organize America's real-capital markets. If some other way were more efficient, that alternative would exist, but it doesn't. The reasons why the existing arrangements dominate makes for an interesting intellectual puzzle, but its solution does no one any good. If something exists, it is as perfect and efficient as it is possible to be—not because we have proved it to be so, but because we know it to be so.

Believing that observed deviations in economic results are produced by random shocks or random misinformation, rational expectationists have only one empirical interest. They want to show that all series of economic data *could have been* produced by some random process. Given the large number of possible random processes and the limited number of observations in most economic data sets, this task is usually not difficult, especially if the burden of proof can be placed on those trying to show that something proceeded systematically, not randomly.

Empirically it is usually impossible to rule out definitively the possibility that a set of observations could have been the product of a random process. To prove that a data series *could have been* produced by some random process does not, of course, mean that it *was* produced by some random process. It is equally difficult to prove that it was produced by a random process and not by some systematic process.

Since economic time series go back only to 1929 and relatively few exist before 1946 (the Great Depression and World War II are also regarded by rational expectationists as peculiar periods where the usual economic rules do not apply), statistical techniques for testing the proposition cannot be used with any degree of confidence. There just aren't enough observations. As a result, statistical tests cannot be used to definitely prove or disprove the validity of the rational-expectationist hypothesis.

Since the radical conclusions of rational-expectations theorists depend not on the introduction of real expectations into economic analysis but on the assumption that markets rapidly reach equilibrium, the rational-expectations school is often seen as a return to the classical economics of the 1920s. Economists of the 1920s would have felt at home in it, though perhaps disturbed by its rejection of the concept of short-run disequilibria and remedial market imperfections. On the other hand, the economists of the 1930s would probably have found it difficult to believe that their economy was as close to equilibrium as it was possible to get.

But even in the case of the Great Depression, you can find no logical reasons why the economy could not just have been hit by very large and persistent adverse random shocks. Given a very substantial random component to economic behavior and events, one would expect large adverse shocks at infrequent intervals. An adverse shock, destined to occur once every thousand years, just happened to hit us in the late 1920s and lasted for twelve years—or so the rational expectationists might argue.

Incomplete Information

In the new classical economics, information is assumed to be less than complete (perfect), while the old classical economics assumed perfect information. For the rational expectationist, the lack of accurate information is a principal cause of large stochastic disturbances, business cycles, and the wide divergence in market results of all kinds.

Without good information, of course, the economy loses its deterministic character. And not having perfect information, the random-walk investor cannot invest with certainty but has to make what are in fact random choices. Having made random choices, he will get random results when the fruits of his investments are harvested, though what he expected was an average crop.

Rational expectationists also assume and strongly believe that the information available to government policy makers is no better than that available to the average private decision maker. Private-market actors, who are just as smart as public policy makers, have access to the same information or models, and quickly learn to anticipate what public policy makers might do. If public policy makers use certain types of econometric models to forecast economic events and then intervene in the economy on the basis of such forecasts, the private economic actors know that is what the public policy makers are going to do. When investors make their private decisions, they make them with the understanding that government will intervene in the economy under certain circumstances. As a result, an actual decision to intervene will have no *new* impact on private decisions. The impact of the intervention has already been built into the initial decisions on an expected value basis.

New information can of course alter decisions, but new information must be generated by unexpected changes in the economy. There is no reason to believe that government authorities will be able to generate any new information about the existing economy not available to private decision makers. Consequently, new information, just like misinformation, is a random event.

For example, the government forecasts a recession and prescribes a Keynesian tax cut as a remedy. The net present expected value of that future tax cut would already have been factored into current consumption plans, and thus have no positive effect on private consumption when implemented. Whatever the impact of the tax cut on stimulating demand, that impact would have occurred much earlier than the tax cut itself. In a Keynesian regime, therefore, countercyclical tax cuts are an essential part of the economic environment and treated as such by the private economy. When the tax cuts actually occur, they have been fully anticipated and bring no new or unexpected stimulus to the situation. Individuals are already consuming and investing based upon the expectation that the taxes will be cut in such a situation.

As a result, the only policies that can affect economic results are those that are unexpected. Any rule by which monetary or fiscal decisions are made with respect to when government should intervene would quickly become known and quickly cease to have any impact on the economy. Policy makers could have effects if they intervened at random, but the last thing they want to do, of course, is to intervene at random to generate random effects. They want to intervene systematically to improve the economy's performance. But this is precisely what they cannot do, say the rational expectationists. Since the economic players know the future course of monetary policies as well as the monetary authorities themselves and have anticipated what they will do, authorities at any given moment can do nothing to affect the future course of inflation or the economy.

But let's consider a little-known corollary of the propositions we've gone over. Even though private decision makers "know" what policy makers will do, the resulting ineffectuality of monetary and fiscal policies does not lead to the conclusion that those policies should be abandoned. If they unexpectedly were, that abandonment itself would have an impact on the economy, since it would constitute a random unexpected event. Thus the decision not to intervene in a recession with monetary and fiscal stimulus could make the recession worse, even though the intervention itself could not eliminate the recession. As a result, policy makers should continue to make the decisions that they were making as if the rational-expectationist hypothesis were not true.

Difficulties

Empirically there are a number of economic realities that rational expectations has a very hard time explaining.[11] For one thing, the sheer duration of the business cycle makes it difficult to believe that the phenomenon is due solely to mistaken information. While some economic actors might misperceive aggregate price changes for relative price changes (all prices and wages are up equally, but employers mistakenly see only higher wages and thus lay off workers) or transitory price changes for permanent price changes (a short-run fall in the demand for a product is mistakenly seen as a permanent fall, and production facilities are shut down), all economic actors should make no such systematic mistakes. And even if they did, the mistakes should be corrected much faster than seems the real case. Unemployment, among other things, is simply too persistent to be interpreted as resulting from mistaken information.

How could everyone have been systematically misinformed for the twelve years of the Great Depression? How could misinformation have produced four years of no economic growth, from the first quarter of 1979 to the first quarter of 1983? How could labor be so systematically misinformed that unemployment rose above 10 percent in 1982, with every prospect of its staying at high levels for a very long period of time? Productivity and real wages rise in a recession when they should be falling if mistakes (for example, that real wages are too high) cause recessions.

The rate at which workers quit their jobs also seems to move contrary to what would be true if mistaken information caused recessions. If mistakes cause unemployment, one would expect to see the quit rate climb in recessions because workers think that higher wages could be obtained from another employer, and are therefore testing the labor market. In fact, quits fall in recessions and rise in booms. Similarly, in periods of low unemployment, real income should fall, inducing workers to opt for more leisure and less work. In fact, real income rises in booms and falls in recessions.

Governments also seem to have the systematic ability to produce a recession whenever they wish. In the past ten years, governments have several times deliberately tightened monetary policies. Each time (1974–75, 1980, 1981) they have succeeded in producing a recession. The rational-expectations school needs to know the how and why because governments should no more have the ability to create recessions than cure them according to the theory.

Rational expectations must also explain why there are so few insurance markets. Why doesn't, for example, private unemployment insurance exist? If there are only random factors and not systematic factors at work, most of the adverse economic experiences suffered by private citizens ought to be privately insurable, but they are not. Why not?

One must also consider the concept of uncertainty (you do not know what will happen) as opposed to risk (you do not know the precise outcome but can place probabilities on all of the various possible outcomes). Rational expectationists seek to translate the future entirely into a framework of expected probability where there is risk but no uncertainty.[12] This cannot be done, however, if the real world is uncertain, with unknown outcomes and unknown probabilities. Because you simply do not know whether government will intervene with a tax cut in a recession, you may take actions to reduce your uncertainty, such as postponing your decisions. But if you do this, government has the ability to alter your behavior by reducing your uncertainty. When government decides whether it will or won't cut taxes in a recession, you will then decide whether you will or won't invest. An uncertain world is fundamentally different from a risky world. But rational expectations, and much of the rest of economics, act as if the world were always risky but never uncertain.

There is also a problem with long-term contracts or commitments that turn what might have been rational expectations at one point into adaptive behavior. What do I mean? General Motors may have changed its expectations about the state of the automobile business after signing its labor contract in 1979, but the company is locked into a contract until 1982. The price of gold may have unexpectedly gone down recently, but gold mines are so expensive to close down or open that operators are locked into operating them over a wide range of prices. In both cases, behavior is adaptive irrespective of how expectations are formed. But it is also behavior and not expectations that government intervention seeks to modify. Models can be built encompassing both rational expectations and adaptive behavior, but such models produce results very different from those based simply on rational expectations and discontinuous adjustments in behavior.

Modeling Expectations

Because none of the major controversial conclusions of the rational-expectations school flow from the role that future expectations actually play, members of the school have not been interested in detailed empirical models of human expectations.

The problem of modeling expectations nontautologically and empirically can be seen in a model of inflation developed by the rational expectationists Sargent and Wallace,[13] who assume that inflation depends solely on inflationary expectations. They assume that businessmen think that inflation is a function of government deficits, even though monetarists and rational expectationists know there is no intrinsic reason to believe that government deficits cause inflation. Because government deficits are *believed* to cause inflation, they in fact cause inflation through upward ratcheting of inflationary expectations. In the reasoning of Sargent and Wallace, higher inflation leads to a tight money policy, which causes interest payments on the national debt to go up. This makes the deficit worse. Whereupon inflationary expectations, and hence inflation, rise once again.

The difficulty here is that a parallel model could be constructed based on any set of expectations no matter how silly. If the monetarists and the rational expectationists are right when they assert that government deficits play no role in causing inflation, then private decision makers should clearly have learned that fact long ago—both the rational expectationists and the monetarists have been proclaiming it publicly for years. Why don't businessmen learn that deficits don't matter and remove them from the list of factors creating their inflationary expectations? The model has no answer, but to be satisfactory, the model must have an answer. Every random thought is not a rational thought: if businessmen are thinking untrue thoughts, it is possible to alter their behavior by showing them the truth.

One can wholeheartedly agree with the proposition that expectations are important and that economists should find better ways of integrating them into their analyses without at the same time believing that markets are as perfect as they can be or that all forms of government interventions are ineffective. In fact, a wide variety of possible alternative expectational models does exist and results depend on which model is used. For example, inflationary expectations based on the Phillips-curve model will be different from those based on a natural-rate-of-unemployment model. Believers in the Phillips curve expect inflation to fall gradually as unemployment rises, while adherents of the natural rate expect inflation to shift suddenly from positive to negative when the natural rate is exceeded.

Conversely, some types of expectations will help to produce a Phillips curve; others, a natural rate of unemployment. Suppose the monetarists are believed, and that inflation is assumed to be a simple function of money-supply changes. Does the individual economic actor believe that larger and larger increases in the money supply gradually lead to larger and larger increases in inflation and smaller and smaller increases in the real GNP, and then adopt appropriate behavior? Or does he believe that the rising money supply reaches a point of discontinuity where inflation accelerates? It makes a difference. One form of behavior produces the Phillips curve, and the other the natural rate of unemployment.

If true, however, the basic conclusions of rational expectations are equally applicable to all of economics. The behavior and decision rules of the monetary authorities are as well known as those of the fiscal authorities. Inflation becomes not a product of past money-supply decisions but a function of expected future money supplies. Monetary authorities cannot affect these expectations, however, unless they do something unexpected. If the high interest rates and tight monetary policies of 1981 have been expected (and rational expectationists believe them to be so), they can have no positive effect on inflation or negative effect on the course of real growth. Inflation may fall and the economy may enter a recession, but both will be accidents and not a product of systematic policies.

Rational expectationists also believe that there is no reason why monetary policies should first produce a downturn in the economy (T) and only then begin to affect prices (P)—the standard monetarist belief. Since the market knows what will eventually happen (it has been informed by the monetarists), a reduction in the money supply would instantly affect prices without the intervening *mistaken* effects on real economic activity.

Similarly, say the rational expectationists, when people made their savings and work decisions they factored in not just current tax rates but all expected future tax rates. So when Reagan lowers taxes, there can be no impact on savings or work effort, because the tax cuts have been expected and are already affecting behavior. Whatever increases the cuts have caused have already occurred, if they are going to occur. Likewise, people factored in the possibility that the Reagan tax cuts will be rescinded in future political battles, and their behavior has already been affected.

What all of this theorizing ignores, however, is the fact that as time passes, tax and other government policies shift from being highly uncertain and almost completely discounted to being certain with definite effects. No expected value calculus can capture that eventuality—the shift from uncertainty to certainty.

Economists have for years tried to model expectations, but all of the models have basically been adaptive where behavior gradually changes as new economic data enter the system. Models of real future-oriented expectations are extremely rare, and what often seems to be such is not when examined closely.

The permanent-income hypothesis is probably the best example of such a disappearing act.[14] According to this theory, individuals consume based not on their current or past income, but on the expected value of their future lifetime income stream. But what is that expected value? In practice, permanent income is estimated as a lagged function of the preceding three years of actual income. This converts the estimate first into a hypothesis that is not distinguishable from the Keynesian assumption (that consumption depends on current and lagged incomes) and second into something that essentially eliminates the future-oriented meaning found in the very word "expectations." So, in effect, future-income expectations became adaptive depending on past income histories. But more important, the model ignores a basic reality; namely, that when it comes to future income, uncertainty is the norm. Professor Thurow and those who might lend money to him are so uncertain about his future income stream that he must consume based on his current income. His actions are thereby forced into an adaptive mode by uncertainty.

Lagged variables are the traditional way to model expectations in econometrics. Decision making slowly changes in response to those lagged variables, which are surrogates for unmeasurable expectations. Thus past rates of inflation become an explanatory variable in a price equation designed to capture rising inflationary expectations as inflationary experience accumulates. Everyone will agree that this is not a satisfactory proposition. Economic actors look into the future as well as into the past and are capable of raising their inflationary expectations in advance of an increase in current inflation. But this is not to say, of course, that past inflation rates have no impact on expectations. In fact, conceptions of both the past and future are important. The problem is to capture that dual reality in economic models.

The second technique for modeling expectations has been to take surveys of household or business intentions.[15] These have not been very useful. Intentions do not seem to project themselves very far into the future and do not seem to be stable over time. Economic actors cannot tell you what they intend to do with their money two years from now, and even in the short run they often alter their intentions in the face of changes in the economy at large. How and why do these expectations change? Perhaps to know intentions is to change them, but systematic factors could also be at work, a possibility not dismissed without empirical evidence.

But, as noted, the current school of rational expectations is generally uninterested in empirical work on how expectations are formed, how they change, and what might be done to influence them. Which is hardly surprising if you really believe that expectations are as perfect as expectations can be expected to be. They are rational and not adaptive, not because it has been proven so, but because they must be so if the individual decision maker is to act as Homo economicus is supposed to act. And he must be acting as Homo economicus, or else opportunities would exist to earn extra profits—something that cannot, by definition, occur in the price-auction model.

Because rational expectationists believe that you cannot measure expectations without changing them, that expectations are subject to discontinuous jumps with new events, and that expectations, like everything else, are subject to large stochastic shocks, the theorists have no interest in finding better ways to model or measure expectations. If you assume, as quantum mechanics does, that the behavior of individual electrons is random, you are not interested in laboratory work tracing the paths of individual atoms, in efforts to predict the future paths of individual atoms, or in a mechanism for attempting to control the paths of individual atoms. All that is a waste of time. Before this conclusion can be justified, however, it must be empirically proved that individual economic behavior in fact resembles an electron of quantum mechanics. Physi-

cists, after all, have excellent empirical evidence backing up
the theory of quantum mechanics. But for the rational expectationist, existing expectations, like the geologically determined
supply of oil, simply must be accepted as one of the constraints
within which our system operates. These expectations cannot
be changed, measured, or controlled. But that robs the expectations approach of all interest, as it becomes a formalism allowing the analyst to say whatever he feels like saying.

Alternatives

There are of course various other alternatives. Economic forecasts have not been as prescient as one would like, but they
have been far better than random guesses or the naïve forecasting models which assume that the next quarter will look
like the present one. Government intervention has not
stopped inflation, but did keep recessions short and mild as
long as they occurred. Some parameters in econometric models have been unstable; others have been remarkably stable.
And the world can of course also be partly deterministic and
partly stochastic. Accordingly, one can believe in stochastic
disturbances without believing that they explain all economic
behavior. And one can believe that some markets—the financial markets, for example—adjust quickly according to rational
expectations while other markets—the labor market for one—
adjust slowly according to adaptive expectations.

Because buying and selling stocks is a liquid activity and
involves no substantial transaction costs either in terms of time
or money, it is easy to believe that financial markets exhibit
rational rather than adaptive behavior. Because you can get in
and out of financial positions very quickly, you don't have to
think about economic fundamentals but about what others are
expecting the market to do. Think of the very high stock-price
multiple given IBM in the late 1960s. To justify such a multiple
in terms of the net present value of future earnings, IBM
would have had to grow so large that no one for a minute could
have believed that it was going to happen. Yet the multiple
existed. Investors could believe that IBM was overvalued relative to the fundamental reality of future earnings, but could
also believe that it was a good short-run investment because
the multiple was going to expand even further—buy or sell to

the "greater fool." Expectations take on a life of their own often divorced from economic reality. Whatever people believe to be true is true, at least for a little while.

By contrast, real investments take time to complete, and once completed, involve enormous transaction costs, for no one can shift resources quickly from one line of activity to another. A legal education once acquired stays acquired. And processes once started are often irreversible. A copper mine temporarily closed fills up with water and is permanently closed. In such markets, expectations and behavior may be knowable and stable for very long periods of time.

The economy has also evolved institutions and practices designed precisely to avoid having to have expectations. With wage indexing, the labor market is essentially saying that it chooses not to have expectations about inflation, but will instead acquire a private insurance policy to protect itself against whatever happens. The impact of inflationary expectations may not be predictable, but the impact of indexing certainly is. One consequence is that any inflationary shock will enter wages in a entirely predictable way.

Similar constraints could be placed on other markets to influence their behavior. The bond market might, for example, be indexed. This would not eliminate uncertainty about the future course of events in the market, but it would eliminate inflationary uncertainty for buyers and sellers of bonds and throw the costs of that uncertainty somewhere else in the system.

Technical constraints may also produce adaptive actions. Think of the transition from oil to gas furnaces induced by an increase in the price of heating oil relative to natural gas. Unless the price differential is very large, it probably wouldn't make economic sense to junk good oil furnaces and replacing them with gas furnaces. But the oil furnaces should be replaced as they wear out in normal usage. The point is that the technical constraint has produced adaptive behavior even if a discontinuous adjustment in expectations occurred as to which was the more economical furnace.

If constraints affect economic behavior—and it is almost an axiom that they do—then a role does exist for government policies. To put matters at their most basic level, government defines property rights without which markets could not exist.

A market with slavery is different from a market without it. Accordingly, an attempt to prohibit the drug trade is not inherently different from an attempt to impose wage and price controls. The argument here being that if government can be even marginally effective in prohibiting the use of certain drugs, it is an open empirical question as to how effective government can be in controlling the prices of general goods and services.

And if government can set constraints that make a difference, it is also an open question as to whether a private institution, let's say unions, can also set constraints that make a difference. Unless a very radical view of governmental impotence is taken, a serious belief in the truth of rational expectations leads not to a conservative position—stay out of markets and let the economy regulate itself—but to the radical, normally leftist, position that government can affect the economy only by altering the fundamental structural characteristics of the economy itself. According to this theory, government cannot fiddle on the margins with either monetary or fiscal policies, but it does possess the capacity to alter the structure of the economy and the constraints under which it operates.

There is another way in which government economic policies can have real consequences even if rational expectations are valid: government can redistribute income from one person to another. It may not be sure exactly what incentive effects will flow from the redistribution, but a shift in the structure of demands will certainly occur. Government may not know how to alter your spending behavior with indirect incentive policies, but it does know how to raise or lower your income with transfers and taxes. Government can collect checks and it can write checks.

Believing what he believes, however, the rational expectationist's debating position is a powerful one if he can throw the burden of proof on those who disagree with him. His opponents have to prove that economic relationships are stable and systematic, while he all himself has to maintain is that they are random until proven otherwise. So the failure of others is his success.

This debating stratagem can be seen in the rational-expectation salvos (in this case those of Robert Lucas) directed at

Keynesians (in this case James Tobin). "Keynesian orthodoxy or the neoclassical synthesis is in deep trouble, the deepest kind of trouble in which an applied body of theory can find itself: It appears to be giving seriously wrong answers to the most basic questions of macro-economic policy. Proponents of a class of models which promised 3½ to 4½ percent unemployment to a society willing to tolerate annual inflation rates of 4 to 5 percent have some explaining to do after a decade such as we have just come through. A forecast error of this magnitude and central importance to policy has consequences."[16]

The implicit argument is that Keynesians have been wrong, therefore rational expectations must be right. But rational expectations do not impose upon themselves Keynesianism's obligation to predict and control the economy, because rational expectations assert that both are impossible. This is hardly a balanced standard of proof or an argument without logical fallacies.

A Gambler's Argument

In the gambler's (Pascal's) argument for God, the gambler faces two choices. If God does not exist and the gambler acts as if he did, little is lost. If, on the other hand, God does exist and the gambler acts as if he did not, much is lost—an eternity in hell. Thus an expected-value gambler—a rational expectationist—will believe in God.

Similarly, a "rational" rational expectationist will always conduct monetary and fiscal policies as if they mattered. If the policies are adopted and implemented, but do not matter, no harm is done. If, on the other hand, nothing is done and they do matter, much damage is done because the policies could have eliminated macro-economic problems and weren't used. And they will also matter if the economy has just one person whose expectations or behavior is adaptive. That person can be affected, and those whose behavior cannot be affected cannot be hurt. Because no one can ever be absolutely sure that no adaptive decision makers exist, the conclusions of rational expectationists must be laid aside and not practiced—just as the beliefs of an atheist will never be practiced by an expected-value rational atheist.

It is also true that, once initiated, monetary and fiscal policies must be continued even if they cannot improve the economy's performance. If monetary and fiscal intervention were to be abandoned, economic actors would be surprised—the government did not intervene when it was expected to—and paradoxically, this itself becomes an unexpected intervention that could adversely alter the path of the economy.

CHAPTER 7

The Labor Market

A Sargasso Sea of Economic Shipwrecks

The basic thrust of labor economics in the 1950s, '60s, and '70s has been to erase the distinction between labor and other factors of production. A unit of labor is comparable to a bushel of wheat, and sold in the same equilibrium price-auction markets. Moreover, the investment calculus employed to understand physical investments is asserted to apply equally to human-capital investments. In labor economics the human-capital approach seemed ready to replace the old institutionalist approach and thus place labor solidly within the price-auction framework.[1] While there has been a powerful movement in this direction, the transition has not completely swept the profession.

Why not? For one thing, human-capital predictions—the relationship between education and earnings—have been far off the mark. And if you want to understand the dominant mode of acquiring human capital, on-the-job training, the human-capital economics does a disappearing act. Just as the economic model of utility maximization is rescued as a theory by the conception of an unobservable variable, marginal utility, which makes any observed consumption decision a "correct" decision, human-capital theory posits a variable, psychic income, which preserves the model theoretically but robs it of all empirical content. Whatever the worker does, he is maximizing income—psychic plus money. The result is a theory possessing an imposing façade upon a much less imposing edifice.

For human-capital economists, the predominant on-the-job

form of training is made into a market phenomenon by asserting that individuals buy training from their employer by working for less than their market wage—their marginal productivity. But without the homogeneous wages—equal pay for those with equal skills—called for in human-capital theory, it is impossible to specify an individual's free-market wage and determine the size of the training payments being made to his employer. And if training occurs on-the-job, it is also difficult to pin down how much training is going on. There is nothing here that can be called equivalent to a year of education not to speak of a direct measure of the skills acquired. In other words, neither the costs nor the benefits of the most significant way human skills are acquired in our economy can be stated in precise numbers.

As a consequence, to force labor market behavior into the human-capital framework, an elaborate tautology has been constructed.[2] If the equilibrium price-auction model is true, the reasoning goes, then educational investments in formal education and informal on-the-job training investments must be in equilibrium and yield the same rates of return. Wage differences over and above those caused by education must therefore represent the returns that can be ascribed to on-the-job training. Given observed relationships between education and earnings and the costs of obtaining the extra education, rates of return can then be calculated for educational investments. By definition the same rate of return must be earned on on-the-job investments. If one can establish this estimated return and the gap between an individual's expected wage, given his education and his actual wage, it is a simple matter of division to calculate the "amount" of on-the-job training that must have occurred to explain observed earnings.

If an individual was earning $10,000 per year more than would have been projected based on his education and if the rate of return on educational investments was 10 percent, he must by this account have received $100,000 ($10,000/0.10) worth of on-the-job training. Accordingly, human-capital-investment theory becomes true by definition, just as unobserved utilities make consumer utility maximization true by definition. But in the process the theory empties itself of all empirical content. Workers simply do what workers do and can never make a mistake in their investments.

The problems with the approach go far beyond tautology. If formal education and on-the-job training complement each other—more formal education leads to greater payoffs from informal on-the-job training; more on-the-job training leads to greater payoffs from education—then it really isn't possible to estimate rates of return for formal or informal training separately. They must be estimated together. That, however, is impossible because, as I have just noted, it is very hard to measure either the costs or benefits of informal training. Human-capital theory also cannot account for the fact that many of the on-the-job training markets where one is supposed to bid for opportunities to acquire informal training don't seem to exist. Employers usually allocate such opportunities not based on a willingness to work for less than one's free-market wage, but on seniority or merit for having performed well in a job previously held.

In general, the attempt to make labor into just another factor of production ignores a wide variety of characteristics that make human investments very different from physical investments. A human-capital calculus can be developed, but in the end it is so different from that for plant and equipment that the similarities are insignificant.[3]

The peculiarities to be found in the labor market spring from a number of sources. First, human beings have preferences—other factors of production don't. Not only do human beings have preferences, they are formed in a social environment where each person's likes and dislikes, satisfactions and dissatisfactions, are highly interdependent.[4] My being satisfied with my economic performance depends not just upon my income (as it is supposed to in the price-auction model) but also on where my income stands in relation to that of my peers and neighbors. Second, the productivity of human labor is not technologically determined, but dependent upon motivation and the effort that each person is willing to supply. Third, human capital cannot be separated from its owners. The owner of physical capital need not accompany his physical capital, but the owner of human capital must necessarily accompany his. To earn a miner's wage one must work in a mine, but one need not do so to earn a high rate of return on mining equipment. Fourth, the same human capital is used by individuals in their role both as workers producing goods and services and con-

sumers consuming goods and services. In contrast, physical
capital is only a producer of goods and services. As a result,
consumption benefits (positive and negative) may occur. Individuals may acquire human capital to produce goods for
themselves that are never sold in the market.

As in other markets, the equilibrium price-auction model
postulates the concept of earnings maximization. But the concept gets into trouble because factors other than money clearly
are important. But if the concept of psychic income (complementary consumption goods) is used to rescue earnings maximization, the latter loses all of its empirical content. People
simply choose the work that they choose, and any choice can
be described as earnings maximization. If this is what it comes
down to, and it does, maximization here has no predictive
value.

The collapse of the distinction between consumption and
production decisions goes beyond the problem of psychic income. Much consumption is self-produced. The services produced by housewives are the most important, but all of our
recreation, do-it-yourself, and personal-services activities require skills. A good deal of the family's standard of living is
provided by the members of the family itself. The ability to
self-produce goods and services constitutes an important current and future stream of benefits, and human-capital skills are
necessary to produce these services. And though these benefits
are never priced or sold in the market, they influence the
human-capital-investment decisions that workers make.

Whether preferences be endogenous or exogenous presents
a general problem in economics, but it poses a special problem
in human-capital theory. Investments are often made for the
express purpose of changing tastes and preferences. For example, prodigious amounts of money are spent on private investments in psychology and psychiatry to alter personal behavior.
And as preferences change, the value of human-capital assets
may also vary greatly. Hence the labor market has little chance
of achieving equilibrium, since another peculiar characteristic
of human-capital assets is that they cannot be sold—only
rented—in a society that prohibits slavery.

An inability to sell human-capital assets also makes them
much more illiquid and riskier than physical assets. In an un-

certain, risky world, assets have value because they are nego-
tiable, and liquidity, of course, increases the value of any asset.
If an emergency arises, physical assets can be sold—perhaps at
a loss but always at some price—and the money used for another purpose. But because human capital is not liquid, it cannot be used as a hedge against risk and uncertainty.
Consequently, it will have a value lower than an equally productive (equal lifetime income stream) investment in physical
capital. So if an investor's human and physical investments are
both earning 10 percent, then too much is being invested in
human-capital assets. Thus the equilibrium of the capital market, human and physical, is not the simple equilibrium of the
auction market.

Because the risks and uncertainties facing the individual also
exceed the risks and uncertainties facing the society, what is
rational behavior for the individual (investing so that returns
are much higher on physical than on human assets) may be
irrational behavior for the society as a whole. Society cannot,
after all, get out of its physical investments any more than it
can its human investments.

With physical assets, maintenance costs and depreciation
charges represent no special problems in making investment
decisions. But with human beings, one is faced with the joint
costs of production and consumption. Man must eat and sleep
both to work and to consume. How are these costs to be allocated? Some human maintenance costs are in the nature of
overhead expenditures so that ignoring them does not distort
investment decisions, but dangerous or very hard physical
work may create large maintenance costs and substantial depreciation of the human machine.

Moreover, a human being, at least in our society, cannot be
bought and then discarded when he becomes economically
obsolete. All of us are interested in preserving our lives—our
most valuable human-capital asset. To use the language of the
economist here: existence represents a stream of future consumption benefits that most of us cherish. Without it, other
streams of consumption goods have little value. Accordingly,
large investments are often made to increase the life expect-
ancy of obsolete human capital.

But most of us do not want just to exist, we also want to be active economic beings with an active role to play. Thus many people make investments to keep economically alive far longer than what could be justified on a simple benefit-cost analysis used for a piece of machinery.

The point is this: the traits and characteristics of the investor matter in human-capital investments and they do not matter in physical investments. Because human beings have a finite life span, the productivity of any investment depends on the age and physical condition of the investor. A particular investment may be a good one for a healthy young man but a poor investment for an old man. The former has many years to use the asset, the latter but a few.

For purposes of discussion, a person may also be regarded as a learning machine whose productive capacity diminishes as he grows older. Both physical and mental abilities to absorb new skills and information deteriorate because of psychological changes and physiological changes. If an individual's economic process declines with age, an important element is introduced into his investment problem. A high premium is placed on making early decisions. To be a figure skater or a ballerina, for example, one must begin training early. By the age of fifteen or sixteen, both lines of work are essentially closed to anyone who has not already started acquiring the necessary human capital. But for the acquisition of physical investments the age of the investor is irrelevant.

While the depreciation of any physical asset depends upon the nature of the asset itself, the depreciation of human-capital assets also depend on the depreciation of the investor himself. If he becomes ill or dies, the asset disappears, while of course this does not happen in the case of physical assets. They become part of the estate. This is another reason why the return on human-capital assets must be higher than on physical assets as far as the individual investor is concerned.

Many human investment decisions also have to be made at an age when the investor himself is not making his own decisions. Parents and society at large often make decisions for children based on their own preferences and not those of the children. Then, too, some decisions take place within a context that makes them very, very risky. Imagine deciding to get a Ph.D. One goes to school for twenty or more years before receiving any return whatever. What physical investment is comparable? Given the time required and the length of time over which the investment must be paying out a return, the risks of finding an economy unlike the one expected are enormous.

Human capital also represents a collection of assets rather than a single asset. One individual possesses many different talents, skills, and pieces of knowledge and information. He may know how to solve mathematical problems, lay a brick wall, sail a ship, or find his way downtown. Though some assets may be complementary, many cannot be used at the same time. A person cannot teach mathematics and lay brick walls simultaneously; whatever skill he uses, the other skill is idle. But with physical assets, the use of one asset does not preclude the simultaneous use of another at a different location.

Each human-capital investment also changes the costs of further human-capital investments. If I am a surgeon, I am making so much money that all other investments are precluded because of the opportunity costs involved. But if I am a physical investor in possession of a very productive investment, I am not precluded from making other investments now or in the future. In fact, that is exactly what I should do if I want to enhance my welfare.

Time constraints extend to matters beyond an inability to use assets simultaneously or to make additional profitable investments sequentially. A human being has a finite amount of time available for consumption, production, and joint maintenance activities. Thus, a time budget, not a money budget, is apt to limit what he can do. But the two are intrinsically different from each other. By borrowing or lending money, income can be redistributed over one's lifetime. Time, however, cannot be borrowed or lent. Consequently, time constraints are much more confining than income constraints, as one faces not just a life-span limit but a twenty-four-hour limit every day.

Human capital is also very unlike physical capital in that not everyone has access to the same set of production techniques. Some people with great natural talent can easily (cheaply) become professional athletes or rock stars. Others are completely unable to acquire the needed skills at any price. Differential abilities are less dramatic in the rest of the economy, but they are substantial.[5]

Given differences in personal ability alone, the human-capital market is not an equilibrium market where each investor earns the same rate of return. Some individuals may face much higher rates of return on investing in themselves than others, but have no time to take advantage of these opportunities because they are busy using skills already acquired. The fiction of an equal rate of return for each and every investor can be maintained by assigning an opportunity cost to each investor's time high enough to equalize financial returns, but this just moves the disequilibrium into the time dimension. The opportunity cost of an hour of time now differs substantially from individual to individual.

Anyone can invest in the drilling of an oil well, but only those with the ability to become a rock star can invest in being a rock star. The investment is not equally open to everyone. In this sense human investments are like natural resources. Some people own a better gold mine than others. But there is an additional complication: the gold mine cannot be sold by one investor to another, and only the original owner can mine for gold. The result is disequilibrium real rates of return and no possibility for buying and selling assets to capitalize the real disequilibrium into a financial equilibrium.

In general, therefore, the attempt to remove the distinction between labor and other factors of production yielded some insights, but in the end the enterprise obscured more real problems than it clarified.[6] Given their characteristics, human-capital investments cannot be made with the same investment calculus as physical investments and hence there is no reason to assume that rates of return on the two types of investments should ever equalize. Then, too, the relevant markets to buy on-the-job training just do not seem to exist. Thus a human-capital model of investments can certainly be constructed, but when it is completed it will have little relation to the model used for physical investments in the price-auction model.

Moreover, in constructing a theory of wage determination, human-capital models have never gone beyond the concept of marginal productivity that is implicit in the standard model. Human-capital models have never tried to explain rigid wages or rigid wage demands that seem to create macro-economic problems.

Conflicting Theories of the Labor Market

Just as archaeologists have two sources of information on ancient civilizations—artifacts and writings—so an observer of economic activity has two sources of information on the labor market: he can examine the observed distribution of wages and employment, or he can turn to the economic literature for a view of how wages and employment are determined. There are problems of a striking mismatch between observed data and theory, but within the theoretical literature is another peculiar phenomenon. At least four different theories of the labor market present themselves. Equilibrium price-auction economics, Keynesian macro-economics, monetarists' macro-economics, and labor economics all have different theories to explain what occurs. The theories are mutually inconsistent, but each has its advocates and economic practitioners.

In the standard price-auction model, the labor market is treated as if it were like any other market in which price (wage) is the short-run market-clearing mechanism. Individuals buy and sell skills and raw labor (time) in a bidding framework in which equilibrium prices clear markets leaving no unsatisfied buyers or sellers. Prices clear markets in the short run and provide investment signals in the long run. Cost minimization on the demand side and earnings maximization on the supply side determine shifts in supply-and-demand curves. Investments in skills (human capital) are equivalent to investments in plant and equipment, with the same decision calculus obtaining in both. Individuals invest until the rate of return to both human and physical investments is driven down to the market rate of interest. The marginal productivity theory of distribution applies—every economic actor is paid a wage equal to his marginal revenue product (the extra output that he produces times the price at which that output can be sold). Wages are flexible in the model, and unemployment is impossible.

In sharp contrast, macro-economics of both the Keynesian and monetary variety treat the labor market as a case of funda-

mental disequilibrium. Disequilibrium must exist, it is reasoned, or unemployment could not exist or persist.

In Keynesian models, money wages are assumed to be rigid
downward—the assumption is not explained, but taken as an
empirical truth. With wages rigid downward, markets cannot
clear in the normal manner. Because flexible wages do not
eliminate disequilibria in the labor market, government must
intervene to eliminate the disequilibria by manipulating aggregate demand. Specifically, government must intervene to
shift the aggregate demand curve for labor so that it crosses
the economy's labor-supply curve at full employment.

In the econometric models of Keynesian macro-economics,
the demand for labor depends upon total output, not upon the
wage rate. Careful calculations are made of the amount of
labor that will be absorbed or disgorged when aggregate output goes up or down. Similarly, the equations used to represent
the supply of labor depend on long-run demographic trends
and job availability, not wages. The labor market, in sum, is a
market where fixed-price models apply.

Monetarist macro-economics similarly depends upon assumptions of rigidity in the labor market. According to the
natural rate of unemployment hypothesis, labor demands a
specific, rigid collective real wage gain for each level of unemployment. Labor demands a real wage gain regardless of the
experience that may have frustrated it in the past—forever
asking for larger and larger nominal wage gains if unemployment is below the natural rate, but forever getting the real
wage gain consistent with productivity growth. Just as in
Keynesian macro-economics, the rigid demanded real wage
gain is an unexplained assumption taken as an empirical truth.
No attempt is made here to derive an unalterable demand for
a collective real wage gain from the equilibrium price-auction
model, because it cannot be done.

The monetarist macro-economic solution is to adjust monetary policies so that the unemployment rate rises or falls to its
natural rate. When the natural rate of unemployment is
reached, society just lives with both the nominal wage gain and
the resulting stable but perhaps high rate of inflation produced
by the gap between the nominal wage demands and the economy's rate of productivity growth. If this is not satisfactory, the
money supply may be used to push unemployment above its

natural rate. If unemployment is pushed above the natural rate, nominal wage demands fall. With lower nominal wage gains and the same rate of growth of productivity, the economy's rate of inflation will fall until it reaches some acceptable level. At that point, monetary policies can be altered to let the unemployment rate drift down to its natural rate. The new induced nominal wage gain then yields a new lower, stable rate of inflation.

No intervention would be necessary except for the fixed-price assumption that labor has a collective real wage gain that is perpetually demands at each level of unemployment. The important point is that both Keynesian and monetary theories of macro-economics leave one wondering about the workings of the equilibrium price-auction model in the labor market. Neither is consistent with it.

In institutional labor economics, inter-skill or inter-industry wage differentials become the focus of analysis.[7] The basic concept here is a wage contour developed by John Dunlop, and the wage relationships various occupations and industries have to one another. The 1974 *Economic Report of the President* states, for example, that 1973 was a year of moderate wage increases because "wages in different industries seemed in good balance."[8] So for this theory, the structure of wages becomes paramount. Except for analysis of how inequities in the structure of wages influence the level of wages, aggregate wages or their rate of increase are ignored. In other words, instead of looking at the determinants of individual productivity, the labor economists' unit of analysis is social or group decision making. In many respects, the thinking here is more closely related to the sociologists' concept of relative deprivation than it is to the equilibrium price-auction model.

Unfortunately, these four theoretical perspectives are often mutually inconsistent. If the price-auction model is correct, the macro-economic problems of unemployment cannot exist, wages are not exogenously set at some rigid money level or some rigid real wage gain, and the labor market is not in perpetual disequilibrium. Conversely, if either the Keynesian or monetarist macro-economic approaches are correct, the conventional model is wrong and economics is left without a theory of wage determination. Wages are determined in some unknown manner exogenous to the micro-economic system.

Labor economics, meanwhile, has a theory of the wage differentials at odds with the price-auction model, but neither does it have a theory to explain the level of wages. The interdependent preferences, relative deprivation, norms of social justice, and wage contours that labor economists use to determine the structure of wages are thoroughly inconsistent with the postulates of the standard economic model. Individuals compare themselves to others instead of looking solely at their own productivity and their own wages. A structure of wages set in accordance with the axioms of the marginal-productivity theory cannot conform to a structure set by patterns of interdependent preferences.

Clearly something is wrong with the economics profession when four mutually inconsistent intellectual approaches are needed to explain what happens in one real-world labor market. Various approaches to a phenomenon exist when the moves being made by the players of the game cannot be explained by any one approach. But in this situation, it is not surprising that unexpected results frequently occur in the economy.

The inconsistent approaches and empirical puzzles of the labor market have not, however, stimulated the economics profession in general to undertake a re-examination of its basic theories. Mostly the inconsistencies and puzzles have been ignored. Belief in the flexible-price world of the equilibrium price-auction market remains undisturbed as if the observed problems of the labor market did not exist.

Coping with Deviant Observations

If Newton and his contemporaries had behaved as the economics profession is now behaving and had had access to the modern computer, it is likely that the law of gravity would never have been discovered. In Newton's day, deviant celestial observations were made that did not fit into the existing epicycle theory of heavenly motion, but each such observation could be and was explained with an addition of another epicycle to the system. Given enough epicycles, all patterns were theoretically explainable. Eventually, however, the computational difficulties forced Newton to rethink the existing theory to obtain a simpler set of results based on gravity. But with the modern computer Newton would never have been forced to look for anything new. The computer would have made short work of the necessary geometric computations, making a new theoretical approach seemingly unnecessary.

Like "deviant" celestial motion at the time of Newton, deviant observations in the labor market keep being reported. But each was and still can be made consistent with the orthodox theory. Usually some market imperfection is hypothesized, and as we shall see, each is posited ad hoc and after the fact. At some point it becomes necessary to examine the weight of the evidence to see the extent to which the labor market is or is not working in accordance with the theories of the equilibrium price-auction model. And if it is not, to develop new micro-economic approaches.

The very nature of the model itself should produce at least some dissatisfaction with it. The rational expectationists are right to point out that whenever market imperfections exist, opportunities exist for someone to exploit them and make extra profits. If some price is being held above its equilibrium level, someone should be able to enter the market, undercut the price, and earn those extra profits. As those profit opportunities are exploited, the market imperfection is eliminated and prices return to their equilibrium level. By this logic, human capitalists argue that economic discrimination cannot exist or persist without the legal backing of government. It is simply impossible in a competitive free market.

As a result, market imperfections should either not exist at all or exist for a very short time only in a price-auction economy. Yet many of the deviant observations in the labor market have a long history, having existed and persisted. Anyone who believes in competitive markets should be extremely reluctant to label anything that has been around for a long time a "market imperfection." If a phenomenon continues to survive, the chances are high that it is an integral and efficient part of the economic game—not a market imperfection. Or at least, this possibility should be seriously investigated.

Of all of the deviant observations, however, none is as important as the existence of persistent unemployment. Unemployment has varied from 1 to 25 percent since 1929. It was high for twelve years during the Depression, low during World War II, high in the 1950s, low in the mid 1960s, and since the

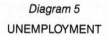

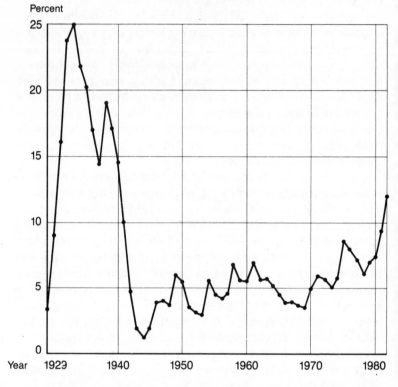

Source: Council of Economic Advisers, *The Economic Report to the President*, pp. 268, 291.

late 1960s, unemployment has cyclically risen to higher and
higher levels as government has repeatedly stepped on the
fiscal and monetary brakes to stop inflation. So the labor market we see in the real world is certainly not the simple full-
employment world predicted by a simple interpretation of the
price-auction model.

Is, then, unemployment explained by the more sophisticated rational-expectations version of the model? It would
seem not. The pattern of unemployment certainly does not
appear to be one produced by random shocks or temporary
misinformation. Can you honestly think that World War II

presented a a case of misinformation that produced low unemployment? No. But when governments tighten fiscal and monetary policies, unemployment also seems to rise as predicted. Moreover, individual spans of unemployment are lengthy—averaging more than twenty-eight weeks in 1981. And 50 percent of those no longer considered unemployed don't find a new job, but simply drop out of the labor force.[9] As a result, the average time spent unemployed, between losing a job and finding a new one, is much longer than twenty-eight weeks. So if unemployment is due to informational mistakes (individual workers think that they are worth more than the market thinks they are), as the rational expectationists maintain, why should the period of unemployment last so long? Individual spells of unemployment should end whenever a worker is willing to face up to the productivity facts of his life and lower his demanded wage. But then, why do quits rise in booms and fall in recessions? If recessions are due to informational mistakes, quits should rise in recessions and fall in booms, just the reverse of what happens in the real world.

According to the price-auction model, anyone can get a job by knocking on the door of some employer and offering to work for less than those already employed. Anyone who has actually looked for work knows this approach is not viable. A theorist can introduce unions as a market imperfection, but less than 20 percent of the American work force is now unionized. Just what is the market imperfection that keeps the door-knocking job seeker from being hired in the nonunion parts of the economy? Whatever it is, any persistent market imperfection, be it created by unions or something else, has to be built into our models of economic behavior. To deny the existence of unions, or to ask that they disappear, is to develop an economic model describing a nonexistent economy.

Consider the evidence we have about the downward inflexibility of wages. After the crash, from 1929 to 1933, money wages fell 25 percent, but prices also fell 25 percent, leading to no decline in real wages—despite massive unemployment. Why didn't wages fall faster to eliminate unemployment? After 1933 wages rose—from 1929 to 1939, prices fell 15 percent, but wages only 10 percent, for a real-wage increase of 5 percent—despite an unemployment rate that had risen to 25 percent in 1933, that was still at 17 percent in 1939, and had only fallen to 11 percent by 1941. How high does unemployment have to go and how long does it have to stay there until wages respond in the manner prescribed by price-auction theorists? The Great Depression seems to prove that to bring wages down, unemployment has to rise to very high levels and stay there a very long time. Why should this be so? What is it about the labor market that prevents wages from falling as conventional theory requires?

The problem confronts not just the historically curious. Since World War II, unemployment has never been high enough to reduce wages. In 1982 unemployment passed 10 percent, but wages still rose 6 percent. The same is true in countries such as Great Britain that have experienced even higher unemployment (13 percent) than the United States. Wages have risen despite sharp increases in unemployment. Again, why don't wages fall in response to unemployment?

The downward rigidity of wages is the key problem in labor economics.[10] If rigidity exists, there is an easy explanation for unemployment. If wages are rigid and too high, then unemployment will result, and any downward movement in the demand for goods and services will produce unemployment. The labor market still clears, but by throwing some labor into unemployment rather than by reducing wages. Unemployment persists as long as wages are "too high."

To sum up: For some reason the unemployed in our economy cannot individually bid themselves back into employment by offering to work for less. Either they don't make the necessary bids low enough or their bids are not accepted. In either case, a mystery is created. Why should this be so? Can something other than market imperfections be behind it?

The labor market exhibits other characteristics that can be readily observed that are very difficult to explain by either the simple or sophisticated versions of the price-auction model. For example, what look like disequilibrium wage differentials between different groups persist for substantial periods of time. Black teen-age unemployment can be many times higher than that of white prime-age males, but relative wages don't seem to fall.

Few systematic attempts have been made to resolve the theoretical contradictions or to explain the empirical puzzles.

The standard procedure is to explain away both forms of deviant observations one at a time, often with conflicting theoretical explanations.[11]

As we saw earlier, the distribution of earnings has not shifted in a way consistent with human-capital theory and the observed changes in the distribution of education. Educational distributions have narrowed; earnings distributions have widened. More and more human capital was also being pumped into the system in the 1970s, yet productivity growth has fallen. A much better-educated labor force should have made it rise. Strong movements toward equality in the distribution of earnings did occur during the Great Depression and World War II without any equivalent changes in inputs, education or otherwise. How does one account for the movement? The distribution of earnings is skewed with too many low-wage workers and too many very-high-wage workers, given what can be predicted from the assumed normal distribution of human abilities.[12] Where do all of those poor people come from? The homogeneous wage categories used so casually in economic theory just can't seem to be found despite strenuous efforts to locate them.[13] Wherever one looks and no matter what corrections are made, a wide dispersion in wages occurs for what look like homogeneous skills and efforts. Moreover, relative wages across occupations change very little over long periods of time despite enormous changes in relative demands. Direct mathematical and econometric tests of the marginal-productivity theory of distribution (people paid their marginal products) fail to confirm the theory.[14] The result: physical capital is paid more than it should be; labor less than it should be. When analyzed, plant designers just do not seem to use, or even know, the relative wages that they should be using to minimize labor costs, if plant design followed the axioms of the price-auction model.[15]

A satisfactory theory of the labor market has to explain the recalcitrance of the world of facts to conform to ideas held in the mind. The real-world behavior of the labor market is not captured by the price-auction model. Hence, I must say again that a powerful case exists for rethinking and reformulating the basic economics of labor-market behavior. As things stand, the labor market is the economist's Sargasso Sea—a dumping ground where the flotsam and jetsam of many economic ship-wrecks collect without having much influence on the active currents of intellectual thought.

Attempted Rescues of the Equilibrium Price-Auction Model

A number of attempts have been made to deal with unemployment—for the price-auction theorist, the central deviant observation in the labor market. But on close examination the attempts are simply not acceptable, because none produces the missing link needed to connect the price-auction model to the macro-economic facts of life.

One approach argues that what appears to be persistent and lengthy periods of unemployment is really nothing of the kind. In other words, unemployment does not really exist. And if it doesn't exist, there is no reason why anyone should expect to see wages fall. No labor market disequilibrium—unemployment—exists to make them fall.

This argument holds that what is measured as unemployment is really "voluntary" rather than "involuntary" unemployment. To use the analytical terms, the unemployed simply have a reservation wage which is above the market wage for workers with their skills and productivity. To use the pejorative terms, they are lazy or foolish. If the voluntarily unemployed were only willing to lower their reservation wage (or in a variant of the argument, were able to lower the reservation wages forced upon them by government programs such as minimum-wage laws), they would find work. Or these people really don't want to work because they are already active in the underground economy, or they really prefer leisure and are simply calling themselves unemployed to collect unemployment insurance.

There are a number of problems with this argument. For one, how does it explain the cyclical pattern of unemployment? Technically, the hypothesis asserts that in 1969 only 3.5 percent of the American work force was unrealistic and possessed reservation wages above personal productivity. But just six years later, in 1975, 8.5 percent of the American work force made unrealistic demands and was left unemployed. Why the sharp increase in foolish expectations between 1969 and 1975? Moreover, once workers become unemployed and are told by the market that they are not employable at their reservation wage, why don't they quickly accept the information and reduce their reservation wage? Why do otherwise intelligent people become stupid or stubborn and refuse to listen to the market's evaluation of their worth?

The "voluntary unemployment" theory must explain concretely how the labor market works, and specifically why these mysterious cycles exist in labor-market psychology. In fact, one can conclude that a real problem (unemployment) is defined away as a semantic (voluntary versus involuntary) problem. But of course, semantic answers never address real problems very well.

Generally speaking, and as noted before, the unemployed are willing to go to work at the wages being paid those employed. This can be seen most clearly in the cases where workers are laid off, and not because they demanded higher wages; other identical workers are still employed at the old wage rates. So those laid off are obviously willing to work at the prevailing wage rates. They proved it by doing exactly that. To make the concept of voluntary unemployment credible, one has to explain why identical workers must work at different wage rates. But no one so far has.

Because most workers are not unemployed forever, voluntary unemployment must also explain why the unemployed accept periodic spells of employment at the current wage rates. The unemployed are not a group of chronically unemployed people but experience recurring periods of unemployment and employment. If voluntary actions explain their unemployment, why do their attitudes toward work change? At one moment they are willing to take a job at the current wage rate; at the next they are not.

According to the price-auction model, you can always bid yourself back into the labor market by lowering your wage demand. The bidding mechanism is, in fact, the method for driving market wages back down to their equilibrium level. But as I said earlier, what would happen if you confronted the employer of your choice with a willingness to work for less than his existing employees are getting? According to the model, he should fire some of them (or force them to take a wage cut), take advantage of your lower wage rate, and increase his profits. We all know that in the real world any em-

ployer would think that you were a nut if you really expected
him to accept your offer. That just isn't the way to get a job,
but by the theory it *should* be the way to get a job. Why isn't
it the way?

That the real labor market ignores the theory is often
blamed on the market imperfections created by minimum
wages or unions. But that explains very little. Most large firms
have minimum wages that are far higher than the officially
mandated legal minimum wage. Every firm has a self-imposed
minimum-wage rate, and offers to work for less than that are
no more accepted at nonunion firms such as IBM than they are
at union firms such as General Motors. What about the costs of
hiring and firing? This might explain why slightly lower wage
bids are not accepted, but cannot be advanced to explain the
absence of the bidding process entirely.

Even the university professors who write about competitive
labor markets work in institutions where no one gets fired
because job applicants have announced that they will work for
less. If they *were* hired, think of the carnage of wage reductions that would occur in fields such as English literature. Vast
numbers of qualified teachers and scholars of English exist and
most would jump at the chance to bid in an auction market for
a teaching job. So academic tenure can be regarded as a market imperfection (although I notice few, if any, economics
professors campaigning for its elimination), but it is not an
aberration or a market imperfection. The protection of tenure
or its equivalent (seniority hiring and firing, offers to work for
less are rejected) seems to exist almost everywhere in the labor
market.

There are two other explanations why employers do not
accept lower wage bids: the existence of unions, and discontent among those workers who are not fired but remain employed at the new lower wage. But neither rescues the
equilibrium price-auction model.

Whatever one believes about unions, they can at most only
be blamed for wage rigidity in the 20 percent of the labor force
they control. What about the other 80 percent of the labor
force? A rigid union wage does not lead to a rigid nonunion
wage. Quite the reverse. If union wages are not flexible, then
all employment competition and resulting wage flexibility is

thrown into the nonunion labor market. If union wages are held above equilibrium levels, nonunion wages will be forced below their previous equilibrium levels as the workers unemployed in the union sector because of high wages are forced into the nonunion sector. Unions cannot produce rigid wages or unemployment unless everyone belongs to a union. Everyone doesn't. In any case, real-world wages seem as rigid in the nonunion sector as they are in the union sector. Patterns of labor-market behavior just do not differ significantly between the two.

Economists often blame unions for economic effects that extend well beyond the direct effects on their own membership. It is asserted, for example, that employers have to meet union wages in order to keep unions out. This may be true, but if so, the economy is not the competitive economy prescribed by the price-auction model. In a free market, employers cannot meet union wages to keep unions out. They have to pay market, not union, wage rates to keep other nonunion employers from driving them out of business.

The propensity for market wage reductions to create discontent among already employed workers is a real issue, about which more will be said later, but such discontent either cannot exist or does not matter in the conventional model. Discontent cannot exist because workers know that in a competitive labor market, wages will rise and fall according to the dictates of supply and demand. Though it is certainly possible to be disappointed, no one can be legitimately discontented if he goes to the local department store and finds that the special sale ended last week, and that this week there are no big discounts. That is just the way the world works.

Moreover, if labor is discontented, it does not matter, because employers do not care. According to the theory, the employer is only interested in whether his work force is delivering the specified level of productivity. Is the individual's productivity consistent with his wage rate? A happy labor force may be a pleasant thing to have, but happiness plays no role in competitive labor markets. Workers are paid because they suffer the disutility (unhappiness) of being kept away from their leisure activities. Discontent and its remedy—interest in promoting better motivation—may be a very important issue in the real world, but taking discontent seriously leads to an economic model very different from the one specified in the price-auction model.

A more sophisticated version of the "voluntary" idea is embodied in "search theory."[17] Here unemployment is not what it appears to be—unemployed workers unable to find work at prevailing wage rates. Instead the unemployed are a group of people searching (a form of work) for work and testing the market as to their real value. They develop and alter their reservation wage as they explore the labor market. And unfortunately, searching takes time.

Search theory also has its problems with the cycles in unemployment. If unemployment is a matter of workers testing the labor market, why should 25 percent of them be doing it in 1933, while only 3 percent in 1953, and 1 percent in 1943? If search is something going on in the real world, why do so many spells of persistent unemployment last for so long? Why do so many spells of unemployment result in people withdrawing from the labor force rather than finding employment? And why does it take people so long to land a job?

All of these are interesting and unanswered questions, but search theory has a more fundamental problem. Studies indicate that most unemployed workers spend very few hours per week actually looking for work.[18] Search theories cannot explain what needs to be explained unless workers *actually spend their time searching for work.* Moreover, it is not necessary to be unemployed to be searching for a new job; most workers move from one job to another without experiencing spells of unemployment. The sensible search strategy is to accept the first job offered but to keep on looking. Whenever a better job is found at a higher wage rate, the sensible searcher quits the first job and takes the second—a process that continues until he is sure no job openings exist that offer him a better wage. In other words, the concept of search in no way has to produce unemployment. This is true both in a deterministic world with homogeneous wages for identical skills and in a stochastic world where individual workers may receive very different wages for identical work. In other words, search theory as it is used to explain unemployment is simply not consistent with income maximization and sensible search procedures.

Minimum wages and unemployment compensation sometimes get blamed for unemployment, but they also fail to explain the phenomenon. We have already examined the leaky sieve called the official minimum-wage rate. Given the loopholes, lack of penalties, and millions of workers receiving wages below the specified level, only a small fraction of unemployment can be attributed to the minimum wage. Moreover, increases in it do not correlate with the cyclical patterns of aggregate unemployment. Two million workers were suddenly added to the unemployment rolls in April and May of 1980, while the minimum wage underwent no change. Then, too, because there was no minimum wage at the time of the Great Depression, something else has to account for the unemployment in the 1930s.

Similarly, unemployment compensation is a bad place to lay blame for unemployment. The cyclical pattern is out of synch —unemployment does not rise and fall with the ups and downs of unemployment compensation. Besides, more than half of those unemployed are not covered by unemployment insurance. In May 1982 only 4.4 million out of 10.5 million unemployed people were receiving unemployment compensation.[19] What causes unemployment for those 6.1 million people not receiving benefits? For people not getting benefits, market wages cannot be less than their unemployment benefits. One can argue the payments are so generous that 4.4 million people voluntarily choose not to go back to work, but if this is so, one would expect to see rapid re-employment when unemployment compensation runs out. That doesn't happen.

An alternative approach is to accept the existence of involuntary unemployment and try to explain it in terms of rigid wages. This approach is followed in the "implicit contract" or the "invisible handshake" hypothesis. Here workers and employers agree to an implicit contract calling for rigid wages, just as an explicit contract between a union and an employer might call for a fixed wage. The models differ substantially, however, depending on reasons for "signing" implicit contracts.

Some implicit-contract models present a fundamental challenge to the price-auction model, while others try to rescue it. Risk-aversion implicit contracts, the most common approach, are attempts at rescue.[20] According to the theory, workers would rather suffer the large risks of unemployment than the small risks of wage reductions; therefore they sign an implicit contract with their employer giving them wage certainty but employment uncertainty. There is no empirical evidence for the existence of this set of preferences, but it also makes no intuitive sense. A sensible risk-averse worker, given the choice between the small risks of occasional wage reductions and the large risks of many weeks of unemployment, would always choose the small risks and flexible wages. Any group of workers that chooses the large risks of inflexible wages could not be described as in any meaningful sense "risk averse."

A more interesting approach investigates the possibility that workers and employers both have an interest in long-run cooperative arrangements that would not be served by wage flexibility. In other words, fixed wages are more efficient and productive than flexible wages. The possibility becomes an axiom for many theorists who accept the existence of implicit contracts. These people, then, immediately attempt to analyze the implications of implicit contracts for macro-economic policies before working out a micro-economic framework of labor behavior that can first explain why long-term cooperative agreements come into existence.[21]

But obviously, one must understand the forces that create implicit contracts more carefully before attempting to build a macro-economics on top of them. The micro-economic hull of the ship has to be built before the macro-economic superstruc-ture can be constructed.

What are the mutual interests that produce agreements to: (a) not lower wages, (b) provide annual wage gains, and (c) not accept the bids of new workers who might offer to work for less. How are these agreements enforced? Why can't a competitor willing to lower wages force everyone else to do so? To answer these questions we have to compare the characteristics of a price-auction market with those of the labor market.

A Behavioral Approach

The price-auction model depends upon four counterfactual empirical assumptions about the characteristics of the labor market.

1. Skills are exogenously acquired and then sold in a competitive auction market.
2. The productivity of each individual worker is known and fixed.
3. Each individual worker's happiness (utility) depends solely upon his own wage.
4. Total output is simply the summation of individual output.

A competitive auction market ensures price flexibility, but skills *must* be exogenously acquired to preserve the independence of the supply-and-demand curves. In other words, workers acquire skills outside the labor market and then bring the skills into the labor market to sell at auction. Moreover, if buyers are to bid intelligently for labor, productivities must be known and fixed. One cannot bid unless one knows the value of what one is buying. Since every individual must be paid his marginal product, workers are equally expensive. The employer does not care whom he hires, since his profits are identical in all cases.

As individual utility maximizers, workers (the price-auction theorists assume) look solely at their own income and wage rate when deciding to work or enjoy leisure. As these individual decisions are made and the consequent individual economic rewards allocated, the Gross National Product will end up as high as it should be, given the underlying preferences of the work force. Total output is simply the summation of individual outputs.

These four assumptions underlie the equilibrium price-auction model, but upon examination they would seem to conflict with the everyday reality we see around us.

Technically, the standard model cannot work whenever there are either economies or diseconomies of scale. With economies of scale, the work force's marginal productivity exceeds its average productivity. A 1 percent increase in factor inputs leads to a more than 1 percent increase in output. As a result, factors of production cannot be paid in accordance with the dictates of the price-auction model, since there isn't enough output to pay everyone according to his marginal productivity. There has to be some rule for scaling back the returns to capital and labor so that they just exhaust what is available to be divided. But whatever that rule is to be, it cannot be derived from price-auction principles.[22]

Similarly with diseconomies of scale, something is left over after all factors of production are paid their marginal products. Who gets it? The necessary rule for allocating the surplus does not exist. As a result, wages are again left indeterminant even if the theory is correct.

One can argue about whether significant economies or diseconomies of scale exist in the aggregate, but a price-auction theorist is forced to argue something that is clearly not true—namely, scale economies don't exist at the level of the individual firm. Yet significant economies of scale are found in many firms and industries, meaning that some subsidiary allocation rule must be advanced before the model can be used.

The key problem, however, is not the prevalence of economies or diseconomies of scale, as widespread as those may be, but the assumption that workers acquire laboring skills exogenously in formal education and training programs and then bring those skills into the labor market to sell. In the price-auction model, the skills that any worker has to sell depends solely upon his willingness to invest in acquiring those skills. There are no other constraints on skill acquisition. Possessing skills, workers bid for jobs that use the skills.

Unfortunately, the underlying assumption does not seem to hold for the American economy. Workers do not bring fully developed skills into the labor market. Most cognitive job skills, general or specific, are acquired informally through on-the-job training after a worker finds an entry-level job and the associated promotion ladder.

More important, the training opportunities are not purchased in the market for human capital but allocated by the employer as he distributes jobs and training opportunities. Almost never does he simply allocate training slots to those who are willing to work for the lowest wage. Training opportunities are awarded on other bases—sometimes on merit but mostly on seniority. This means that the markets for buying skills are severely atrophied if not entirely nonexistent. The worker cannot simply decide to buy some training opportunities; he must acquire it in a very complicated job-acquisition process that effectively removes much of the control of the skill-acquisition process from the person who will ultimately possess the skills. First an entry-level job must be found. Then the individual has to demonstrate that he has enough merit or seniority to be eligible for training. Finally he has to be lucky enough to be in a firm that is growing and needs more labor of the very kind in which he wishes to receive training. Hardly a simple market procedure where one buys whatever skills one wishes from one's employer.

The dominance of on-the-job training is very clear in the American economy. In the 1960s the President's Automation Commission undertook extensive surveys of how workers learned the actual cognitive job skills they were using.[23] It turned out that only 40 percent of the work force reported that they were using any skill that they had acquired in formal training programs or in specialized education. And most of that 40 percent reported that some of the skills that they were using had been acquired on the job. The remaining 60 percent of the work force acquired all of their job skills through informal, casual, on-the-job training. They were taught how to do some new job by older, already trained workers. Even among college graduates, over two thirds reported that they had acquired their skills informally.

When the surveys asked workers to list the form of training that was most useful in acquiring their current job skills, only 12 percent of them put down "formal training" and "specialized education." Some of this was also done at their place of work, and subject to the allocation procedures of the employer rather than of the market.

Although the results may seem surprising, they are easily explained. Most skills are best taught in conjunction with the job itself because training and production are complementary products. Goods and services produced as training occurs can be sold to lower the costs of training. Only actually doing or making something creates the realism needed to polish working skills. Workers also come to learn only what they need to know to perform a specific job, making the process efficient. Surgeons learn surgery by doing surgery, first under the eye of an experienced surgeon, but then by doing lots of surgery themselves. Although training is quite formalized in medicine, how one learns to be a doctor does not differ that much from what happens in the rest of the economy. Informal on-the-job training—from one worker to another—is simply the cheapest method of conveying skills.

So one has to conclude that the labor market is not a place where people with fully developed skills bid for jobs. Rather, it is primarily a market where supplies of trainable labor are matched with training opportunities, which is to say, with the number of job openings that exist. And job openings, in turn, means that demand exists for the skills in question.

The effect of this chain of events on the labor market is profound. There is not, as is conventionally assumed, an independent supply of skills coming into the market to be auctioned among potential employers. On the contrary, because most skills are acquired on the job, they are only created when demand exists for labor with those skills. So people are trained only when job openings exist; or put another way, the supply of trained labor depends on the demand for trained labor.

Let's extend the argument here and try to establish some theoretical clarity. Take the extreme case, one not found in the real world, where *all* skills are acquired on the job. This should produce a supply curve of skills lying on top of the demand curve. This means that every job created would lead to the creation of a skilled worker. Moreover, given identical supply-and-demand curves, it is obviously impossible to determine an equilibrium wage rate where the two curves intersect, which is what price-auction economics calls for. The two curves cannot intersect, because they coincide. There is no supply curve. in the normal sense of that word, and a demand curve alone cannot determine wages. Wages, therefore, become indeterminant and must be set elsewhere in the economic system.

To continue the scenario: for every wage rate, the demand curve determines how many job openings will exist and how many workers will be trained, but this makes training endogenous rather than exogenous. If that is the case, the characteristics of an auction market must be greatly altered to promote efficiency. Instead of being structured to allocate skills to the most productive uses, the market must be structured to maximize the creation of skills. The market characteristics required to maximize skill creation are quite different from one required to allocate already existing skills most efficiently. In one case I have to worry about the production and allocation of training, and in the other case I have only to worry about allocating existing skills to the highest bidder.

Let's now look at another problem with the price-auction view of the labor market. Anyone who has tried to assess individual productivity in the real world can tell you that it is not fixed and known, but variable, unknown, and perhaps unknowable. Each worker undoubtedly has some maximum level of productivity that he can bring to the work place, but depending on motivation, he can also provide his employer any productivity between his maximum and nothing.

But the word "motivation" is strangely absent from the vocabulary of the price-auction theorist. Wages, it is assumed, do not motivate workers but rather compensate workers for their productivity. Yet for people who own and run real-world businesses, motivation is a crucial matter. In fact, what we now commonly hear is that the Japanese economy is outperforming ours because it has a better-motivated and more cooperative work force. Here the argument is that labor motivation is the soft underbelly of American productivity. Because they are better motivated, the Japanese can get more output from the same physical facilities than their American counterparts. To raise American productivity, the argument continues, managers have to concentrate on the "soft" sources of productivity gains like motivation rather than the "hard" sources of productivity gains like more investment or research and development.

None of this makes any sense to the price-auction theorist. Neither does an intellectual discipline like industrial psychology, which studies ways to improve workers motivation, nor do quality control circles, which are springing up everywhere. The price-auction model simply denies that problems of motivation can have any meaningful existence. Since all workers are paid a wage equal to their marginal product, all workers are equally efficient as far as an employer is concerned. But if motivation has no meaningful existence, why is the business community so worried about creating and maintaining it?

There are a number of reasons why. Employers find it both difficult and expensive to determine how much productivity each of their employees provides. In a complicated interdependent industrial operation, how does a manager know which one of two employees is shirking? And even if he does know, it is hard to change individual wage rates or to fire an employee. To lower a wage rate is perhaps to induce an even lower level of productivity. To fire an employee can mean losing a valuable source of human capital that has been trained at great expense.

Accordingly, every industrial operation requires a substantial amount of voluntary cooperation. If employees choose to withhold that voluntary cooperation (work only to rule), any industrial operation can be brought to its knees. Think of the examples where workers have not struck but simply decided to "go by the book" and withhold voluntary cooperation. Within a short time production drops radically. Like motivation, voluntary cooperation over and above what is required in the rule book is foreign to the economist's vocabulary, yet that cooperation is vital in the real world of production.

Motivation and voluntary cooperation introduce another large lump of indeterminancy into wage determination. Each individual has not just one marginal product, but many potential marginal products, depending on his motivation. But with many marginal products there is no one equilibrium wage rate.

The price-auction model also assumes that within a group of workers an individual worker looks only at his own wages and productivity to determine whether he is being fairly paid. Yet a worker often looks at his neighbor's wages, because human preferences are in fact interdependent rather than independent: satisfaction depends upon relative rather than absolute income. But if this is true, the sociology of wage determination becomes important because workers can become unhappy, lose their motivation, and reduce their productivity if they do not feel fairly paid relative to other workers. The wage-structure theory advanced by institutional labor economists becomes important.

A great deal of evidence points to the existence of interdependent preferences. On and off for the past three decades, the Gallup poll has asked: "What is the smallest amount of money a family of four needs to get along in this community?" The seventeen responses lie slightly above the average income in the year in which the question was asked (between 53 and 59 percent), but grow in absolute terms as average incomes grow.[24]

People who study consumption behavior use relative position to explain why savings rates do not rise over time. They should, since average incomes are rising and high-income people have a higher savings rate than low-income people. But what is a high family income relative to the national average, and hence a high-savings family at one period of time, is later a low family income relative to the national average, and hence a low-savings family, though the two absolute incomes are identical. In sum, keeping up with the Joneses, not absolute income, dominates savings behavior.[25]

Lee Rainwater has shown that when people are asked to categorize others as "poor, getting along, comfortable, prosperous, or rich" they do so rather consistently relative to average incomes.[26] Richard Esterlin has reviewed the evidence as to how happiness is related to income in different countries of the world.[27] He finds that a person's happiness (utility, as the economist has it) is almost completely dependent on his relative income position within his own country and almost not at all dependent on his absolute income.

Actual utility or happiness functions seem to be heavily, if not completely, determined by relative incomes and interdependent preferences rather than absolute incomes and independent preferences. Sociologists call it interdependent preferences[28] and "relative deprivation"; labor economists talk about wage contours; psychologists speak of envy. But whatever the name, interdependent preferences seem to be a widespread phenomena.

While price-auction economists usually deny the existence of interdependent preferences, they also go on to deny their importance even if they do exist. If individuals have fixed marginal products that they sell in the labor market, unhappiness can play no role in economics. Happy or unhappy workers have the same productivity to sell. My preferences (utility function) may be highly interdependent—my happiness may depend on my income relative to yours—but I cannot exercise my interdependent preferences in the labor market. Like it or not, each individual is paid his marginal product.

But if marginal products are variable depending on motivation, an unhappy worker can in fact exercise his interdependent preferences because he can lower his productivity in a way difficult to detect and expensive to correct. Hence employers are required to set not just individual wages but a structure of wages that elicits voluntary cooperation and motivates their labor force. The net result is an avenue whereby interdependent preferences can influence the wage structure.

If an employer attempts to establish a structure of wages running contrary to the interdependent preferences of the group, the employer creats a completely different set of marginal products from what he initially had. In short, workers change their productivity in response to different wages. What is worse, an employer who attempts to impose an alien structure of wages on a contrary set of interdependent preferences may find that total productivity drops substantially. The point is that because interdependent preferences exist, the performance of both the group and the individual depends on having a set of relative wages that the group regards as fair and equitable. Therefore, when it comes to wage determination, the observed behavior of nonunion employers is indistinguishable from that of union employers. In setting wages, equity becomes important for efficiency.

In practice, most production processes also require a degree of teamwork that can only be acquired through common on-the-job experiences, a high degree of internal harmony, and a substantial period of practice working together. Team and not individual productivity dominates industrial processes.

The nature of the issue here is clearly evident on the newspaper's sporting pages. We read that some member of a team feels unfairly paid. He then disrupts the team by leaving or not cooperating to the fullest degree possible. The net result is a fall in team productivity much larger than the difference between the best productivity of the unhappy worker and the best productivity of his replacement. What is true on the sporting pages is no less true on the business pages. A production team with a revolving membership unhappy with its wage structure has a lower productivity than a team satisfied with its wage structure and a stable membership.

The best analytical evidence for team productivity can be found in learning curves. These first emerged after World War II to explain the rapid rise of productivity in shipyards and aircraft factories. Observers noted that the hours of work needed per unit of output fell dramatically as time passed, although the factories had been using the best available workers from the beginning (having effective priority, the factories essentially drafted the most skilled workers). Though these people kept working in the same factories with the same equipment, the labor time necessary to produce a unit of output was typically more than cut in half over the first three or four years of production in shipyards and aircraft factories.[29] Since then the same observation has proved to be true in civilian industries.

The labor-cost reductions spring from two interrelated factors.[30] Workers learn by doing, honing their existing skills and acquiring related specialized skills needed on this job but not on previous jobs. (Although in wartime the best possible workers were hired, few of them had the requisite skills to step right in and work as efficiently on their first Liberty ship or B-29 as they could after some experience had been gained.) In addition, workers learn to work together as a team. Gradually production becomes so organized that the existing skills and capital equipment can work together efficiently to produce the maximum output.

If endogenous skills and teamwork are important, however, workers cannot be regarded as the interchangeable parts of the equilibrium price-auction mechanism. If they become unhappy with the wage structure and quit, the extra costs are more than the replacement costs of hiring a new worker. Production falls or costs rise until the new worker has acquired the needed skills and teamwork has been restored.

Team productivity creates a real problem for the price-auction theory because a simple distribution of individual marginal products is not possible. There is, instead, a lump of output produced by a team. How is it to be divided among the members of the team? Technically speaking, the marginal-productivity theory of distribution has no rule determining how a team's marginal product should be distributed among members of the team.

To sum up: Variable individual marginal products, team marginal products, and interdependent preferences all lead to a substantial degree of indeterminacy in setting wages. The market forces of supply and demand do not react with each other to produce a distribution of marginal products, because no one unique distribution of marginal products exists. Many distributions are possible.

Meanwhile, employers are as eager as employees to establish wage structures that employees regard as equitable, since profits depend on it. There may be a profit-maximizing wage structure (more likely there are apt to be several), but instead of depending upon individual marginal products that structure is a function of the real-world structure of worker's interdependent preferences and the team's marginal product. Moreover, bargaining about relative wages is at least as pervasive as bargaining about absolute wages. Not so long ago, college-educated workers in Sweden struck to increase their pay relative to noncollege workers. Their demand was not for more income but for a wider wage differential.

Finally, employers do not encourage direct wage competition, since wage increases for one worker may show up as welfare (utility) reductions for another. If such a loss is perceived, workers lower their own productivity and disrupt the team's activities. Thus, wages are set on a team rather than on an individual basis, which is something unions formalize and perhaps strengthen but do not cause in the first place. In any case, little wage flexibility exists in either instance, and neither union nor nonunion employers seem interested in allocating their jobs to those who are willing to work for the lowest wage rates.

Team wages lead to the observed phenomena of different wage rates for the same skill—one of the major deviant realities, as we know, found the labor market. Here's why: some workers with certain occupational skills play on high-productivity teams, whereas others play on low-productivity teams. In other words, wages vary for the same work depending on whether he plays for IBM or some marginal manufacturing operation. In this case the two workers, having exactly the same skills, are effectively segregated from each other. The high-wage worker gets a team bonus plus his basic wage, while the other worker is simply not allowed to bid for the job at IBM. In this context, who you work for heavily affects how much you make, something that can't happen in the price-auction model. The net result is a structure of wages often more homogeneous within firms or industries than it is within occupations, something which again defies price-auction theory by being the reverse of what it predicts.

All this, however, does not prevent productivity from playing an important role. Marginal productivity effectively becomes a theory of employment rather than a theory of wage determination. In other words, given some exogenously determined wage rate, productivity determines how many workers will be trained and hired. But workers are not hired unless their productivity—including their team bonus—is expected to exceed their wage rate. Obviously, at $20 per hour many fewer machinists will be hired than if the wage rate is $10 per hour. Consequently, markets clear with changes in training and employment rather than wages. This leaves open, however, the question of where wage rates come from.

Analytically, the problem of wage determination can be defined as trying to pin down what factors produce and alter interdependent preferences and group norms of industrial justice. Sociologists who study relative deprivation find that people feel strongly that economic benefits should be proportional to costs (effort, hardship, talent) but that equals should be treated equally. Since there are various costs and rewards (income, esteem, status, power) in any situation, the problem of course is how equals are defined and how proportionality is to be determined.

This takes us to something called a "reference group." To what group do you belong and to what groups do you compare yourself as you try to determine whether you're being treated equally and proportionally? In any concrete situation, it is relatively easy to point to the various reference groups that exist, but it has proved to be difficult, or even impossible, to find the general principles that govern what creates one in the first place.

Reference groups seem to be both stable and restricted. A member of a group usually compares himself to members of other groups that are in close socioeconomic proximity; he then defines what constitutes relative deprivation, and to change that definition requires great social shocks like war and economic depression. Thus conceptions of what constitutes equality and proportionality are heavily influenced by history and culture. In other words, the money distributions of the past are considered fair until proven unfair. This explains why inequalities in the distributions of economic rewards that are much greater than inequalities in the distribution of personal characteristics seem to cause little dissatisfaction. The legacy of the past also explains why people tend to ask for rather modest amounts (about 10 percent) when asked how much more money they would like to be making.[31] And in general, the happiest people seem to be those who do relatively well within their own reference group rather than those that do relatively well across the entire economy.

The importance of social shocks can be seen in the income changes induced by the Great Depression and World War II. In both cases a major shift toward equality occurred in the distribution of earnings without any change in economic fundamentals. Presumably norms of justice simply changed under the pressure of events, but engineering such a change or predicting how it will occur has proven difficult or impossible.

Labor economics deals with the concepts of relative deprivation under the title of wage contours. Here workers see themselves as belonging to a particular wage contour which has some fixed wage relative to workers in other contours. Over time, relative wages are very stable across contours. So wage inflation can break out if the wage structure accidentally gets out of line with historical contours. If one group improves its historical position, other groups attempt to re-establish that historical position, or even to better the status quo ante to "get even" for the initial violation of "equity." As with the concept of relative deprivation, Dunlopian wage contour theory runs into problems because it can't find the general principles that explain why specific wage contours exist and how they might change over time. This failing makes it very hard to know how to alter wage contours.

If utility functions are interdependent and conditioned by experience and history, relative wages may be rigid regardless of changes in underlying supplies and demands. Why? Because the historical wage differentials have the sanction of the past and are assumed to be just until proven otherwise. The longer they are around, the more they condition workers' beliefs as to what constitutes justice and injustice, and the more stable the distribution of preferences and hence wages are apt to be.

None of this is to say that relative earnings are immutable. Slow changes in relative earnings might be accepted because they never appear to challenge the established norms directly. Industries faced with extinction, such as the American automobile manufacturing business, may be able to reduce wages. But wage changes shift from being a short-run market clearing mechanism to being a long-run or emergency market clearing mechanism, which in effect reverses the assumed process of the price-auction model.

To understand the structure of earnings and the factors that can alter it, economists need to combine a sociological and psychological theory of interdependent preferences with an economic theory and to show how they interact to produce the realities of the world we can readily see and measure. Alas, such a cooperative endeaver has not excited the general interest of the economics profession.

In any case, interdependent preferences and variable marginal products do create problems for the standard theory if the labor market is viewed as a market to allocate and maximize training opportunities rather than as an auction market to sell skills. A training market must structure incentives to maximize the willingness of people already working to transmit their knowledge to the newly hired, and to minimize every worker's (including the trainer's) resistance to acquiring new skills and accepting new technologies.

It is for this reason that wage and employment competition is limited to entry-level jobs. If workers feel that they are informally training potential competitors who will bring about a reduction in their wages or increase their chances of becoming unemployed, they have every incentive *not* to show others how to do their job. Every worker trained produces just that much more potential downward pressure on wages or creates just that much more chance that the trainer will become unemployed during the next cyclical downturn.

If wages are really flexible and allocated in a bidding auction, each worker would try to build his own little monopoly by hoarding specific labor skills and labor information in an effort to make himself indispensable. What happens in the real world? To encourage training, employers repress wage competition and build employment security. Seniority systems of hiring and firing emerge to ensure that no trainer will be displaced by one of his trainees. Lower outside wage bids are not accepted, because if they were, workers already on the payroll would feel threatened and bring training to a halt within the enterprise.

Because of business cycles and the normal job turnover,

some unemployed workers may have acquired the necessary
skills to complete for a given job. But can they bid themselves
back into employment by offering to work for lower wages?
Once again, on-the-job training would stop within the firm
because those already working would quickly learn that every
worker trained was a potential competitor for their job regardless of previous assurances. Once again, every worker would
try to create a local monopoly in his skills, and would refuse to
train new workers. Accordingly, for the employers the short-
run gain to be had from being able to pay lower wages would
be more than offset by the long-run loss from a self-inflicted
deterioration in the training process.

Wage and employment competition in the real world would
also mean that every worker has a vested interest in resisting
any technical change that might reduce his wages or employment opportunities. Because training opportunities in the new
skill might be allocated to someone else, the new technologies
would have to be opposed. Conversely, if no one is trained
unless a job is currently available (which is what on-the-job
training means), if strong seniority provisions limit employment insecurity to a clear minority (the newly hired), if new
learning opportunities are allocated to those with the most
seniority, and if no danger exists that some trainee now with
the requisite skills is going to be allowed to bid down wages,
employees are going to be willing to pass along information to
new workers and to accept new techniques and technologies.
So if anyone is to be made redundant, it will not be the teacher.
The teacher never injures himself by being willing to teach.

Given the need to train and to promote the acceptance of
new technologies, employers also agree to share the gains from
those new technologies with their labor force. If productivity
rises, wages can rise regardless of what is happening in the
external labor market. You don't need an aggregate shortage
of trainable labor before wages can go up. Wages can do just
that even when unemployment is climbing.

Consider the market for construction labor in the United
States. Of all of the American labor markets, this one most
closely embodies the principles of the equilibrium price-auction model. Actual job shape-ups exist, so that workers do not
have permanent jobs. In most places substantial short-run
wage fluctuations occur. If unionized labor is in short supply,

premiums will be paid in excess of union scales to get workers. If unionized labor is in surplus supply, union workers will leave the unionized sector and work for lower nonunion wage scales in nonunion construction. But what does the resulting wage and employment competition produce?

For starters, severe restrictions are placed on training, and the resistance to technical change is legendary. Let me suggest that construction workers exhibit the same responses and motivations as the rest of the population. Their attempts to build countervailing monopoly positions and their resistance to technical change are just what the rest of us would do if we were really faced with wage and employment competition. We don't resist training and technical change to the same degree because we don't live in a world where our skills are sold in an auction market at fluctuating wage rates.

The lack of wage and employment competition is not limited to the United States, which probably has the dubious distinction of being the industrial country where it is the easiest to fire labor and reduce wages. It is typically much more difficult to fire workers in Europe than it is here. In Japan, large firms extend formal tenure to their employees. Moreover, Japanese wages are heavily conditioned by age and seniority, not personal skill and merit. But Japanese workers are held up as the very models of those willing to accept technical change and cooperate with one another to raise productivity. This is not surprising if you remember that under Japanese norms an employee can only raise his own income if the productivity of the entire enterprise rises. Japanese workers, therefore, have a direct incentive to intensify and increase training of others and to accept technical change.

The wage and employment competition that constitutes the essence of efficiency in the equilibrium price-auction model may not be the essence of efficiency in a real-world dynamic (changing) economy where the primary function of the labor market is to maximize training and allocate trainees to potential training ladders. Moreover, wage and employment competition when found in the real world retards the introduction of new techniques and technologies.

No one quarrels with the theoretical proposition that flexible wages are necessary for an economy to reach its current production frontier in a static economy (no training necessary) with independent preferences. But in a dynamic economy with interdependent preferences, an effort to maximize static efficiency with flexible wages is counterproductive—engendering a slower rate of growth of efficiency over time. Because the potential gains from maximizing long-run growth always prevail over the potential gains from maximizing short-run efficiency, employers find it profitable to structure the labor market to maximize long-run growth, even though that may mean accepting some short-run cost inefficiencies.

The proposition here is that in the long run fixed wages are more efficient than flexible wages. Wage rigidity, therefore, is not a "market imperfection" producing inefficiency, but is instead a functional market adjustment producing long-run efficiency: more output is produced with it than without it. But if repressing wage and employment competition becomes a tool to increase long-run productivity, the model of labor behavior in the real world is very different from that presented by the price-auction theory.

In fact, the labor market does not show the four characteristics needed for an auction market to exist and to operate, but precisely their opposites:

1. Labor supplies are endogenously acquired and the labor market is not an auction market based on price, but one that is structured to maximize the transfer of knowledge (training) over time. Static efficiency is relatively less important than dynamic efficiency.

2. The productivity of each individual worker is unknown and variable. Motivation is important, since individual workers control their own productivity and can offer a wide range of productivities.

3. Happiness (utility) is heavily conditioned by interdependent preferences. If violated,these preferences can lead to reductions in productivity—team and individual.

4. Total output is heavily determined by team as opposed to individual productivities. But with team productivity an indeterminacy is created in individual wages, since there is a team bonus to be allocated.

Wages in a modern industrial economy are set within a social process that is far removed from a simple supply-and-demand auction framework. For the employer the process is statically inefficient because he cannot adjust wages to individual productivities and short-run changes in circumstances, but the same process is dynamically efficient, since his production team is not disrupted by dissatisfied workers and training can occur at less cost than it otherwise would. In short, the gains from fixed wages are simply greater than the gains from flexible wages.

With downward rigidity in wages, demands for annual real-wage gains reflect the sharing of higher productivity, and fixed relative wages. Labor markets, therefore, cannot clear via wage reductions or shifts in relative wages, but instead clear through worker qualifications (level of education, experience).

But this leaves the economy with unemployment and inflation. Workers are willing to work at current wages but cannot find work, because wages do not fall. Because wages don't fall prices cannot fall. Rather than reducing prices in times of falling demand, firms cut production, exacerbating unemployment and forestalling the price declines that should be offsetting inflationary shocks such as those administered by OPEC. Put another way: when oil prices rise, other prices do not fall. If anything, other prices and wages rise in an effort to catch up.

With wage rigidity, the nature of the labor-supply curve also changes. Rather than the traditional labor-supply curve sloping upward, we have a horizontal portion at the bottom imposed by the rigid wages (see Diagram 6). Individual workers would be willing to work at even lower wages but given real world business firms lower wage bids will be accepted. For those workers represented by the horizontal portion of the labor-supply curve, one can in fact pursue macro-economic policies—monetary or fiscal—to ensure that the demand curve of the economy cuts the supply curve of the economy as close as it can to the point where the labor-supply curve starts to rise. Until this point is reached, employment expands without an increase in wages.

Because of the inertial effects of indexing (see Chapter 3) and the agreed upon sharing of productivity gains between workers and employers, the labor-supply curve also continually moves up over time even if unemployment exists. Once such an upward movement gets under way there is no reason to believe that increased unemployment can easily stop it.

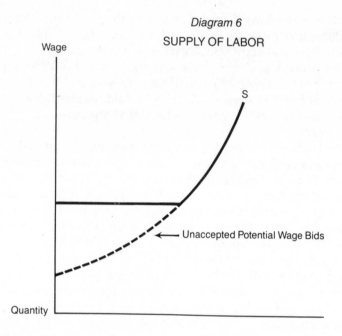

Diagram 6

SUPPLY OF LABOR

Wage

S

Unaccepted Potential Wage Bids

Quantity

Accordingly, to reduce inflation with higher unemployment, you would need to force unemployment so high that it would push the industrial structure to the edge of bankruptcy and collapse. In other words, unemployment has to reach devastating levels to undo the existing structure of interdependent preferences and the structure of wages it has created. Just *how* devastating can be seen in 1982.

No one knows just how high unemployment would have to climb to bring about a reduction in wages. Twenty-five percent unemployment rates during the Great Depression did not bring about real wage declines, and there is every reason to believe that the structure of implicit contracts is stronger now than then. Eleven percent wasn't enough at the end of 1982 to bring money-wage gains anywhere close to zero. No prudent person should even play with the idea of trying to crack the structure of wages because no one knows what would happen to a society when you destroy the implicit contracts on which individuals have based their lives and their willingness to participate in the economic system.

Some economists, I among them, have tried to build models

of labor behavior on sets of assumptions other than those embedded in the equilibrium price-auction model, but none of
them have swept the profession.[32] None are widely accepted
and none have so shaken the profession to get it to rethink just
how the rest of economics is built on the foundations of labor
behavior. The alternative models may have been inadequate,
but the real problem is that the mainline practitioners of economics refuse to believe that labor behavior, though un-
charted and not understood, profoundly affects all of the
economy that we directly observe. Instead labor-market behavior is ignored and labor economics has been compartmen-
talized, often literally, in separate university departments, so
the rest of the profession does not have to think about it.

Conclusion

Economics needs a new micro-economics of the labor market.
Too many deviant observations and contradictory theories are
running around for anyone's comfort. Until such an economics
is built and labor behavior is integrated into general economics, no one is going to develop a successful macro-economics.

If one were ranking various economic markets along a continuum by the extent to which they reflected the postulates of
the price-auction model, financial markets would probably be
placed at one end and labor markets at the other. Most other
markets would be arrayed between the extremes. Commodity
markets (grain, metals) would lie near the financial end of the
continuum; real-capital investment markets might lie near the
labor end. Ultimately we'll need to know where every market
lies to determine the economy's average operating characteristics—the degree to which it fits a flexible- or a fixed-price
model of behavior. But the economy's center of gravity is
going to be determined by the labor market. It is by far the
largest market, accounting for 85 percent of domestic income
in 1981.

CHAPTER 8

Rebuilding the
Foundations of Economics

Catching the Trade Winds

One of the peculiarities of economics is that it still rests on a behavioral assumption—rational utility maximization—that has long since been rejected by sociologists and psychologists who specialize in studying human behavior. Rational individual utility (income) maximization was the common assumption of all social science in the nineteenth century, but only economics continues to use it.

Contrary behavioral evidence has had little impact on economics because having a theory of how the world "ought" to act, economists can reject all manner of evidence showing that individuals are not rational utility maximizers. Actions that are not rational maximizations exist, but they are labeled "market imperfections" that "ought" to be eliminated. Individual economic actors "ought" to be rational utility maximizers and they can be taught to do what they "ought" to do. Prescription dominates description in economics, while the reverse is true in the other social sciences that study real human behavior.

Besides, the world is a complicated place, which means you can see pretty much what you want to see. An industrial psychologist, Douglas McGregor, once constructed what he called theory X and theory Y.[1] A theory X person believes that people are rational utility maximizers motivated by a calculus of individual economic costs and benefits. As in the child's nursery tale, man is basically a grasshopper with a limited, short-time horizon who, liking leisure, must be forced to work and save enticed by rewards much greater than those he gets from leisure. Wherever a theory X person looks, according to

McGregor, he sees people who confirm his prior belief that harsh economic whips and large economic carrots are required to keep individuals working and saving.

A theory Y person believes that man is basically a social, working, tool-using animal. It is possible to create disincentives big enough to stop him from working and saving, but relatively mild rewards and punishments will keep him at work in a world of social interaction. Man, for a theory Y person, is a beaver living in a colony with other beavers—a social animal motivated by many factors other than self-interested utility or income. Wherever a theory Y person looks, he sees social, industrious people having a variety of motives, who work without harsh whips and large carrots.

Proponents of both theory X and theory Y can easily observe real people who confirm their theories. There are lazy, self-interested individuals and also industrious social beings. The basic problem is one of proportion, and according to McGregor, top business managers (and economists?) are programmed to see mostly grasshoppers wherever they look, even if they happen to be looking at a colony of beavers.

Behavioral Assumptions

Utility maximization in economics survives despite the lack of empirical support for it. Why? Because it has assumed a sophisticated form in which it has been emptied of empirical content. Every elementary economics textbook has several chapters on the theory of consumer choice. The utility maximizing consumer must insure that the marginal utility of the last dollar spent on each good and service is equal if individuals are to maximize their total utility, given some budget (income) constraint. Yet when it comes to empirical analysis of consumer choice, economists retreat to the doctrine of "revealed preferences" and do not attempt to specify the procedure by which marginal utility is determined or measured. Revealed preferences, however, is just a fancy way of saying that individuals do whatever individuals do, and whatever they do, economists will call it "utility maximization." Whether individuals buy good X or good Y they are still rational individual utility maximizers. By definition, there is no such thing as an individual who does not maximize his utility.[2] But if a theory can never be wrong, it has no content. It is merely a tautology.

The same problem exists on the earnings side of individual behavior. Income maximization is postulated, but then vanishes via a presumed nonobservable variable, psychic income. This notion tautologically makes everyone an income maximizer whatever his observed behavior. A person takes a job that pays less money than some other job, but economists still describe that person as a rational utility maximizer, since his total income (money plus psychic income) must be greater than jobs paying more money, or he wouldn't have taken the job. Again, by definition, no one can ever make a mistake and accept the wrong job.

Attempts have been made to rescue the postulates of consumption and income maximization with analogies based on natural selection—economic Darwinism. Firms and individuals who survive economically must be better maximizers than others, or they would not have survived. "Survival of the fittest" makes maximization a reasonable postulate.

But as recent work on the biology of natural selection shows, "survival of the fittest" is not synonymous with "individual maximization." Survival is instead a group process where random changes in the environment can turn survival into random good or bad luck. To prove that a species is optimal, you must be able to point to the specific characteristics that permit one to survive and another to become extinct. And this no one has been able to do. Whenever a given characteristic is asserted to be the reason for a species' becoming extinct, another species that survived can be found with that same characteristic. Survival, therefore, cannot be taken to mean maximization.

And even if survival approximated maximization, the theory of the second best has shown that simply being somewhere close to a maximizing path does not permit you to use deductive reasoning based on maximizing price-auction theory.[3] What would make for "market imperfections" on an optimal path may not be that on something less than optimal. In other words, the best actions in the world of the second best cannot be deduced from the theory of the first best, but need empirical justification.

Among economists, the failure or inability to move from rational optimization to a concept more refined and complicated reflects a number of realities within the profession. But probably none is more important than the fact that maximization can be mathematized while the alternatives—often labeled "satisficing"—cannot.[4] There is a seeming intellectual rigor to individual maximization, and a seeming "softness" to social satisficing. But the appearance of rigor is useless if economic actors don't maximize in the manner called for by the theory. Perhaps economic actors could be taught to be individual maximizers and forget social factors like relative income, but that is irrelevant unless the transformation actually takes place.

"Satisficing" may not be the right word, but each of us knows that we have made mistakes in our own decisions to spend money and often knowingly fail to be maximizers. Moreover, individual and group actions dictated by habit rather than optimization are pervasive. Many of our decisions are large irreversible decisions rather than the small reversible marginal decisions assumed by economic analysis. Ignorance is often greater than knowledge, and human preferences are not exogenous, given unchanging reference points, but continually form and re-form as people engage themselves in economic activity. The basic problem of economics is to find a way to model this reality, even if the model cannot be neatly mathematized.

As things now stand, the price-auction model is silent about how preferences are formed. In theory they simply exist—fully developed and immutable. This of course in no way tells us anything about how the real world works. What we want and like constantly evolves as we experience life. We will often do something deliberately, take a music appreciation course, for example, to explore or even alter our preferences. So some real theory of preference formation has to lie at the heart of the rebuilding effort in economics. No one knows where a reformulation of the behavioral assumptions of economics would lead, but it is clear that the current assumptions neither conform with what we know about human behavior nor produce models with much predictive power.

Consider a deliberate and pervasive effort to alter preferences: advertising. Not wanting to recognize what is happening, the economics profession has a very ambivalent attitude toward it. Advertising is divided into good advertising (informational) and bad advertising (persuasive), but most advertising is clearly designed to persuade, not to inform. Some economists see advertising as a pernicious attempt to distort perfectly good "home-grown" preferences, while others consider it a not very successful attempt to alter those same perfectly good "home-grown" preferences and therefore not anything worth worrying about. In either case, if true preferences are being "distorted," advertising is a market imperfection that must be eliminated.

Neither view of advertising confronts the real problem. Preferences are not being distorted by advertising, but are instead being formed endogenously in the market by a wide variety of *social* forces that include deliberate advertising. There is no such thing as "true" independent individual preferences. Human preferences are like an onion, because when the layers of social influence are peeled away, nothing is left. So the rock of stable preferences on which equilibrium price-auction markets are founded is in fact little more than quicksand.

If we concede that advertising is effective (and if it isn't, why does anyone bother with it?), the problem of preference formation becomes visible to anyone interested. If the demand for cigarettes is man-made, then human beings can unmake that preference, and rules that require health warnings on cigarettes become as legitimate as the advertising that created the initial demand. No one is distorting true preferences; it is just a matter of who has the *power* to create individual preferences. On the other hand, if preferences are fixed and fully formed, a clear argument exists for limiting any government intervention that tries to distort those fully formed preferences. But if we use social preferences to alter individual preferences, we immediately admit that the real world is much more complicated than the one traditionally studied by economists.

The desire for power, economic and otherwise, clearly motivates many people, but the desire for power is also left out of economic analysis because in the price-auction model there is no such thing as economic power. And a rational man cannot desire what cannot exist. Yet in the world most of us live in, we see many people working to get economic power, to get rich, and some are thought to have it, both by those who possess it and those who don't.

If you do not admit to economic power, problems are created for the conventional analysis of capital (wealth) accumulation. According to the dictates of the price-auction model there is only one reason for accumulating wealth—future consumption. A person saves to consume in the future. So eventually everyone wakes up one morning and starts to "dissave" because no one wants to die with a lot of unused consumption privileges.

If the rational individual knew when he was going to die, if he had, in the language of the economist, "perfect knowledge," he would die with zero assets. Lacking such knowledge, the rational individual buys annuities to yield the same result, which is to say, bringing lifetime consumption and production into equilibrium. But this model is at variance with the facts —many people die with a very substantial accumulation of wealth; at no age above sixty-five are Americans on average dis-saving (the average American saves until the day he dies), and the society at large is gradually accumulating a larger capital stock (something it would not do if everyone's lifetime consumption equaled his lifetime income). Why?

The standard way out of the problem expands consumption desires to take into account the bequest motive. But the desire to make consumption gifts to your children after you are dead constitutes an ad hoc addition to the theory that only seems sensible because we have heard it so often. It means you have to believe that a person gets more pleasure from providing for his children's consumption after he is dead than he would get from watching them consume while alive. Also ignored are American tax laws under which less tax is paid if income is given away before one dies rather than after one dies. So if a person has a strong desire to provide for his children, why doesn't he give his money away, in a way minimizing the tax bite? But those who choose low gift taxes over high inheritance taxes are few.

Moreover, children who know that they will receive bequests will usually accumulate less themselves. If all are arranging their lifetime consumption possibilities optimally, a bequest can neither change that pattern of consumption nor increase savings at any point in time. A bequest can only have an effect if it is unexpected and alters individual estimates of lifetime budget constraints. And even here the effect is only short-run. No increase in capital accumulation results over time. The bequest motive is also peculiar in a world without "power" motives because it effectively transfers income from the poor (this generation) to the rich (the next generation). Why should a rational individual utility maximizer want to shift money from someone presumably having a high marginal utility of income (the poor, himself) to those with a low marginal utility of income (the rich, his children)?

You can get a realistic model of capital accumulation more in line with what happens in the real world if you assume that human beings want to accumulate economic power. But as we've said, the standard economic model rules that out because there is no such thing as economic power in an equilibrium price-auction economy, within which no individual can affect market outcomes. No individual decisions to buy or sell can affect the market rate of return.

But even if market economic power does not exist, presumed wealth undeniably allows one to exercise power within the family and the society at large. Studies show that people don't take advantage of the gift tax because they feel that with fewer resources they will lose authority and respect within the family. Upon death you will give your money and assets to your children, but until that time you will keep them so that you can use them to wield family power. Economic clout also gives one access to the political and cultural affairs of a society that one would not otherwise have. At the extreme, economic power can be used to buy political power to change the rules of the economic game. In short, one can become a very important person with the judicious use of economic resources. Individuals want to become wealthy for many reasons other than considerations of future consumption.

Social Interactions

To reconstruct a theory of economic behavior, a more complex vision of the interaction between society and its citizens is paramount. Societies are not merely statistical aggregations of individuals engaged in voluntary exchange but something much more subtle and complicated. A group or a community cannot be understood if the unit of analysis is the individual taken by himself. A society is clearly something greater than the sum of its parts despite what the price-auction model would maintain.

Consider the price-auction view of criminal behavior. Here sanctions exist only to create a structure of costs and benefits that persuades the average individual that the expected costs of criminal behavior are greater than the expected benefits.[5] While that purpose exists, it is far less important than another. We have laws against criminal behavior to inculcate a set of values or preferences. By saying that something is illegal, society is saying that it would like its citizens to form preferences to avoid that product or activity *voluntarily*. Ideally, individuals won't engage in criminal activity even if there is little chance of being caught because avoiding that kind of behavior creates both a "good" society and an efficient society.

A society that has to spend a lot of its money for locks, burglar alarms, policemen, courts, and jails to raise the cost-benefit ratio of crime is simply an inefficient society. An efficient one can inculcate honest behavior without incurring great expense. No society can enforce laws, no matter how good, to which the vast majority of its citizens do not voluntarily subscribe, as prohibition and now the drug laws seem to show. But just as firms require a well-motivated cooperative labor force to be efficient, so do societies need a well-motivated cooperative citizenry if they too are to be efficient. In both cases, an individual calculus of costs and benefits has to come second if social cooperation and maximum economic efficiency is to be obtained.

Many environmental regulations are in fact expressions of social preferences that seek to alter contrary individual preferences. Laws that prohibit pollution are chosen over the more "efficient" effluent charges beloved by the economist because prohibitions are felt to better inculcate the values of environmentalism than the cost and benefit calculus of effluent charges, which allow you to pollute if you are willing to pay the "right" price.[6]

In the final analysis, human preferences are not individually but socially determined, involving an intense interaction between society and the individual. In the extreme case, an individual will sacrifice his life defending his country. That is never the rational optimizing behavior of Homo economicus, but is sometimes necessary if Homo sapiens is to live in a rational society. To convert real altruism into self-interest ("I feel good because I am altruistic, and therefore altruism is really selfishness") is to not understand altruism. Self-esteem, power, duty, reciprocal altruism, trust, security—all influence economic actions. Narrow individual economic self-interest constitutes a powerful motive, but not the only human motive to be found.

Consider questions of equity or fairness. Are matters of equity, whatever they might be, part of economics? Should social preferences about equity be permitted to interfere with individual income maximizing opportunities? In short, should income ever be taken from one person and given to another?

To answer these questions, let's ask another. How do you go about designing democratically the rules of a "fair" economic game? People have what I will call private-personal preferences and individual-social preferences.[7] I might, for example, try to become the country's richest person if the only game the country were playing was the economic game called "unfettered individual capitalism." I might at the same time still think that a better game would be one in which progressive taxes and transfers limited how far anyone could rise or fall, even though both would lower my own income. The first preference, to get rich, expresses my private-personal preferences about playing the existing economic game, and the second, my individual-social preferences, expresses my beliefs about the optimal rules of the game. Individual preferences are still totaled up in a democracy to get a given social preferences, *but the relevant individual preferences are of a different type.*

Imagine that you were asked to devise the rules of a football game. You must specify the conditions under which the ball can be advanced, but you must also specify the size of the field, the initial starting score, and how often the game starts over. All of these decisions have to made about the economic rules of the game.

We must specify the rules of what we take to be a fair economic game. The rules may or may not contain provisions about bonus points for those that fall behind. We also have to specify the initial distribution of economic resources, which is an equity decision. We can decide to ratify the arbitrary initial income distribution given to us by history, but that in no way alters the fact that we have made an equity decision. Then, too, we have to decide how often the game starts over with a redistribution to zero-zero or whatever we take as the fair starting score for the next game. Societies could decide to make such a judgment only once in all of human history, but no one that I know of has chosen specifically to do that. Though at Oxford University there is a rowing race where every boat starts where it left off the year before—a game that never starts over.

The general point is that the rules of the economic game, the starting score, and how often the game starts over cannot be deduced from the equilibrium price-auction theory, but exist apart from that theory. Fair lotteries can be played with many different distributions of prizes. The rules of a fair market game are not axiomatic but *must be set* by each society.[8]

To construct the optimal distribution of economic prizes, the real-world structure of preferences makes for a big difference. If preferences are interdependent rather than independent, the economy by that reality alone becomes something quite unlike a random collection of individuals. Because economic satisfaction or dissatisfaction depends on relative position, no one's economic position can be independently assessed either by itself or by others, but as it stacks up against gradations found in the rest of the society at large.

With interdependent preferences, words such as "motivation" and "voluntary cooperation" have to re-enter the vocabulary of the economist because theories that deny the importance of such realities can hardly hope to say anything meaningful about human behavior. If economic structures and incentives have to be built to elicit teamwork, voluntary cooperation, and motivation, then economic theory has to reflect the reality of such structures and incentives. If the auctioning of jobs based on the willingness to work for less cannot exist if long-run efficiency is to be obtained, economic theory cannot be constructed on the presumption that a labor auction exists.

An economics assuming interdependent preferences is very different from assuming independent preferences. Given the latter, more output is unambiguously good regardless of its distribution because it raises someone's utility. Given the former (more output) might lower welfare. Suppose everyone were envious of the person above him on the income-distribution ladder. So his happiness would go down as the income of the person above him goes up. Here individual utility (taken singly or in toto) might fall as incomes rise.

As a result, it is rational to let our social preference about the right rules of the game prevail over our individual preferences of envy. If we don't rule the preference of envy out of bounds and illegitimate, we are left with an outcome (under some circumstances zero income produces the maximum utility in an envious world) that we all realize is absurd. This leads us into difficult questions about irrational preferences and overruling individual preferences, but such questions are real and cannot be avoided by postulating a model where they do not exist. One can build an economics of interdependent preferences, but it cannot be deduced theoretically, since the model would depend on the exact interdependencies that exist in the real world. It is much simpler, but it is also ultimately misleading, to pretend that preferences are independent and that real-world human interactions do not have to be taken into account.

Similarly, real-world human behavior depends upon the expectations a person has about the future. Psychology, sociology, and politics all have theories that might produce a set of expectations very different from those ascribed to Homo economicus. Patterns of socialization, cultural and ethnic history, political institutions, and old-fashioned human will power all affect our expectations. All this cannot be assumed away as irrelevant, which is what the price-auction economist does.

A realistic model of "rational" choice will take into account a strategic view of the world where there is not enough time to maximize on every margin. Some decisions will be made by habit because that is the most efficient thing to do, absent a major change in the environment. What is rationality in the short run (hire the cheapest workers) may not be rationality in the long run (informal training grinds to a halt). We need to develop a real, empirically based theory of expectations. And here economics will have to draw on other disciplines for help. Economics cannot be, as some would want, a self-contained deductive mathematical science.

The price-auction model also assumes that economic events never have social consequences and that social events never have economic implications. But both assumptions are absurd.[9] If high unemployment leads to rioting in the United Kingdom, the social consequences are much greater than the simple economic consequence—lower income for those unemployed. And it is obvious that poor economic performance in general tends to produce political consequences: governments are thrown out of office. It is clear to everyone but the strict price-auction economist that since economic events exert influence on social and political events, economic activities are not going to occur in a world free of social and political concerns or constraints.

Imagine the Russian military threat intensifying. The armed services need strengthening, which generates a new set of economic demands: taxes must be raised; civilian expenditures cut; production shifted; the distribution of earnings altered. Give such interactions between political and economic events, political interventions in the economy will of course occur. In short, economic markets are obviously not allowed to operate free of political intervention, because they are needed to serve social and political purposes and because economic outcomes have an impact, sometimes a heavy one, on social and political events.

Consider what has been regarded as the strictly economic issue of under-savings. According to the Reagan Administration, productivity has stopped growing because Americans are saving and investing too little. When productivity was growing at more than 3 percent per year from 1948 to 1965, Americans invested 9.5 percent of the GNP. Yet recently, from 1977 to 1981, productivity fell even while Americans were investing 11.8 percent of the GNP. Investment rose, yet productivity fell because of the baby boom in the 1950s and early 1960s, which was a social and demographic event. The baby boom sharply accelerated the growth of the labor force in the late 1970s. Since $50,000 in capital investment is necessary to equip every new American worker to produce like the average American worker, capital investments that produced a rising capital-labor ratio in the 1950s and 1960s produced a falling capital-labor ratio in the late 1970s. With less capital available per worker, productivity not surprisingly fell—a market result.[10]

What does economic theory tell us about how the economy would deal with a baby boom? An increasing supply of labor lowers the relative price of labor. So when managers calculate the cost-minimizing techniques of production, they find that they should use more labor and less capital. The result is increased employment but reduced output per hour, since the average worker is now working with less capital. With lower productivity—output per hour—wages should fall.

What really happened? With a rising supply of workers, the price of capital rose relative to that of labor. Whereas the price of labor was rising relative to the price of capital at 2.9 percent per year from 1948 to 1965, the price of capital fell relative to that of labor at 5.8 percent per year after 1972. The market sent a signal to employers to invest less per worker, and employers responded to that signal. Economic theory calls for what happened to happen.

Yet there are many social reasons for not letting the economy take its natural course, which means a falling standard of living both in absolute terms and compared to the standard of living in countries that did not experience as large a baby boom. Meanwhile, the baby boomers themselves have a standard of living lower than either their parents or their children. All this strains the social fabric. The baby-boom generation votes and does not like its diminishing economic circumstances—who would? With an income falling behind that of the rest of the industrial world, the United States finds it harder and harder both politically and economically to play the international role that it desires. Accordingly, perfectly good social, even geopolitical reasons exist for intervening in the economy to push savings higher. But instead of dealing with the real social and political issues facing us, the debate gets set up around the issue of whether there is or is not a "market imperfection" leading to too little savings.

But by price-auction economic theory, there is no such thing as too little savings. Americans can save too little to ensure rapid economic growth, but they cannot save too little as long as they are saving to bring their lifetime consumption patterns into balance with their lifetime incomes. Savings is an individual decision, and if the aggregate of all of those individual decisions produce a 6 percent savings rate in the United States, a 14 percent savings rate in West Germany, and a 20 percent savings rate in Japan, so be it. Standards of living in Japan and Germany will eventually surpass those in the United States, but that does not justify government interventions to force Americans to save more.

Many economists concerned about the problem advocate government policies to stimulate capital investment, and argue that the inadequate investment was caused by a market imperfection—namely, tax laws that discouraged investment and are holding it below where it would have been in a free market. By labeling the problem a "market imperfection," these economists can plunk for a set of policies without having to admit that what they want means that government has to intervene in the market to alter private decisions.

But to regard taxes as a market imperfection strikes me as peculiar. Everyone knows that taxes have to be collected and that all taxes have incentive effects. Accordingly, taxes are a constraint, but they are not market imperfections. They cannot be removed; they must be lived with. So our tax system can be designed to discourage consumption and favor investment or the reverse, but in either case the structure of the system will reflect *a deliberate social decision that cannot be deduced from economic theory.* The neutral tax system with no effects just does not exist.

The point is, our productivity and investment problem stems not from a market imperfection, but from a historical and demographic event—the baby boom—that produces severe economic, political, and social consequences if nothing is done to mitigate them. Rather than speaking to the real issues, the debate gets structured around whether or not a "market imperfection" exists that holds savings below where they should be in a perfectly functioning equilibrium price-auction economy.

But to look at the problem that way means that only some of the possible remedies are considered within the realm of legitimate public discourse. If there are only social mistakes—bad tax laws—and no private mistakes, such as a system of management that encourages a very-short-time horizon (a peculiar view if you remember that the same individuals are making both the social and the private decisions), then all of the remedies lie within the public domain. Tax laws are debatable, but private management incentives (large bonuses for the top brass based on current profits) are not.

To admit that there are social reasons for intervening in the economy to raise investment, however, opens the door for other forms of intervention to achieve some other social goal. Pursuing social goals by intervention affecting private decisions thereby attains an across-the-board legitimacy. Not wishing to admit the legitimacy of other social goals, inadequate investment must be seen as a market imperfection.

Institutional Constraints

Because the price-auction model maintains that institutions automatically evolve into their most efficient form, advocates of the model down play any effort to improve the institutional structure of the economy. No one need worry about its reform because private institutions take care of themselves.

But if we take a look at the savings rate in various nations, no natural savings rate seems to exist. Instead a wide variety of savings rates exist depending on a wide variety of institutional arrangements. The savings rate in a society where tax-deductible consumer and mortgage credit is widely available and requires little or no down payment will be lower than the savings rate in a society employing consumption taxes where nontax deductible consumer and mortgage credit requires large down payments. Neither arrangement presents a market imperfection. Both simply use different economic constraints that produce different savings rates.

One can think of a "fat farm" analogy. Here a person pays a lot of money in order to imprison himself to lose weight. Homo economicus would never need to go, because he would just eat less, not needing anyone to stop him. But Homo sapiens knows he often has to force himself to do what he knows he should do but is incapable of doing without external constraints.

In any case, to say that institutions are important is not to be antitheoretical, but to say that any theory must be based on descriptive reality and that reality will vary depending on the institutional structure of the society analyzed. Another way to put is that there is no such thing as a market operating without constraints. The economic outcome of a society allowing slavery will be very different from the outcome of a market in a society that does not. And in general all markets require a specification of property rights. Without such rights clearly understood and enforced, nothing could be bought and sold. If somebody wanted something from somebody else, he would club him for it.

Meanwhile, arguments go on and on about what are legitimate and illegitimate constraints on economic activity. Most of us think that a prohibition against slavery is a legitimate constraint; many think that the minimum-wage constraint is illegitimate. Others want to stop the market activity of abortion, while still others want to create legal market activity in the selling of marijuana.

The point is that none of these constraints can be deduced from economic theory, though adoption of one or the other can produce a very different market outcome. The constraints themselves are a result of pressure from society and culture on economic activity. When people like or dislike some outcome, they attempt to constrain the system to produce or avoid that outcome. Some of the issues involved are debated as ethical matters (abortion), but others (minimum wage) are treated as if they were economic problems with technical economic judgments at issue. In fact, they are both ethical and economic issues. An economy with a minimum wage will produce a slightly different distribution of income from an economy without a minimum wage, just as a society that allows abortion will produce a slightly different distribution of income from a society that does not. Preservation of an individual's right to a decent existence can extend to the living through the minimum wage, as well as to the unborn through the right to be born. An economist, speaking technically, cannot say whether a society is better off with or without legal abortion or the minimum wage.

In the price-auction model, institutions are neutral, or perhaps more accurately, the constraints they impose are formed by the market. Because institutions are nothing but voluntary collections of maximizing individuals, it is reasoned, they exist if and only if they help individuals to maximize. Moreover, because inefficient institutions are driven out of business by efficient economic institutions, no voluntary institution can have an impact on economic output. At all times the market forces institutions to evolve into their most efficient form.

If the equilibrium price-auction view of the world is regarded as an appropriate way to look at some markets, but inappropriate for others, and then adjusted to fit a specific real-world set of conditions, that view can produce a good many useful insights. But taken literally, the price-auction model assumes that all goods are a homogeneous bushel of wheat that can be easily auctioned, but many are not. Information is assumed to be complete, but in the real-world it is often far from it. All risks are assumed to be insurable, when many are not. Disequilibrium paths matter, and the time lags required to adjust to new equilibria can be so long in some markets that for all practical purposes they do not adjust. And finally, as the labor market shows, what is efficient in a short-run static environment may be inefficient in a long-run dynamic environment. None of the modifications needed are antitheoretical. They merely show that for any theory to be valid and fruitful, its foundations must correspond with an external reality and not an internal mathematical rigor or tractability.

The voluntary social institution called unions were not imposed by government but were generated in workings of the economy. Do they matter? Are they a market imperfection? Or are they simply a social fact of life—a constraint—within which the economy must operate? The economics profession is not sure whether unions matter or not. Some traditionalists regard them as just another institution that cannot significantly affect economic behavior. Over long periods of time, unions seem not to have led to higher wages for their members than they would have had without the unions. Other economists see unions as important "market imperfections" that should be eliminated. For short periods of time, such as during recessions, union and nonunion wage behavior differs noticeably.

I think unions should be seen as a social institution or constraint that affects economic behavior, which means they are neither market imperfections nor irrelevant. Unions are therefore simply one of many social constraints and institutions that affect our behavior and must be taken into account by economic theory that seeks to model reality. Some effects of unions are economic (wages are not what they might otherwise have been), some are social (norms of industrial justice may have been influenced by them), and some are political (unions may form political parties to elect labor representatives).

Consider again the real structure of American savings behavior. In theory households save; businesses borrow. But in fact something quite different occurs in the United States. In 1980, household savings amounted to $104 billion, or precisely equal to the $104 billion in residential investment. If residential investment is included in the household sector, as it should be, the household sector is essentially self-financing but provides no net saving for the business sector. So business investment must be financed with internal savings. In 1980, gross business savings totaled $332 billion, or $33 billion more than the $299 billion in private nonresidential investment. The business sector was not only self-financing but a source of savings for the rest of the economy.

But because the American capital market is not marked by the large flow of funds from the household to the business sector called for in price-auction theories, American firms face a problem in meeting foreign competition. Institutionally everyone has come to expect and demand low debt to equity ratios—far below those that normally occur in Germany or Japan. Japanese firms sometimes get as much as 95 percent of their capital in the form of debt, while a 60 percent debt capital would be considered normal in Germany. Debt-to-equity ratios anywhere near these levels would be regarded as unsafe, too risky, and evidence of bad management in the United States, even though they are precisely what is called for by standard economic theory. Because these ratios are regarded as "too risky," businesses that cannot generate sufficient internal funds also find it impossible to borrow heavily and expand capacity in anticipation of market demand, which is what their foreign competitors do.

American firms are often heard to say that they must raise prices to increase earnings in order to undertake new investments. The justification makes no sense in economic theory and is dismissed by economists as a pricing decision made for other reasons entirely. In economic theory, today's profits do not need to go up to raise tomorrow's investment. If tomorrow's expected rate of return is equal to or above the market rate of interest, tomorrow's investment can be financed with today's borrowing regardless of the rate of return today on yesterday's investments. If investment must be self-financed, however, the justification for higher prices is both sensible and correct.

If financial markets have been structured so that they are not led to loan money based on expected rates of return, financing problems and inflationary pressures are created that simply do not exist in the standard economic model.

In any case, business firms typically save to invest their savings in their own operations. They may save more than they need to invest today, but they are only short-term lenders. Sooner or later they want their money back to undertake investments under their own management, because only investments within the firm maximize the opportunities for the managers making the savings decisions.

Absent a stable source of long-term debt from either the personal sector or the rest of the business sector, it is not surprising that the financial markets frown upon debt finance. It is regarded as too risky in the institutional environment of the United States, though it might not be so regarded in other countries or in the world of economic theory.

The ability and need to rely on internal financing in turn produces managerial capitalism in the United States. Because managers must save to provide their own investment funds and don't depend on the capital markets, they don't need to behave like servants of the shareholders but gain a substantial degree of independence. Which raises the question, Just what kind of capitalism, if any, is managerial capitalism, and what kinds of theories do we need to understand it? Whatever the answer, managerial capitalism is not the capitalism of the standard model.

Other institutional arrangements compound the problem. Under U.S. banking and antitrust laws, financial institutions and industrial corporations must maintain an arm's-length relationship. A major lender, for example, cannot place its representatives on an industrial firm's board of directors. But in Germany no such sharp distinction is drawn between debt and equity capital. The provider of debt capital has a right to his representatives on the management team, and in Germany financial institutions can follow their money with hands-on control. Given this knowledge and control, they are willing to lend much more than their American counterparts.

Such constraints limit how fast firms and industries can grow, which is not what you would find in a perfectly functioning capital market. Time horizons are also altered, as companies that depend on the stock market for financing end up with a much shorter time horizon than those using investment banks. Inflationary pressures are magnified because shortages occur that would not take place if firms were building production facilities further in advance of market demands and because pressures exist to raise prices to increase cash flows to undertake those needed investments. What is the cure? One could adopt policies to force private savings up, to force business savings down, and to undo the sharp separations between industrial and financial firms. But all of these involve structural changes in the nature of the economic game, well beyond the traditional recommendations of price-auction economic theory.

Similarly, personal economic mobility—labor-force turnover—is unambiguously good in the price-auction model. It moves workers to where they are most needed and maximizes individual income. Individuals should move to new jobs whenever a new employer is willing to pay more than their old employer. Yet businesses cannot function if everyone is always thinking about jumping ship and no one takes responsibility for the long-run success of the institution. With many fewer opportunities for economic mobility, the Japanese have a much greater attachment to the firm for which they work. This attachment produces dynamic efficiency. Mobility is not unambiguously productive, as the standard model would have it. With a labor-force turnover rate of 4 percent per month, perhaps the United States has too much mobility.

Uncertainty

The real world is marked by uncertainty and not risk. As I've said, genuine uncertainty as opposed to risk exists when it is impossible to assign probabilities to the different possible outcomes or where all of the different possible outcomes are unknown. But because it is the only assumption that is mathematically tractable, economists work almost entirely in terms of risk where all decisions can be made on an expected value basis. Economists act as if the world were risky but never uncertain. But the world is fundamentally uncertain, not risky, and this needs to be built into economic analysis. Often risk aversion is advanced to explain phenomena that are better explained by uncertainty. I hold some of my wealth in the form of money, for example, not because I am risk-averse but because I am uncertain and there are very few liquid markets for selling other assets.

In any case, most decisions are made in at least a partial state of ignorance or uncertainty.[11] The impact of uncertainty is compounded in the real world because many decisions are not reversible. In an auction market all decisions are reversible, and any product bought can quickly be sold with little change in price. But a factory built cannot be unbuilt or quickly sold at anything like its cost of construction. Moreover, lengthy time lags make the problem even trickier. Major investment projects such as nuclear power plants take well over a decade to complete, but who knows what the demand for electricity will be in 1990s?

The problem with uncertainty is that someone has to bear it. We need to know who does and how the damage can be minimized if a market economy is to work successfully. But no answers will be forthcoming from price-auction advocates who with their expected value analysis basically deny the existence of uncertainty.

Conclusion

Where does all of this leave us? Economics is in a state of turmoil. The economics of the textbooks and of the graduate schools not only still teach price-auction model but is moving toward narrower and narrower interpretations. The mathematical sophistication intensifies as an understanding of the real world diminishes.

Nevertheless, one can see signs of countercurrents beginning to develop. Economic models are being constructed that are designed to better reflect the world as we can see and measure it and also enhance possibilities of exercising economic control. This alternative way of thinking does not reject conceptual analysis. On the contrary, almost every paragraph of this book has used the ideas and categories of economists. But it is my hope that the ideas presented here derive their shape and their life from the world we all live in, not the world of Homo economicus. Economics cannot do without simplifying assumptions, but the trick is to use the right assumption at the right time. And this judgement has to come from empirical analyses (including those employed by historians, psychologists, sociologists, and political scientists) of how the world *is*, not of how our economics textbooks tell us it *ought* to be.

The transition from one mode of thought to another is difficult, since it involves abandoning a beautiful sailing ship—the equilibrium price-auction model—that happens to be torn apart and sinking in a riptide. So a raft must be built to catch whatever winds may come by. That raft won't match the beauty or mathematical elegance of the sailing ship, although it has one undeniable virtue—it floats.

Notes

Introduction

1. The 1982 International Conference on Economics and Management. Tokyo, Japan, July 1982.
2. Jack Barbash, "The Guilds of Academe." Presented at the December 1981 meetings of the American Economics Association.

1 Fixed versus Flexible Prices

1. Daniel Bell and Irving Kristol, eds., *The Crisis in Economic Theory* (New York, Basic Books, 1981).
2. K. S. Arrow and F. H. Hahn, *General Competitive Analysis* (San Francisco, Holden, 1971).
3. Arthur Okun, *Prices and Quantities: A Macroeconomic Analysis* (Washington, D.C., Brookings Institution, 1981).
4. Named after Arthur Okun, who developed it for use at the President's Council of Economic Advisers.
5. Council of Economic Advisers, *The Economic Report of the President, 1982*, p. 278.
6. H. S. Hauthakker and Lester C. Taylor, *Consumer Demand in the United States* (Cambridge, Harvard University Press, 1970).
7. Christopher Jencks, *Inequality* (New York, Basic Books, 1972).
8. R. E. B. Lucas, "Hedonic Wage Equations and Psychic Wages in the Returns to Schooling," *American Economic Review* (September 1977), pp. 549–558.
9. U.S. Department of Commerce, *The National Income and Product Accounts of the United States: Statistical Tables 1929–1976*, pp. 258, 318.
10. This develops some ideas first presented in Lester C. Thurow, "Economics 1977," *Daedalus* (Fall 1977).
11. Alan S. Blinder and Robert M. Solow, "Analytical Foundations of Fiscal Policy," in *The Economics of Public Finance* (Washington, D.C., Brookings Institution, 1974), p. 3.
12. Edward M. Gramlich, "Impact of Minimum Wage on other Wages, Employment and Family Income," in *The Brookings Papers on Economic Activity*, No. 2 (Washington, D.C., Brookings Institution, 1976).

2 Economic Failures

1. Council of Economic Advisers, *The Economic Report of the President, 1982*, p. 261.
2. *Ibid.*, pp. 234, 268, 291.
3. Example: Gary S. Becker, "A Theory of Marriage: Part 1," *Journal of Political Economy.* (July–August 1973), p. 813.

4. *Economic Report of the President, 1982*, p. 291.
5. Blinder and Solow, "Analytical Foundations." See Note 11, above.
6. Council of Economic Advisers, *The Economic Report of the President, 1970.*
7. E. F. Schumacher, *Small is Beautiful* (New York, Harper & Row, 1973).
8. *Economic Report of the President, 1982*, pp. 234, 268, 291.
9. *Crisis Investing, How to Profit from the Coming Collapse*, etc.
10. Office of Management and Budget, *Fiscal Year 1982 Budget Revisions*, March 1981.
11. Verbally recounted to me when I was working on the staff of the Council of Economic Advisers in 1964.
12. Franco Modigliani and Richard A. Cohn, "Inflation, Rational Valuation, and the Market," *Financial Analysis Journal*, No. 3 (March–April 1979).
13. U.S. Department of Commerce, Bureau of the Census, *Current Population Reports: Consumer Income. Money Income of Families and Persons.* 1948, 1950, 1980.
14. Robert M. Solow, "Technical Change and the Aggregate Production Function," *Review of Economics and Statistics*, No. 39 (1957); Edward F. Denison, *The Sources of Economic Growth in the United States and the Alternatives Before Us.* (New York, Committee for Economic Development, 1962).
15. John W. Kendrick, "Survey of the Factors Contributing to the Decline in U.S. Productivity Growth," in *The Decline in Productivity Growth.* Conference series No. 22 (Boston, Federal Reserve Bank of Boston), p. 1.
16. Richard Eckhaus, *Estimating the Returns to Education* (New York, Carnegie Commission, 1973); Gary Becker, *The Economics of Discrimination* (Chicago, University of Chicago Press, 1957).
17. See: The Seattle & Denver Income Maintenance Experiment, *Journal of Human Resources*, Vol XV, No. 4 (Fall 1980). Entire issue.
18. Steven Kelman, *What Price Incentives?* (Boston, Auburn House, 1981).
19. Robert S. Pindyck, "Optimal Policies for Economic Stabilization," *Econometrica* (May 1973); William Poole, "Rational Expectations in the Macro Model," in *The Brookings Papers on Economic Activity*, No. 2 (Washington, D.C., Brookings Institution, 1976).

3 Inflation

1. Keizai Koho Center, *Japan 1981: An International Comparison* (Tokyo, 1981), pp. 12, 63.
2. Stanley Fischer, "Relative Shocks, Relative Price Variability, and Inflation," in *The Brookings Papers on Economic Activity*, No. 2 (Washington, D.C., Brookings Institution, 1981), p. 381. And "Towards an Understanding of the Costs of Inflation." Mimeo.
3. Joseph J. Minarik, "The Size Distribution of Income During Inflation," *Review of Income and Wealth* (International Association for Research in Income and Wealth); Lester C. Thurow, "Stagflation and the Distribu-

tion of Real Economic Resources," *Data Resources Review* (December 1978), p. 1.11.

4. In 1982 the public opinion polls witnessed a shift from inflation to unemployment as public enemy number 1.

5. Council of Economic Advisers, *The Economic Report of the President, 1982*, p. 342.

6. *Ibid.*, p. 286.

7. Milton Friedman and Anna Schwartz, *A Monetary History of the United States, 1867–1960* (Princeton, N.J., Princeton University Press, 1963).

8. The best example was the Carter Administration in April 1980.

9. Richard G. Lipsey, *Government and Inflation.* Paper prepared for the December 1981 meetings of the American Economics Association.

10. This view depends upon the Fisher equations where interest rates are seen as a relative constant real rate plus a variable expected rate of inflation. In 1982, short-term interest rates exceeded 10 percent and did not seem to be following the Fisher equations.

11. Franco Modigliani and Albert Ando, "The Relative Stability of Monetary Velocity and the Investment Multiplier" *American Economic Review* (September 1965). Reply by M. Frieman and D. Meiselman and Jejoinder, same issue.

12. Council of Economic Advisers, *Economic Indicators*, June 1982, pp. 23, 26, 30.

13. Milton Friedman, "Monetarism: A Reply to the Critics," *Times* of London (March 3, 1980), p. 19.

14. Nicholas Kaldor, "Origins of the New Monetarism." The Page Fund Lecture, December 3, 1980. (University College Cardiff Press.

15. Paul Davidson, *Money and the Real World* (London, Macmillan, 1978).

16. A. W. Phillips, "The Relationship Between Unemployment and the Rate of Change of Money Wages in the U.K.," *Economica* (November 1958).

17. J. M. Keynes, *The General Theory of Employment, Interest, and Money* (London, Macmillan, 1936).

18. M. Friedman, Presidential Address, *American Economic Review* (March 1968); Edmund S. Phelps, "Money Wage Dynamics and Labor Market Equilibrium," *Journal of Political Economy* (July–August, 1968); *Microeconomic Foundations of Employment and Inflation Theory* (New York, Norton, 1970).

19. U.S. Department of Commerce, *Statistical Abstract of the United States, 1981*, p. 411.

20. P. Diamond, "A Search Equilibrium Approach to the Micro–Foundations of Macro Economics." Wicksell Lecture No. 1 (Stockholm, June 1982).

21. In the 148 occupations compared between 1959 and 1969, 94 percent of the variance in 1969 wages can be explained knowing 1959 wages. Lester C. Thurow, *Generating Inequality* (New York, Basic Books, 1975), p. 58.

22. A Gold Commission under the leadership of Anna Schwartz was investigating the possibility of returning to the gold standard for the Reagan Administration in 1982.

23. Thomas J. Sargent, "The Ends of Four Big Inflations." Conference Paper Series No. 90 (New York, National Bureau of Economic Research).
24. Barry P. Bosworth, "Inflation and Relative Wage Rates." Paper delivered at a conference on the supply-side aspects of stagflation sponsored by the Ontario Economic Council, Toronto, November 25, 1980.
25. Question asked at meeting of *Time* Magazine Board of Economists, 1981.
26. Otto Eckstein, *Core Inflation* (Englewood Cliffs, N.J., Prentice-Hall, 1981).
27. Joan Robinson, *The Economics of Imperfect Competition* (London, Macmillan, 1933); Edward Chamberlin, *The Theory of Monopolistic Competition* (Cambridge, Harvard University Press, 1933); William Fellner, *Competition Among the Few.* (New York, Knopf, 1949).
28. Pratt, Wise, Zeckhauser, "Price Differences in Almost Competitive Markets," *Quarterly Journal of Economics,* No. 93 (1979), pp. 189–212.
29. J. K. Galbraith, *The New Industrial State* (Boston, Houghton Mifflin, 1967).

4 Econometrics

1. The major macro-models are those of Data Resources, Chase Econometrics, Wharton, the Georgia Institute of Technology.
2. Robert W. Fogel and Stanley L. Engerman, *Time on the Cross* (Boston, Little, Brown, 1974).
3. Paul Samuelson, *Foundations of Economic Analysis* (Cambridge, Harvard University Press, 1947).
4. T. F. Cooley and S. F. LeRoy, "Identification and Estimation of Money Demand," *American Economic Review* (December 1981), p. 825.
5. Stephen K. McNess, "An Evaluation of Economic Forecasts," *New England Economic Review* (November–December, p. 3.
6. MIT-FRB, *Quarterly Econometric Model Equations* (January 1973). Equations XI through XIII.2.
7. Richard Eckhaus, *Estimating the Returns to Education* (New York, Carnegie Commission, 1973).
8. Lester C. Thurow, "A Fiscal Policy Model of the United States," *Survey of Current Business* (June 1969).
9. Gary S. Becker, *Human Capital* (New York, Columbia University Press, 1964).
10. Calculated based on data from U.S. Department of Commerce, Bureau of the Census, *Current Population Reports.* Series P-60, 1970–1978.
11. Richard Freeman, *The Over Educated American* (New York, Academic Press, 1976).
12. J. Meyer and E. Kuh, *The Investment Decision* (Cambridge, Harvard University Press, 1957); Dale W. Jorgenson, "Anticipation and Investment Behavior," in J. S. Duesenberry, E. Kuh, G. Fromm and L. Klein, eds., *Brookings Quarterly Econometric Model of the United States* (Chicago, Rand McNally, 1965); Robert Eisner and M. I. Nadiri, "Investment

Behavior and Neoclassical Theory," *Review of Economics and Statistics* (August 1968).

13. Marvin Kosters, "Effects of Income Tax on Labor Supply," in A. L. Harberger and M.J. Bailey, eds., *The Taxation of Income from Capital* (Washington, D.C., Brookings Institution, 1969).

14. Martin Feldstein, "On the Optimal Progressivity of the Income Tax." Harvard Working Paper No. 309.

15. Lester C. Thurow, "Psychic Income: A Market Failure," *Journal of Post-Keynesian Economics* Vol. III, No. 2 (Winter 1980–81), p. 183.

16. Edwin Kuh and J. Neese, "Econometric Model Diagnostics," in *International Symposium on Criteria for Evaluating the Reliability of Macroeconomic Models*, Gregory Chow and Paolo Corsi, eds. (London, John Wiley, 1982); Edwin Kuh, David Belsley, Roy Welsch, *Diagnostics in the Linear Regression Model: Identifying Influential Data and Sources of Collinearity* (London, John Wiley, 1980).

5 Supply-Side Economics

1. George Gilder, *Wealth and Poverty* (New York, Basic Books, 1981).

2. Milton Friedman, "Painless Revenue," *Newsweek* (April 5, 1982), p. 63.

3. Office of the White House Press Secretary, *The Economic Plan.* February 18, 1981.

4. This was done on the grounds that the money would, after all, ultimately be invested.

5. Closed-circuit TV debate sponsored by the National Association of Manufacturers, 1981.

6. Norman B. Ture, "The Economics of the Reagan Recovery Program" (Paris, Institut August Comte, September 12, 1981), p. 10.

7. *Ibid.*, p. 29.

8. *Loc. cit.*

9. William Fellner argued this view in a joint appearance before a CIA seminar on national economic issues.

10. Gilder, *Wealth* p. 226.

11. Sheldon Danziger, Robert Haveman and Robert Plotnick, "How Income Transfers Affect Work, Savings, and Income Distribution," *Journal of Economic Literature*, Vol. XIX, No. 3 (September 1981), p. 975.

12. Professor Laffer of UCLA wrote the original Laffer curve on a napkin that was not preserved for referencing.

13. Council of Economic Advisers, *The Economic Report of the President, 1982*, p. 321.

14. Jerry A. Hausman, "Labor Supply," in *How Taxes Affect Economic Behavior*, Henry J. Aaron and Joseph Pechman, eds. (Washington, D.C., Brookings Institution, 1981), p. 27.

15. Gilder, *Wealth*, p. 87.

16. *Ibid.*, p. 114.

17. *Ibid.*, p. 151.

18. *Ibid.*, p. 259.

19. Martin Feldstein, "Social Security and Savings: The Extended Life Cycle

Theory," *American Economic Review* (May 1976), p. 77; Dean Leimer and Selig Lesnoy, "Social Security and Private Savings: A Reexamination of the Time Series Evidence Using Alternative Social Security Wealth Variables." Working paper, Office of Research and Statistics, Social Security Administration, Washington, 1980.

For a discussion of the controversy and a listing of the following charges and countercharges, see: Danziger, et al., "How Income Transfers," p. 980.

20. *Economic Report of the President, 1982*, p. 262.

6 Rational Expectations

1. Brian Kantor, "Rational Expectations and Economic Thought," *Journal of Economic Literature* Vol. XVII, No. 4 (December 1979), p. 1422.
2. Robert E. Lucas, Jr., "Expectations and the Neutrality of Money," *Journal of Political Economy*. (April 1972), p. 102.
3. Such as mistaking absolute price changes for relative price changes.
4. Thomas J. Sargent, "Rational Expectations and the Reconstruction of Macroeconomics." Paper presented at 100th Anniversary of Hosei University, Sept. 17, 1980.
5. In the simple model of perfect competition there is no real unemployment, inflation either does not exist or does not matter, and growth is occurring at the maximum rate consistent with labor-leisure and present-future consumption preferences.
6. Eugene Fama, "Efficient Capital Markets: A Review of Theory and Empirical Work," *Journal of Finance*. (May 1970).
7. Benoit Mendelbrot, "The Variation of Certain Speculative Prices," *Journal of Business*, No. 36 (October 1963), pp. 394–419.
8. Lester C. Thurow, *Generating Inequality* (New York, Basic Books, 1975), p. 129.
9. A. Tversky and D. Klahneman, "Judgement Under Uncertainty, Heuristics and Biases," *Sciences*, No. 185 (1974) pp. 1124–1131); R. Nisbett and L. Ross, *Human Inference: Strategies and Shortcomings of Social Judgement* (Englewood Cliffs, N.J., Prentice-Hall, 1980).
10. F. E. Brown and A. R. Oxenfeld, *Misperceptions of Economic Phenomenon*. (New York, Sperrand Douth, 1972).
11. Arthur Okun, "Rational-Expectations with-Misperceptions as a Theory of the Business Cycle," *Journal of Money, Credit, and Banking*, Vol. XII, No. 4 (November 1980), p. 817.
12. Technically, the sum of the expected probability of all possible events must equal 1.
13. Thomas J. Sargent and Neil Wallace, "Some Unpleasant Monetarist Arithematic" Federal Reserve Bank of Minneapolis *Quarterly Review* (Fall 1981), p. 1.
14. Milton Friedman, *A Theory of the Consumption Function* (Princeton, N.J., Princeton University Press, 1957).
15. The Michigan Survey Research Center has been a pioneer in this effort.

16. Robert E. Lucas, Jr., "Tobin and Montarism: A Review Article," *Journal of Economic Literature*, Vol. XIX, No. 2 (June 1981), p. 559.

7 The Labor Market

1. Gary S. Becker, *Human Capital* (New York, National Bureau of Economic Research, 1964).
2. Jacob Mincer, "On-the-job Training," *Journal of Political Economy*, No. 70 (October 1962 supplement).
3. Lester C. Thurow, *Investment in Human Capital* (Belmont, Cal., Wadworth, 1970).
4. Edward E. Lawler III, *Pay and Organizational Effectiveness* (New York, McGraw-Hill, 1976).
5. S. Rosen, "The Economics of Superstars," *American Economic Review* (December 1981), p. 845.
6. Models have been developed modifying the basic model to account for each of these differences individually, but not to correct for all of these factors simultaneously. If such a model were developed, it would be so far away from that for physical investment as to be unrecognizable.
7. John Dunlop, *Wage Determination Under Trade Unions* (New York, Kelley, 1950).
8. Council of Economic Advisers, *The Economic Report of the President, 1973.*
9. Kim B. Clark and Lawrence H. Summers, "Labor Market Dynamics and Unemployment," The *Brookings Papers on Economic Activity*, No. 1 (1979), p. 13.
10. The pattern may differ from country to country. See: Robert J. Gordon, "Wages and Prices Are Not Always Sticky: A Century of Evidence from the U.S., U.K. and Japan." National Bureau of Economic Research Working Paper No. 847; William H. Branson and Julio J. Rotemberg, "International Adjustment with Wage Rigidity," *European Economic Review* Vol. 13, No. 3 (May 1980). Money wages may be rigid in the United States while real wages are rigid in Europe.
11. Lester C. Thurow, *Generating Inequality* (New York, Basic Books, 1975), Chapter 3, p. 51.
12. Herman P. Miller, *Income Distribution in the United States.* Bureau of the Census, Washington, 1966. p. 21.
13. Christopher Jencks, *Inequality* (New York, Basic Books, 1972).
14. George Hildebrand and Ta-Chang Liu, *Manufacturing Production Functions in the United States* (Ithaca, N.Y., Cornell University Press, 1965; Lester C. Thurow, "Disequilibrium and the Marginal Productivities of Capital and Labor," *Review of Economics and Statistics*, No. 45 (February 1968), p. 25.
15. Peter B. Doeringer and Michael J. Piori, *Internal Labor Markets and Manpower Analysis* (Lexington, Mass., D. C. Heath, 1972, Chapter 6.
16. Franklin M. Fisher, "The Existence of Aggregate Production Functions," *Econometrica*, No. 3 (1971), p. 553.

17. E. S. Phelps, *Microeconomic Foundations of Employment and Inflation Theory* (New York, Norton, 1970).
18. Kenneth Burdett, "A Theory of Employee Job Search & Quit Rates," *American Economic Review*, No. 68 (March 1978), p. 212; Matthew Black, "Pecuniary Implications of On-the-job Search and Quit Activity," *Review of Economics and Statistics*, Vol. 3, No. 62 (May 1980) p. 222; Peter J. Mattila, "Quit Behavior in Labor Market," *American Statistical Association Proceedings*, Economics Statistics Section (1969) p. 697.
19. Council of Economic Advisers, *Economic Indicators*, June 1982, p. 13.
20. C. Azariadis, "Implicit Contracts and Unemployment Equilibria," *Journal of Political Economy*, No. 83 (1975), p. 1183.
21. Arthur M. Okun, *Prices and Quantities: A Microeconomic Analysis.* (Washington, D.C., Brookings Institution, 1981).
22. Martin Weitzman, "Increasing Returns and the Foundations of Unemployment Equilibrium Theory," June 1981. Mimeo.
23. U.S. Department of Labor, *Formal Occupational Training of Adult Workers.* Manpower Automation Research Monograph, No. 2, 1964, pp. 3, 18, 20, 43.
24. Lee Rainwater, "Poverty, Living Standards and Family Well-Being." Joint Center for Urban Studies of MIT and Harvard. Working paper No. 10, p. 45.
25. James Duesenberry, *Income, Saving and the Theory of Consumer Behavior* (Cambridge, Harvard University Press, 1949).
26. Rainwater, *Poverty*, p. 49.
27. Richard Esterlin, "Does Money Bring Happiness?" *Public Interest*, No. 30 (Winter 1973), pp. 3–10.
28. Walter Garrison Runciman, *Relative Deprivation and Social Justice* (London, Routledge & Kegan Paul, 1966).
29. A. D. Searle, "Productivity Changes in Selected Wartime Ship Building Programs," *Monthly Labor Review*, Vol. 61, No. 6 (December 1945); Asher Harold, *Cost-Quantity Relationships in the Airframe Industry.* R-291 (Santa Monica, Calif., Rand Corporation, 1956).
30. Steven Sheffrin and Lester C. Thurow, "Estimating the costs and benefits of on-the-job training," *Economie Appliqué*, Vol. XXX, No. 3 (1977).
31. Esterlin, "Does Money . . . ?"
32. Thurow, *Generating Inequality*; Doeringer and Piori, *Internal Labor Markets.*

8 Rebuilding the Foundations of Economics

1. Douglas Murry McGregor, *The Human Side of Management* (New York, McGraw-Hill, 1960).
2. For an attempt to break out of this dilemma, see: Lester D. Taylor, "A Model of Consumption and Demand Based on Psychological Opponent Processes." Mimeo; and Tibor Scitovsky, *The Joyless Economy* (London, Oxford University Press, 1978).

3. R. Lipsy and K. Lancaster, "The General Theory of the Second Best," *Review of Economic Studies*, Vol. 24 (1956–57), p. 12.

4. Herbert Simon, *Models of Man: Social and Rational: Mathematical essays on Rational Human Behavior in a Social Setting* (New York, John Wiley, 1957).

5. Richard M. McGahey, "Labor Market Structure: The Economic Choice Model, and Crime." Presented at the December 1981 meetings of the American Economics Association.

6. Steven Kelman, *What Price Incentives: Economists and the Environment.* (Boston, Auburn House, 1981).

7. Lester C. Thurow, "Toward a Definition of Economic Justice," *Public Interest*, No. 31 (Spring 1973), p. 56.

8. John Rawls, *A Theory of Justice* (Cambridge, Harvard University Press, 1971).

9. M. Harvey Brenner, *Estimating the Social Costs of National Economic Policy; Implications for Mental and Physical Health, and Criminal Aggression.* Joint Economic Committee of the U.S. Congress, 1976.

10. Lester C. Thurow, "The Productivity Problem," *Technology Review* (November–December 1980).

11. C. Alan Garner, "Uncertainty, human judgement, and economic decisions," *Journal of Post-Keynesian Economics*, Vol IV, No. 3 (Spring 1982), p. 413.